BOOKS BY LOUIS D. RUBIN, JR.

Thomas Wolfe: The Weather of His Youth

No Place On Earth: Ellen Glasgow, James Branch Cabell, and
    Richmond-in-Virginia

The Golden Weather: A Novel

The Faraway Country: Writers of the Modern South

The Curious Death of the Novel: Essays on American Literature

The Teller in the Tale

George W. Cable: The Life and Times of a Southern Heretic

The Writer in the South: Studies in a Literary Community

Black Poetry in America: Two Essays in Historical Interpretation
    (with Blyden Jackson)

William Elliott Shoots a Bear: Essays on the Southern
    Literary Imagination

Edited

Southern Renascence: The Literature of the Modern South
    (with Robert D. Jacobs)

The Lasting South *(with James J. Kilpatrick)*

Teach the Freeman: The Correspondence of Rutherford B. Hayes
    and the Slater Fund for Negro Education, 1881-1893

The Idea of an American Novel *(with John Rees Moore)*

South: Modern Southern Literature in Its Cultural Setting
    (with Robert D. Jacobs)

The Hollins Poets

A Bibliographical Guide to the Study of Southern Literature

The Experience of America: A Book of Readings
    (with R. H. W. Dillard)

The Yemassee Lands: Poems of Beatrice Ravenel

Southern Writing, 1585-1920 *(with Richard Beale Davis
    and C. Hugh Holman)*

The Comic Imagination in American Literature

Thomas Wolfe: A Collection of Critical Essays

William Elliott Shoots a Bear

William Elliot

Shoots a Bear

Essays on the Southern Literary Imagination

LOUIS D. RUBIN, JR.

LOUISIANA STATE UNIVERSITY PRESS / BATON ROUGE

ISBN 0–8071–0160–5

Library of Congress Catalog Card Number 75–5352

Copyright © 1975 by Louisiana State University Press

Manufactured in the United States of America

This book was composed in VIP Baskerville by Graphic World, Inc.,
St. Louis, Missouri, printed by Edwards Brothers, Inc., Ann Arbor,
Michigan, and bound by Universal Bookbindery,
San Antonio, Texas.

I should like to express my gratitude to the following parties for
permission to reprint some of the material appearing in this book:

University of Georgia Press, for " 'The Begum of Bengal': Mark Twain
and the South," "Fugitives as Agrarians: The Impulse Behind *I'll Take
My Stand,*" and "Second Thoughts on the Old Gray Mare."

Southern Review, for "Uncle Remus and the Ubiquitous Rabbit."
Prentice-Hall, Inc., Englewood Cliffs, New Jersey, for "Thomas Wolfe
Once Again," from Louis D. Rubin, Jr., *Thomas Wolfe: A Collection of
Critical Essays* © 1973.

Mississippi Quarterly, for "Southern Literature: A Piedmont Art."

Hollins Critic, for "Everything Brought Out into the Open: Eudora
Welty's *Losing Battles*" and "William Styron and Human Bondage."

Georgia Southern College, *Symposium '74,* for "William Elliott Shoots a
Bear."

For Eva, Robert, Billy—

"Dear love, these fingers that had known your touch,
And tied our separate forces first together,
Were ten poor idiot fingers not worth much,
Ten frozen parsnips hanging in the weather."

Contents

Preface

These essays, written for various occasions over the course of a decade, all have to do in one way or another with the same problem: why do southern writers write the way they do? If one grants that there is and has been a body of literature identifiable as southern, then what is there about the place and the time that has played so noticeable a role in shaping the literature? The discussions that follow are attempts to discover, at points here and there along the line, some of the things that might be involved in the answer.

In terms of the writers being discussed, these essays fall into three groups. "William Elliott Shoots a Bear," the title piece, is an inquiry into one quite minor antebellum southern writer, in an effort to search out some of the reasons why—given the fact that he was working with very much the same material that the greatest of twentieth-century southern writers, William Faulkner, used in one of his finest short stories—he managed to do so little with it. On the surface this might seem an unprofitable avenue of inquiry to pursue; why, after all, is any third-rate writer not as good at using his material as a first-rate writer? But there is more to it than that, as I have tried to show. William Elliott had an unusual imagination; he was no hack writer. What factors were at work in his situation that kept him from realizing his talent? I have attempted to suggest what some of them might have been.

The second group of essays deals with the local-color period—those years after the Civil War when southern authors briefly moved into the center of the national literary stage, only to lose favor when the vogue declined for writing that emphasized the oddities, peculiarities, and quaint surfaces of provincial life. The paradox here is that the one southern author of the period whose reputation as a major American writer has survived, Mark Twain, is usually not even thought of as a southern writer at all. I have sought to show how and why Samuel L. Clemens' literary imagination was deeply involved in the time and place of his origins. What is involved, I think, is that Mark Twain has customarily been thought of as other than a southern writer for precisely the same reasons that account for the distinction of the literature of the twentieth-century southern renascence—qualities of detachment as well as loyalty, a way of focusing the complex relationship of writer and region into a dialectic of the inner moral imagination. In other essays I have attempted to show how, in writers of lesser importance, the South has played its shaping role.

Finally, there is a group of essays on writers and writing of the twentieth-century South. I confess that I chose these few from among many that might have fit into the design; I have been writing about the twentieth-century South and its writers for more than a quarter century, and the inquiry is not yet concluded. I have included a piece on Thomas Wolfe even though it might appear to bear less upon Wolfe's experience as a southern writer than upon the reader's experience in encountering Wolfe. I have placed it here because I felt that Wolfe's response to the South in *Look Homeward, Angel* represents a way of feeling and writing that tends to get overlooked in much discussion of southern literature precisely because most of those who write about the subject have passed beyond the stage at which they care to write about Wolfe—for reasons given in my essay. But Wolfe has appealed to the imagination of too many good southern writers to be left out of any account of why southerners write as they do.

These are occasional essays; most were commissioned. Beyond disposing of an incidental shaky or redundant passage, I have not attempted to give them more unity or progression than they merit by attempting to eliminate repetition, revise inconsistencies, or furnish transitions. I have appended to each a note on how it got written, except for a couple that were written only because I felt like writing them.

I am aware of the fact that my concern for why southern writers write like southern writers is not exactly a major preoccupation in literary circles today. Unfortunately for my bank account, however, it happens to be what I am interested in. A few years ago I wrote a book about such authors as Cervantes, Stendhal, Proust, James, and Mauriac, and a reviewer was good enough to remark favorably upon my having at last entered the larger arena of literature. I have not, I am afraid, gone on to justify that congratulation; I keep turning back to the South and its writers because, for better or for worse, that is where my obsession lies.

All of these pieces were written while I have been a member of the English faculty of the University of North Carolina at Chapel Hill. Such merit as they possess is in large part ascribable to the advantages of working daily in a building in which C. Hugh Holman, Carroll Hollis, Blyden Jackson, Lewis Leary, and William Harmon are all available to read one's manuscripts, and with George Tindall installed in another building just across the way and Arlin Turner six miles down the road at Duke University. For anyone studying southern literature it would be difficult to improve on such consultative privileges.

Louis D. Rubin, Jr.
Chapel Hill, N.C.
January, 1975

William Elliott Shoots a Bear

William Elliott Shoots a Bear

One of the earliest and best known of all books about outdoor life in the South is William Elliott's *Carolina Sports by Land and Water*. Originally written as newspaper sketches, it appeared in 1846 and in an illustrated edition in New York in 1859. The book has been recurrently in print ever since. It was reissued as late as 1967 in the Abercrombie and Fitch Library series.[1] The book is divided into two sections: one involving accounts of fishing, signed by "Piscator," and the other on hunting, the sketches in which were first published over the pen name of "Venator." Though the fishing episodes, in particular those having to do with "devil-fishing," are the best known and most often cited, the hunting stories are actually more interesting, in that, however obliquely, they suggest Elliott's role in his society and his attitudes toward his times. William Elliott is an interest-

This essay was first presented at a symposium on "The Southern Mystique: Myth or Reality?" at Georgia Southern College, Statesboro, February 21, 1974, and printed in the proceedings, *Symposium '74: The Southern Mystique: Myth or Reality?* (Statesboro, Ga., 1974), 1–19.

1. William Elliott, *Carolina Sports by Land and Water* (New York, 1967), x. Page citations throughout are to this edition and are given parenthetically.

ing and moderately significant man.[2] He was a native of Beaufort, South Carolina; his estate, Oak Hall plantation, remained in the family until the 1920s. He was born in 1788, educated at Harvard, served in the state legislature and for one term in the United States House of Representatives, and generally managed his plantations in the South Carolina Low Country, but primarily he engaged in the practice of writing and hunting. As a writer he reviewed for Hugh Swinton Legaré's *Southern Review*, wrote a poetic drama, contributed to the sporting magazines, and produced numerous political and agricultural pamphlets. Though a wealthy Carolina planter, William Elliott was no proslavery zealot. He was a devoted Unionist, an opponent of nullification, and later of secession, an advocate of manufacturing and scientific farming, and among his closer friends were James Louis Petigru and William John Grayson, the former of whom never admitted to the right of secession and remained a Unionist in Charleston during the war, and the latter a vigorous opponent of secession as well as author of a noted proslavery poem in heroic couplets, "The Hireling and the Slave."

William Elliott's skill as a fisherman and a hunter was well known. In *Carolina Sports* he describes killing two bears with one shot of a heavily loaded shotgun. His grandson Ambrose E. Gonzales recalls his prowess.

A few weeks before his death [in February, 1863], when I was five and a half years old, a servant came up to the house to say a covey of partridges was in the briar thicket near the pond, two hundred yards away. He called me, took his gun, walked up to the birds and killed one with each barrel. I picked them up and we were back at the house within five minutes. He was a very fine shot to the last, and in his seventy-third and

2. There is no full-length biography of Elliott. The most informative single biographical source is Lewis Pinckney Jones, "William Elliott, South Carolina Nonconformist," *Journal of Southern History*, XVII (1951), 361–81. In *The South in American Literature, 1607–1900* (Durham, N. C., 1954), Jay B. Hubbell discusses Elliott as a man of letters. See pages 564–68.

seventy-fourth years made some remarkable bags—partridges, snipe and woodcock, which at the close of the day's shooting were always spread upon the big silver waiter and brought in to the hall by the butler, as was the custom, for the ladies to see. About this time, too, I remember seeing three beautiful bucks laid out at the back steps, two of which my grandfather had killed with two barrels—a double shot.[3]

The sport of "devil-fishing," for which Elliott was best known in his time, was a rather dangerous affair. Elliott and his party would have themselves rowed out by black slaves into Port Royal Sound, between St. Helena Island and Hilton Head, and would wait until manta-rays drew near. The manta-ray, or "devil-fish," was a formidable beast, which could attain a breadth of twenty feet or more and a weight of more than two tons. At the proper moment they would sink a harpoon into one of these, and for the next several hours they would be towed all over the area at great speeds. If one did not know that *Moby-Dick* was published four years after the first edition of *Carolina Sports*, one might suspect that Elliott had drawn heavily on Herman Melville for some of his descriptions. The audacity of Melville's Queequeg, Tashtego, and Daggoo, for example, does not much surpass that of "May," a Negro slave.

Staff in hand, he planted his foot firmly on the bow of the barge. He stood there but a second when, grasping his staff in both hands, he sprang into the air, and descended directly on the back of the largest Devil-fish, giving the whole weight of his body to the force of the stroke! The weapon sunk deep into the body of the fish, and before he had tightened the rope, "May" had already swam to the boat, laid his hands on the gunwales, and been dragged on board by his fellow blackies, who were delighted at his exploit (9).

Another bout with a devil-fish elicited this description by Elliott of a dying manta-ray:

3. Ambrose E. Gonzales to James Henry Rice, February 3, 1922, quoted in James Henry Rice, *The Aftermath of Glory* (Charleston, S. C., 1934, 243–44.

The turbid waters of the river have now given place to the transparent green of the sea, through which objects are distinctly visible for feet below; and look! he is rising again from his depths! every struggle and contortion of the agonized monster is clearly to be seen, as he shoots upward to the light! He is upon his back,—his white feelers thrown aloft above his head, like giant hands up raised in supplication! There was something almost *human* in the attitude and the expression of his agony,—and a feeling quite out of keeping with the scene, stole over me while I meditated the fatal blow.

But Elliott quickly adds, "It passed away in an instant; and as he emerges from the water, the harpoon cleaves the air and is driven home, into his head. A shout of exultation bursts from the crew!"(41)

There are many such carefully composed scenes in the devil-fishing episodes, but I shall content myself with only one more example, which I hope will recall to you a passage from *Moby-Dick*. A devil-fish has been captured and killed:

The winds were hushed, and the wide expanse of water on which we floated was smooth as a mirror. The tender, with her Devil-fish in tow, was before us. The tide, still flood, was drifting her up the river, and out of her desired course. See! she has let go her anchors, hauled her fish close up under her stern, and the boatmen are beating off with their oars the sharks that, having scented the blood, as it flowed from many a ghastly wound, can scarcely be deterred by blows from gorging themselves on the immense but lifeless mass! Farther from shore glides the "Sea-Gull"—the first energies of the monster fish that impels her have been tamed down, and she tacks across the channel, like a barge beating to windward! Jests, merriment and laughter are rife on board of her; and the mirthful echoes are borne to us over the still waters (29–30).

Though the devil-fish episodes are the best-known elements of *Carolina Sports*, it is to a series of hunting tales that I would now turn. Elliott's favorite form of hunting was for deer, and this in the traditional southern way, whereby the hunters take up stands, and a pack of dogs with a driver or two is set to work to raise the deer and drive them through the woods toward the waiting hunters. The hunters on this occasion have horses ready, and once a fleeing deer is hit, they spring to the saddle and join in the chase. The wounded deer is then pursued through fields and along woodland trails until it can be brought down. This is pretty much the same method described by William Faulkner over a century later in "The Bear."

William Elliott's deer-hunting descriptions make up four sketches, "A Day at Chee-Ha," "Another Day at Chee-Ha," "A Business Day at Chee-Ha," and "The Last Day at Chee-Ha." Chee-Ha is the name of a river—the modern-day spelling is Chehaw—which flows into the Combahee River about ten miles to the east of Beaufort, and it is there that Elliott's plantation was located.

On the first day's hunt Elliott and his friends raise a deer and pursue it. One of the hunters is a novice, and he brings down the deer.

We all rode to the spot, to congratulate our novice on his first exploit in sylvan warfare,—when as he stopped to examine the direction of his shot, our friend Love-lcap [Thomas Rhett Smith the younger] slipped his knife into the throat of the deer, and before his purpose could be guessed at, bathed his face with the blood of his victim. (This, you must know, is *hunter's law* with us, on the killing a first deer.) As our young sportsman started up from the ablution,—his face glaring like an Indian Chief's in all the splendor of war paint,—Robin the hunter touched his hat and thus accosted him.

"Maussa Tickle, if you wash off dat blood dis day,—you neber hab luck agen so long as you hunt" (94).

Later that day the author wounds another deer and with his slave pursues the deer to a marsh canal. The deer swims across and into the marsh beyond, and the dogs follow and corner it. The slave climbs a tree to observe, and the writer urges him to come down, swim across the canal, and get to the spot where the deer has been cornered, to save it from being torn to pieces by the dogs. The slave is skeptical. The author then accuses him of being afraid. To which the slave replies, "Got maussa . . . if he be water, I swim'um—if he be bog, I bog'um,—if he be briar, I kratch tru'um,—but who de debble, but otter, no so alligator, go tru all tree one time!"

Whereupon Elliott continues as follows: "The thought was just stealing its way into my mind, that under the excitement of my feelings, I was giving an order, that I might have personally hesitated to execute" (96–97). It turns out just then, however, that the deer has gotten free and is swimming in the canal; the chase resumes, and ultimately the deer is killed.

So much for the first day's hunt. Note, however, that in it we have encountered a ritual—the daubing of the novice hunter's face with the blood of his victim—and also the motif of *noblesse oblige*—the author may order his slave to do something only if he himself is not fearful of doing so.

The second day's hunt is prefaced by an apologia:

The sportsman, who gives a true description of his sports, *must be an egotist.* It is his necessity. The things, which *he* has seen or done, are precisely those which make the liveliest impression; and with none other, but such as are thus brightly enshrined in his memory, should he attempt the difficult task of interesting the careless or pre-occupied. Let this be my apology for speaking of myself;—and if in my narrations there is (as some friendly critic may suggest,) a *want of repose;* it is as well for me candidly to confess, that the *want* is intentional. I sin through design. . . . Could I rouse you an elephant, gentlemen critics, you should have a grave and stately march: I'd give you *repose* with a vengeance. But, for your lighter game,—dash, splash on, with whip and spur! *Celerity of movement* is the play,—whether in the field or in the narrative! (100)

Note what he says there. The author should write of what *he* knows—his own experience. And he must be an egotist. (One thinks of Thoreau's remark in *Walden*: "In most books, the *I*, or first person, is omitted; in this it will be retained; that, in respect to egotism, is the difference. . . . I should not talk so much about myself if there were anybody else whom I knew as well."[4]) But at the same time, the emphasis throughout is to be on descriptive action, not contemplation.

The second day's hunt is successful, and the author and a companion kill three deer and a turkey gobbler as well, whereupon Elliott delivers a peroration to northern-born hunters, "Ye city sportsmen" who "marshal your forces for a week's campaign among the plains of Long Island, or the barrens of Jersey,—and in reward of your toil, bag one brace of grouse, or enjoy a *glorious* snap at some straggling deer." He jests at sportsmen of metropolitan regions who must import quail from South Carolina to be released in the fields of Long Island. "What think ye of sport like this? Ours was no *preserve* shooting! We were not popping over our own nurselings! They were wild deer, of the wild woods, that we slew, this day at Chee-Ha!!" And he invites them to come down and enjoy the sport as it should be pursued (107–108).

The third day's hunt is delayed by business. Like most of his fellow planters Elliott has been living in the city during the hot weather because of the malarial climate of the Low Country. Now it is October, and he must inspect one of the family's plantations to see how things have been faring in his absence. The overseer is there to greet him, "pale and still feeble from the inflictions of the autumnal scourge; and yet this man had done no bodily labor,—he had not toiled under our burning skies; but rode habitually to the fields to superintend the work of the blacks, and was sheltered from sun and rain by an umbrella!" For Elliott this is the occasion for a political observation: "And is it *this* region, which the

4. Henry David Thoreau, *Walden*. Introduction by Brooks Atkinson (New York, 1961), 2.

philanthropic abolitionist would people with white
laborers?" The malaria of the Low Country would be
more deadly for white men than the Asiatic cholera, he
declares, while the blacks can take it in stride: "What a
contrast to the bloodless, fever-striken being who was
placed there to superintend their labor! The dank va-
pors of the swamp, so baneful to him—had they served to
nourish *their* grosser bodies?" Clearly the slaves were
well fed on the planter's rice: "Could they have stolen it?
'The theft of a slave is no offense against society;' says a
high legal authority; and these slaves had possibly acted
on the principle, and had not been looked to over
closely in so doing; for there is a precept better known
to the Southern planter, than to the philanthropist who
condemns him,— 'Muzzle not the ox that treadeth out
the corn'"(111-12).

In the midst of sketches on deer hunting, the political
and social concerns of the antebellum South have in-
truded. Elliott must point out the economic justification
for slavery and also the essential benevolence of the
slaveowner. If he has any qualms about either, they are
not to be aired here, however; he goes on to describe his
interviews with his slaves. The blacks ask him for cloth,
for shoes; one of them reports that the overseer has told
her that the master, "him no care a dam!" because her
shoes are cut too short. But he is anxious to get back to
the hunting and promises redress later. Before leaving
he checks to see how the sick are being cared for. The
slave woman in charge refers to him as "ole maussa." He
is indignant:

" '*Old Maussa!*' you shall not say that. No," said I, as some
unpleasant memories flashed across my mind,— "not for two
years to come!"
    "Tink of dat now!" said the disappointed nurse, as she
hobbled back to her bed, to sleep out the remnant of her nap;
"he hair 'gin to run gray, and he bex caus I call um ole!" (115)

There is almost no defensiveness or sensitivity here, so far as I can see; not for a minute does Elliott seem to feel any need to show himself in an idealized relationship with the slaves. They are, in his view, no more than children, and his relationship with them is forbearing and responsible, but he does not examine it or go to any pains to display it. He is anxious to be off. He and Love-leap rejoin the hunt. Twice they pursue fleeing deer, without success. He bids Love-leap go ahead, and stops to rest alongside an old abandoned colonial fort near the Ashepoo River, where he falls into meditation:

And, as the leaves, fanned by a gentle southern air, fell rustling from the surrounding trees to mingle and be lost in the earth which received them, I mused, and bethought me, that they were but too apt emblems of human fortunes. Where were the original lords of this soil, whose dark forms glided in by-gone days, through these forests; intent like ourselves, on the pleasures of the chase? Gone like those bubbles! scattered like the leaves of a former season by the blast of the whirlwind, or buried (as those now falling about me, were soon to be,) undistinguished beneath the soil! their musical dialect every day upon our tongues, and they— forgotten as though they had never been! And where were they, who dispossessed them? the early white colonists?— gone like themselves! The spreading oaks hard by, marked their traditionary graves: but their histories, their very names, already indistinct from time, are fading day by day from human memory! Shall we too pass away and be forgotten? Must the like oblivion rest on us, and on the race to which we belong? What unthought of page in the unsearchable book of futurity, might yet be ours! (117–18)

At this point, far off, he hears the report of a gun, and his reverie is interrupted. A deer comes, is hit, falls, escapes into the river; Elliott orders his slave Robin to swim in after him, and, when Robin demurs, Elliott prepares to do so himself. Then Love-leap comes up and pretends to wish to go in his stead; he does not, however, for he has already killed a handsome doe, and there is no need to go after the one in the stream. Thus ends the third day's hunt.

In many ways the fourth sketch, "The Last Day at Chee-Ha," is the most interesting of all. The hunters assemble; Elliott describes them, gives their initials, recounts their setting forth. He takes up his stand near some ponds. As he listens to the hounds off in the distance, he catches sight of some unfamiliar objects. To his great surprise, there are no less than four bear, visible just ahead, emerging from a nearby thicket. The leading bear stops not twenty yards away. A second moves directly behind the first, rears, and looks over the first bear's shoulder. Elliott fires one barrel of his gun, which is loaded with heavy shot. He believes he has hit both of them with the single blast. "Riding to the spot, imagine my surprise at seeing the large bear motionless, and in the same upright posture which he maintained before I had fired; his head, only, had sunk upon his knees. *He was stone dead!*—two shot had pierced his brain. His death, apparently, had been instantaneous, —and the slight support of a fallen tree, had enabled him to retain a posture, by which he yet simulated life!" (126) Elliott sets off in search of the second bear he is sure he has wounded, and meanwhile the deer hunters come up. Informed of Elliott's fortune, they are astounded. They go to see; when the dogs smell the bear, their hair bristles in fright: "There he stood before them!—not fallen, but crouching, as if prepared to spring,—yet, as we have said, *stone dead!*" Elliott then tells about the second bear. His friends refuse to believe: " 'Now we know you joke,' said they in a breath; 'you fired but one barrel!' " (129) They go looking for the second bear, though the hounds are panic-striken and will not pick up the trail. Sure enough, they find the second dead bear. A fellow huntsman taunts Elliott as being *the luckiest man I ever saw in my life!*" (130) Elliott declares that skill is more at issue than luck. There were yet two more bear, however, and it is time to go after them. "We cheered on the hounds, but they would not respond. In vain the drivers brought them to the trail,—they would follow the horsemen, but would not advance a step before them,—such was the instinctive dread they entertained of the bears, which none of them had seen before that day. Oh, for a bull terrier, or some other dog of bolder nature!—even a cur of low degree, would have yelped in pursuit, and enabled us to add two more bears, perhaps, to the list of slain!" (131)

The huntsmen give up the pursuit of the remaining bears and get back to the pursuit of deer. One man, called the Laird, is sure he winged a deer, but not a trace can be seen. Presently the Laird claims to have found a bit of marrow from the deer's leg. No one believes that, however, and for the rest of the day he is royally teased about it. They do not find the deer, and they return home for dinner.

Elliott has a theory, which he now proposes: "His seeming to be shot, yet moving as if unhurt!—his losing a leg, yet running off without it!—his bloodlessness!—*his disappearance at 'May's Folly'*—the confusion of the hounds,—and the unaccountable dispersion of the pack!—impress upon my mind the possibility of this being no deer of flesh and blood,—but the 'Spectre Buck,' of which we have heard traditionally, but which I never supposed had been met by daylight!" (133) He then recounts a story of how a German, named May, had long ago owned the land they have hunted. Suffering financial loss, he had become sour and embittered, retreating into himself, sometimes hunting with desperate energy, at other times relapsing into despondency. "He grew still more unsocial and secluded, as he advanced in life; and men began to whisper strange stories of him" (134). It was said that he had been tainted by the atheism of the French Revolution, had mocked at sacred things, denied the sanctity of the Bible. "Others said, that in his moody fits, he had treated his slaves with barbarity; and had shrunk back from the public scorn, which such cowardice is sure to provoke, into the seclusion we had noticed." Whatever the cause, he became more and more the recluse. Upon his death, his slaves, in accordance with his instructions, buried him secretly in the woods, leveled his grave and covered it with leaves, so that no one might discover the place of his burial. No headstone marked his grave; without prayer or hymn, he was buried at night. Ever afterward, Elliott relates, the slaves have viewed the area as haunted ground (134–35). Sometimes a gush of air, hot against the passerby's face, causes cold shivering, as if a spirit were nearby:

Sometimes a milk-white buck is seen, by glimpses of the moon, taking gigantic leaps,—then shrouded in a mist wreath, and changed, in a twinkling, into the likeness of a pale old man, swathed in his grave clothes,—then melting away slowly into air! At other times, the "Spectre Buck" starts up before his eyes, pursued by phantom hounds, which rush maddening through the glades,—yet utter no sound, nor shake the leaves, while they flit by like meteors! It is the ghost of May, doing penance for the sins done in the flesh, under the form of the animal which he most persecuted while living!" (135)

They discourse upon ghosts for a while, but then the Laird interrupts to discount the story of the "Spectre Buck." Old May, he says, was a drunken sot. The Laird himself, when hunting in the area, had once stumbled upon his grave and found there a skeleton, "and at its head and feet, by way of head-stone and foot-board, lay—a bottle of *brandy,* and another of *rum,*—corked, sealed, and deposited for convenient use, in another world—if haply, in that world, *drinking* were a permitted enjoyment!" (137) Thus the spell is broken. Meanwhile the hounds have disappeared, far off in pursuit of the deer and will not be recovered again for days to come, and the four days of deer hunting at Chee-Ha are done.

Elliott was a South Carolina gentleman, sportsman, and a man of letters. He published the four sketches of the deer hunt at Chee-Ha in the 1840s. Almost one hundred years later, in 1942, another southern author, who was also a member of a distinguished family in his state, and who was sportsman as well as author, published his deer-hunting sequence in a book called *Go Down, Moses and Other Stories*. William Faulkner entitled his story "The Bear." I hope that it has become obvious why I have gone into such detail in describing William Elliott's tale of deer hunting in coastal South Carolina. The fact is that in Elliott's narrative, published long before the Civil War, is contained, implicitly and sometimes even explicitly, almost every ingredient, every motif, every sequence of action that may be found in "The Bear." We remember the symbolic blooding of Isaac McCaslin by Sam Fathers; the novice sportsman is blooded by Love-leap after shooting his first deer. The Indian motif, exemplified in Sam Fathers' heritage, is touched on when Elliott sits and muses on the former Indian inhabitants of the Chee-Ha region. There are two bears slain in Elliott's narrative, and Elliott makes much of the way in which the first bear stands lifelike in death, as if he were a sentinel of the wilderness. Indeed, the statuesque quality of the slain but still upright bear, "*stone dead*" and erect, reminds us momentarily of the way in which, for Ike McCaslin, the tableau of Boon Hogganbeck astride the great bear, and the dog Lion, his jaws gripping the bear's throat, hanging on, seems frozen in timeless statuary. Elliott longs for a bull terrier or "some other dog of bolder nature . . . even a cur of low degree" to go after the remaining bears; we recall the little fyce dog that heads straight for Old Ben in

"The Bear" and has to be restrained by Sam Fathers. "'You's almost the one we wants," Sam Fathers tells the fyce. " 'You just aint big enough. We aint got that one yet. He will need to be just a little bigger than smart, and a little braver than either.' "[5] The story of the "Spectre Buck" in Elliott's narrative suggests the mythical qualities of the bear Old Ben in Faulkner. And so on. If what happened at Chee-Ha comes out of Elliott's own experience, then that experience furnished him with every bit as much material for fiction as Faulkner's experiences with his famous hunting group in the Delta provided. The potentialities for high drama were certainly present.

But the account of the hunt at Chee-Ha remains on the level of hunting sketches. Nothing in Elliott's account is pointed toward the great wilderness theme of "The Bear"; the deaths of the bear and of the various deer are not made into the symbol of the passing of the woodlands before the coming of civilization. We know that Elliott was aware of the inevitability of what was going on; in a postscript to *Carolina Sports* entitled "Random Thoughts on Hunting" he remarks, "Sportsman as I am, I am not one of those who regret the destruction of the forests, *when the subsistence of man is the purpose.* It is in the order of events that the hunter should give place to the husbandman; and I do not complain of it" (166). It is obvious, from his description, that the sight of the slain bear, erect in death, has moved him profoundly, but he makes nothing further of it. He does not see, in the killing of the great bear in his story, its potential symbolic relationship to the passing of the woods, even though he notes that it has been some time since bear have frequented the area he hunts. Earlier he has meditated briefly on the ephemerality of the gener-

5. William Faulkner, "The Bear," *Go Down Moses and Other Stories* (New York, 1942), 212.

ations of men on the land, the disappearance of past civilizations; he has wondered whether similar oblivion is in store for his own; but he does not think to link this with the disappearance of bears from the region.

In the story of the old German landowner and his mysterious burial at night in an unmarked grave, Elliott goes so far as to associate the wilderness and the legend of the "milk-white buck," seen in the moonlight "taking gigantic leaps" and "pursued by phantom hounds," with the institution of slavery; the German has reputedly mistreated his slaves and denied the sanctity of the Bible, and his ghost was doing penance for his sins. But that is all. Faulkner made Sam Fathers, with his mixed Indian and Negro blood, a priest of the woods, and what he taught Isaac McCaslin caused Isaac to attempt to take upon himself the guilt of slavery and of the ownership and mistreatment of human beings by his grandfather, old Carothers McCaslin.

When Ike recalls the way Sam Fathers' face had looked on the day the dog Lion was discovered, he thinks: *"He was old. He had no children, no people, none of his blood anywhere above earth that he would ever meet again. And even if he were to, he could not have touched it, spoken to it, because for seventy years now he had had to be a Negro. It was almost over now and he was glad."*[6] Elliott, when the old Negro nurse alludes to his own age, makes a joke of it. There is no sense of the huntsman feeling himself growing old amid the wilderness, or of the possible existence of a deeper kind of knowledge, beyond that of the skilled use of the rifle, as having accrued to one who has grown to manhood and to middle age out in the open, in the woods. The apprenticeship theme, which provides the central development of "The Bear" as young Isaac McCaslin learns the ways of the woods from Sam Fathers and comes toward a moral decision upon

6. *Ibid.*, 215.

his maturity, has no counterpart in Elliott's narrative, even though we know that he was the son and grandson of sportsmen. Nor is there a deeply felt historical sense. Elliott did not look for ties with his region's past. The account of the slave leaping on the back of the devil-fish with his harpoon happened not during one of his own expeditions, but when his grandfather was the lord of the land. The Elliott family ancestry in the Beaufort area was at least as distinguished and as long-lived in its lineage as that of William Faulkner in Mississippi; its roots went back as far or farther; Elliott's father grew one of the first crops of the sea-island cotton that enriched the agriculture of the Carolina Low Country, and he had served with distinction during the Revolutionary War. As Elliott notes, after the last day's hunt at Chee-Ha the dogs chased the remaining deer onto the scene of the last Revolutionary War battlefield at Tar-Bluff on the Combahee River, where the patriot John Laurens fell (138). Surely there was nothing missing in the way of historical tradition in Elliott's own background; and as a youth growing up amid such surroundings and with such a heritage, he must have seen himself in the apprentice role of heir-presumptive to a long sequence of planters and sportsmen. But nothing is made of it; the deer hunt is presented in time present, without important antecedents.

Of course William Elliott was no Faulkner; he was a planter who dabbled in writing; that is the sum of it. But we cannot stop there. For we know that Elliott *wanted* to write, that he had serious, if intermittent, literary ambitions. Not only did he contribute critical essays to the *Southern Review,* but he produced a verse drama, *Fiesco,* which he published privately. Based on the narrative of Cardinal de Retz, it recounts the Genoese conspiracy of Luigi Fiesco in 1547. In 1831, Stephen Elliott, Jr., the son of William Elliott's uncle, the noted naturalist Stephen Elliott, wrote urging his cousin to devote his talents and energy completely to literature.[7] Such a prospect must have had some appeal for Elliott, though he did not pursue it. A literary reputation mattered to him. "I think that if any thing that I have written will live after me it will be these 'Sports,'" he wrote to his wife toward the end of his life. "At the worst they can only drop into oblivion, but should they acquire notoriety, it will be a sort of legacy of honor to my posterity who need not then be ashamed of claiming descent from old 'Venator.'"[8]

If as a writer Elliott remained a dilettante, author of some interesting but superficial hunting sketches, a privately printed verse tragedy dealing with the theme of justice, and various agricultural and political writings, we cannot ascribe it to the want of imaginative observation. I cannot help but feel that there was in the quality of Elliott's imagination a potentiality for important literary accomplishment. *His eye recognized what most mattered.* For we have seen how, in the hunting tales, he did pick up so many of the motifs that might have been developed. The fact that they are included in his stories shows that he did sense the relationships. But he did not develop them, make anything of them; he did not do with the superb material of his own experience what he attempted to do with his verse drama of sixteenth-century Italy: weave the material into formal unity, search out and delineate the human consequences of events described, give definition, and pronounce meaning. His single surviving work is a record of surfaces.

In part, of course, what we are dealing with is a matter of literary convention. Nothing in the literature being produced around him, whether by his friend William Gilmore Simms or others, would have caused William Elliott to think that the hunting experiences he so

7. Jones, "William Elliott, South Carolina Nonconformist," 379.
8. William Elliott to Phoebe Caroline Elliott, October 9, 1859, quoted *ibid.*, 381.

cherished could be made into the stuff for serious literature. We might recall what he said about the sportsman
who would write having to be an egotist, having to make
use of those experiences that actually happened to him
in order to create the liveliest literary impression. The
only models for writing about hunting that Elliott knew
were just such sketches as his own, whether published in
newspapers or in the sporting magazines. But clearly he
did not see a similar requirement for self-knowledge as
existing for genuine literature; when he chose to write
tragedy, he turned away from deer, bear, and devil-fish
to chronicle secondhand literary experience: intrigue
and justice denied in Renaissance Italy. The "want of
repose" in his hunting and fishing sketches, he declares,
is intentional; were he hunting elephants instead of
deer, he informs the gentlemen critics, he would give
them a grave and stately march, repose with a vengeance, but for lighter game "*celerity* of movement is the
play,—whether in the field or in the narrative!" (100). If
we take the hunting reference as a literary metaphor, as
he seems to be doing, he would seem to be likening
serious literature, perhaps a play like his *Fiesco,* to
elephant hunting. In such work, there must be thoughtfulness, contemplation, ideas—but not in tales of Low
Country field and stream. There we have it: one did
not, in 1846, write about American deer hunting and
devil-fishing in the way that one wrote about palace
intrigues in Genoa. Local things were not worthy of
thoughtfulness, contemplation; they possessed no potentiality for the definition and meaning that genuine
literature could afford. A hundred years later, in
Faulkner's day, it was different.

But that will not quite suffice to explain it, either.
Herman Melville was a contemporary of William Elliott;
earlier I quoted several passages from Elliott's "devil-
fish" sketches in order to show that some of the same
motifs were present as appeared in Melville's great ro-

mance of the white whale. Once again, the potentialities were there—and Elliott's imagination instinctively singled them out in his fishing sketches. But he did nothing with them. He did not see in the duel with the great manta-ray any of the significance that his own contemporary Melville espied in the pursuit of Moby-Dick.

Let me make it clear that it is not that one might ask or expect William Elliott of South Carolina to have written a *Moby-Dick* or "The Bear," or that his failure to have done so is in any way remarkable. Elliott was *not* a Melville or a Faulkner; he was not even a William Gilmore Simms. But Elliott wanted to write well and memorably; Elliott knew how to use the language, and he knew what great writing was. He had the imagination and the observation of a writer. And the question we must ask—on its answer rests one explanation for the mediocrity of the literature of the Old South—is: Why would a William Elliott fail to discern, in the life that he knew so well and which lay all about him, the potentiality for literary ordering and meaning that he sought to discover in Cardinal de Retz's account of political intrigue in sixteenth-century Genoa? Pointing to the inhibiting influences of the literary conventions of the day is not enough; they did not hold back a Herman Melville or a Nathaniel Hawthorne. To put it another way: Why was it, apart from literary conventions and the like, that the wilderness and the men who hunted it were available as a literary theme for William Faulkner in the 1930s, as they clearly were not for William Elliott in the 1830s?

The first and most obvious explanation that must occur to us, of course, is the existence of slavery. Elliott's position as a planter and slaveowner automatically ruled out the material in the fourth section of "The Bear," in which Ike McCaslin comes to terms with the history of guilt and shame, his heritage from old Carothers McCaslin, and chooses to relinquish his patrimony. Not only did Elliott see no reason to question his position as laird of Oak Hall plantation and Chee-Ha, but it would never have occurred to him to do so. Thus we get, instead of the deep, searching inquiry into man's relationship to man and to the land, a brief dismissal of abolitionism and a vignette of the slaveholder as patriarchal master of a childlike race of black peasants. The old German whose ghost retributively stalks the wilderness in the shape of a white deer was being punished, it is true, for cruelty to his slaves, but only for that; there is no suggestion that the very act of owning human beings and living on their involuntary toil, and of participating in a system that made possible what the old German did, might entail sin and demand remission. So far as William Elliott was concerned, slavery was not an institution that importantly involved soul-searching on his part. And in Elliott's time there was no shock of military defeat, no collapse of society, no heritage of military occupation and sense of tragic destiny that was William Faulkner's birthright and that could lead him to have Ike McCaslin think of God's relationship to his southern people in these terms: " 'So that He said and not in grief either Who had made them and so could know no more of Grief than He could of pride or hope: *Apparently they can learn nothing save through suffering, remember nothing save when underlined in blood—.*' " [9]

But the existence of slavery itself will not do as an explanation. We must ask why it worked as it did, not only in Elliott's case but in Simms's and Cooke's and Timrod's and all the other antebellum southern writers —even Poe's. In the late nineteenth century Thomas Nelson Page, himself an aristocrat and heir of slaveholders, wrote of the literature before the war:

The standard of literary work was not a purely literary standard, but one based on public opinion, which in its turn was founded on the general consensus that the existing institution

9. Faulkner, "The Bear," 285–86.

was not to be impugned, directly or indirectly, on any ground or by any means whatsoever.

This was an atmosphere in which literature could not flourish. In consequence, where literature was indulged in it was in a half-hearted way, as if it were not altogether compatible with the social dignity of the author. Thought which in its expression has any other standard than fidelity to truth, whatever secondary value it may have, cannot possess much value as literature.[10]

Page was suggesting, among other things, that the office of man of letters was itself suspect in the Old South, and there is abundant evidence to bear him out. Jay B. Hubbell notes that while William Elliott could publish his hunting sketches under his own name, he chose anonymous publication of his verse tragedy: "It was not desirable that a great planter should be known as the author of a poetic drama."[11] And it is true, too, that as Page and many others have pointed out, the South was a beleaguered aristocracy, and its energy and intelligence went chiefly into political defense. "What might the eloquence and genius of [Henry Clay] have effected had they been turned in the direction of literature[?]," Page asks.[12] Very well, but why were they not thus turned? It is not enough, or even entirely accurate, to say that the profession of letters was itself suspect; I think this has been somewhat overstated. One only has to look at the political career of William Gilmore Simms, attained not only while he was an author but *because* he was an author, to realize that southerners did not automatically suspect all literary men of essential public unsoundness. Simms not only served in the legislature, but with only a modicum of energy expended to make it come about, he might easily have been lieutenant governor or United States congressman if he had so chosen.

---

10. Thomas Nelson Page, "Authorship in the South Before the War," *The Old South: Essays Social and Political* (New York, 1919), 71.

11. Hubbell, *The South in American Literature,* 565–66.

12. Page, "Authorship in the South Before the War," 66.

The idea of the writer having been a pariah in the Old South, though it has its justification, has been rather too narrowly applied. I doubt that anyone would have seriously considered electing Simms's friend Henry Timrod to political office, but Simms was of a different sort. To an extent, then, it depended upon the particular author and his personality. Simms's public role, to repeat, came as a result of, and in recognition of, his literary distinction.

I do not believe, therefore, either that Simms suffered from lack of public recognition because he chose authorship, or that had he lived elsewhere he would have been a major rather than a relatively minor literary talent. He would have prospered more as an author had he lived in New England, perhaps, but that was not what kept Simms from being Hawthorne or Melville. Simms's *talent* was limited. I would turn the matter around, and phrase the question this way: What was there about the Old South and its life that did not attract the attentions of a first-rate intellect and really perceptive imagination? Or that did not permit such intelligence and imagination to fulfill themselves in literature? For an answer, let us look again at William Elliott. What prevented Elliott—who, to judge from what he saw in his hunting sketches, might have produced major literature—from developing, and what kept him a genteel sportsman and dabbler in the arts?

In the year 1849 Simms took over the editorship of the *Southern Quarterly Review* and set out to enlist the support of certain possible contributors. Among those whom he approached was William Elliott. On March 7, 1849, he wrote to Elliott in connection with this, and in the course of his letter he remarked as follows: "Did I not venture to hint to you that all that was necessary to make our Carolina Sports popular was such an incorporation with its details of the Social and Domestic Life of the Parishes, as would absolutely carry the reader to the scene, and supply the relief which is always essential in works whose chief object is exciting event and lively action?" In his writings for the new magazine, Simms told Elliott, he might get at such things: "Note the falling off in our social tone, indicate the causes of degeneracy—the evil influences of the Revolution—the abolition of the rights of Primogeniture—the suicidal practice of intermarriages—in direct hostility with the practice—that of the aristocracy marrying the commoner—thus crossing the breed—by which the British nobility has been made the most splendid race of men in the world.—The subject is a pretty one & the study highly interesting."[13]

Now Simms was correct; in *Carolina Sports* Elliott had not grounded his portrayal of life in field and stream in the social texture of his society. There is, however, one sketch in Elliott's volume that I have not thus far mentioned—one entitled "The Fire Hunter." Unlike the others, this one is not drawn directly from Elliott's own adventures; it is, Elliott says, "illustrative of life," rather than " 'a sketch from life.' " It is not nonfiction, but a short story. He writes it, he declares, in order to expose to public attention "the dangers to property and to life" attendant upon the illicit practice of hunting deer by "fire-hunting" (149). This species of hunting involved lighting a fire, carrying it to where deer were accustomed to feeding at night, and, when the illumination from the fire was reflected in the eyes of a deer, shooting the helpless animal where it stood.

Elliott's sketch tells of an overseer on a plantation who enlisted, half through encouragement and half through fear, the help of a slave in going fire-hunting. The overseer is described as "short, of sinewy frame, with

13. William Gilmore Simms to William Elliott, March 7, 1849, in Mary C. Simms Oliphant, Alfred Taylor Odell, and T. C. Duncan Eaves (eds.), *The Letters of William Gilmore Simms: Vol. II: 1845–1849* (Columbia, S.C., 1953), 495.

high shoulders, lank whitish hair, sallow skin, and vulgar features" (139). Pompey, the slave, is reluctant to
help him: " 'Maussa count pun dem buck for heself,' "
he objects. But the overseer replies as follows:

"Fat or no fat, I have one of them tonight—I'll do it, by jingo,
if I have to walk for it. Here he's been writing to me, as if I
was a nigger, telling me to keep them bucks, till he comes over
with his friends to hunt them. Dang me, if I do. Who gave
them to him? were they born in his cattle pen? have they got
his mark and brand upon them? all that have white tails are in
my mark, and I'll shoot them as I please, and ask no
odds"(140).

The overseer and Pompey go fire-hunting, and they
shoot a deer—and also a colt, by mistake. The overseer
then sends Pompey to the stage house, where he is to
deliver the haunches and loins to a stage driver, who will
sell them for him. This the slave does, but on the way
back, riding with a torch in his hand, he notes where
someone else has been fire-hunting, and then he comes
upon a riderless horse. Pompey rides ahead, and what
he discovers is a dying slave, his own brother. He learns
that his brother has been accidentally shot, while riding
a mule on an errand to buy sugar for his sick wife, by
another fire-hunter, who had seen the lights of the
mule's eyes in the darkness and fired, hitting the rider.
The fire-hunter had made the wounded man promise
not to reveal his identity before placing him on the
mule. When Pompey came in sight with his torch, the
fire-hunter allowed the wounded man to fall from the
mule and rode off to escape detection. The dying slave
gasps out his last words: " 'Maussa musn't say I die like a
tief!—tell um all bout it! If he been here; de firehunter
neber bin shoot me! Feel in me pocket, brudder,—take
out de paper wid de sugar. Oh! me blood upon it. Neber
mind!—gib it to me poor wife; tell 'um to 'member
me!—tell um, for him sake I get me death! I'm cold,—
draw me to the fire'" (148).

William Elliott may have intended for his story to illustrate the dangers "to property and to life" involved in fire-hunting, but it suggests considerably more than that. Clearly it gets directly into the matter of class and caste. The overseer is indignant because in forbidding him to hunt, the master is treating him "as if I was a nigger." Who owns the deer? the poor white asks. What right does the planter have to mark the deer for his own, merely because he holds title to the land? What *is* ownership? the implied question rises. In what sense can one be said to own land, and deer? Why should an absentee landowner have the privilege of preventing those who live on the land from taking its fruits?

And consider the slave. Elliott attempts to show that it is the poor white who corrupts Pompey into helping him. He has the wounded black die with the wish that his brother exonerate him in his master's eyes. But he also has the dying slave remark that *if the master had been there,* he should not have been killed. Because the landowner will not guard his own property, the helpless slave must die. And the slave dies when on an errand of mercy: getting sugar for his sick wife. If the master had been there where he should have been, the slave would not have needed to borrow the mule and ride to the distant store for sugar.

If we will consider these questions, and what they imply, we can begin to understand why it might have been that William Elliott of Beaufort County, South Carolina, preferred to write his sketches of Low Country life in terms of their surface action, and to avoid "repose"—which is to say, contemplation, while turning to sixteenth-century Genoa for literary effort which involved contemplation. I do not suggest that the decision was conscious; in Elliott's instance I simply do not know. But it is obvious that it would have been tremendously dangerous for a man who lived on the land and made his life, livelihood, and recreation out of his relationship

to the land to try to write about that relationship in ways
that would lead him to search out the moral implications
and underlying meanings. To have done what Simms
suggested—attempt to ground his hunting tales in "the
Social and Domestic Life of the Parishes"—could have
turned up far too much that William Elliott of Beaufort
County could not have afforded to discover. Even in a
brief work of fiction designed to show the dangers of
fire-hunting, we have seen what at once presented itself
to his imagination. Simms wanted him to write pro-
southern propaganda; but Elliott's literary imagination
did not work that way.

There is no doubt in my mind that Elliott recognized
some of the social implications. In the note that he
appends to *Carolina Sports,* he discusses the disappearance of deer and game from the Low Country. It comes
about because of the destruction of the forests, he says,
and because of "the demand which has grown up, in our
cities, for the supply of hotels, and of the private tables
of luxurious citizens, with venison"; this has caused professional hunters to slaughter the deer. "It is too much
to expect this class of men to refrain from 'fire hunting,'
though forbidden by law," he says (167). Furthermore,
the average citizens of the region will not observe property lines; they consider it their right to hunt, whether
or not they own land, and have no respect for the rights
of landed proprietors. More than that, the politicians of
the day flatter the prejudices of the electorate and will
not enact laws protecting such property, nor will juries
made up of average citizens convict such poachers; "the
prejudices of the people are against any exclusive property in game, as everyone feels who attempts to keep it
to himself" (171). The average citizen has been infected
with the attitudes toward such property held by "the
laboring immigrants from England," with their resentment of the English game laws. "The preservation of
game is thus associated, in the popular mind, with ideas

of aristocracy,—peculiar privileges to the rich,—and oppression towards the poor!" (172)

As an aristocratic landowner and hunter, Elliott was indignant over such attitudes. But as a writer of fiction—the author of the sketch entitled "The Fire Hunter"—he could not help but recognize another viewpoint: " 'Who gave them to him? were they born in his cattle pen? have they got his mark and brand upon them?'" The imaginative sympathy works directly against what as landowner Elliott wishes to demonstrate. Clearly that kind of insight could not conveniently be brought to bear upon the "Social and Domestic Life of the Parishes" without results that would be profoundly subversive of the comfortable arrangements of the planter society in which William Elliott lived and of which he was so distinguished a member.

He could not, in short, afford to examine himself in relationship to *the land.* Whenever he wrote about it, as we have seen, he kept turning up motifs and insights that would have been deeply disturbing had he allowed himself to follow them up. He could not ground his writing in what he knew, the life of a planter and sportsman in the Low Country of South Carolina, because the result would have been a searching scrutiny of a social structure all too flawed in its design and grounded upon an attitude toward a certain segment of the population that involved grave injustice and inhumanity. Given Elliott's imagination as demonstrated in *Carolina Sports,* this would have been the inescapable outcome of such an inquiry; and William Elliott and his friends did not intend to see it that way. But that way was the inevitable direction in which imaginative fiction would have led him, and no doubt certain others as well—others like him, men of education, refinement, talent, possessed of a deep involvement in the life of their time and place. Thus it was that antebellum southern literature remained an affair of surfaces.

"The Begum of Bengal":
Mark Twain and the South

Of all the southern writers who produced books in that long period between the end of the Civil War and the beginnings of the southern literary renascence of the twentieth century, only one, Mark Twain, was able to escape the cultural shock of defeat in war. So much so, indeed, that many readers do not think of him as a "southern" writer at all—which was precisely what he would appear to have desired, for a while a least. He came onto the postwar American literary scene by way of the Far West. He joyfully published the memoirs of General Grant. He denounced the "United States of Lyncherdom," and he filled the later pages of *Life on the Mississippi* with scathing comments on southern romanticism and southern addiction to the chivalric nonsense of Sir Walter Scott. Twain was born in the South, he

This essay was originally published in Kenneth H. Baldwin and David K. Kirby (eds.), *Individual and Community: Variations on a Theme in American Fiction* (Durham, N.C., 1975), 64–93, a *festschrift* in honor of Charles R. Anderson. Much of the material also appears in Louis D. Rubin, Jr., *The Writer in the South: Studies in a Literary Community,* Mercer University Lamar Memorial Lectures, No. 15 (Athens, Ga., 1972).

28

used to say, but he almost always insisted quickly that he had since learned better.

Yet the matter is not so easily disposed of as that. Not only was he born there: he grew up in the South, he even enlisted in the military defense in 1861, and he wrote his greatest books about the life he had known there. Furthermore, his style of humor came directly out of a literary genre that reached its greatest popularity in the South, and his art remained throughout his life strongly marked by his southern experience. It is this experience, as it relates to his writings, that I wish to consider here.

Discussions of whether Samuel Clemens' literary imagination was importantly southern or not tend too often to get involved in what are really irrelevancies. Was Hannibal, Missouri, a southern or western town when Clemens was living there? Was a pilot's life on the Mississippi before 1861 southern in its forms, or was it western? How serious was Clemens' ideological involvement with the Marion Rangers? Does Mark Twain use the English language the way William Faulkner does, or more as Sherwood Anderson and Ernest Hemingway do? Is the theme of the revolt from the village a southern or a midwestern theme? And so on. These matters have their bearing on the problem, but are not central to it. What is central is the forms that the imagination took, and how the imagination was formed.

We tend, when we begin speaking about the South as a social entity, to think in terms of a part of the South, and then to treat that part as the whole. Politically there has been some justification for doing this, though it seems to be vanishing, but in most other respects it is a dubious business. C. Hugh Holman identifies three distinct modes of southern consciousness, related to three distinct subregions, and he cautions us that "however shadowy the lines of demarcation among them may be and however similar many of their attitudes were, they dreamed different dreams, formulated different social structures, and worshipped different gods. These differences have persisted for a century and a half and they give evidence of being qualities permanent to their various locales."[1] Mr. Holman defines these subregions as the Tidewater, the Deep South, and the Piedmont South. In the last-named, he says, the "society is in many ways more nearly American and less distinctively Southern, except for its grotesquerie," than in the Tidewater and the Deep South; and he points out that unlike the writers of the other two locales, the writers of the Piedmont have judged their homeland by a standard which, "whether it be that of social justice, or religious order, or of moral imagination, has always been an outer and different standard from that embraced by the local inhabitants." He notes Thomas Wolfe's use of the standards of the middle western writers. "Freed from the deep emotional commitment typical of the Tidewater and the Deep South," he declares, "Wolfe could look calmly and critically at his region, deplore its weaknesses, and love its strengths, without indulging in the emotional upheaval over this ambivalent attitude that Quentin Compson suffers in *Absalom, Absalom!*"[2]

Though Mr. Holman would not include Samuel L. Clemens within the geographic boundaries of his southern tryptych, he has given us an interesting access to Mark Twain. The farmlands of eastern Missouri are not part of the Piedmont, but in the days when Samuel L. Clemens was growing up there, they were surely the border South. Hannibal, Missouri, was settled by southerners, it was linked economically to the river and was dependent upon the trade up and down the river, it was a slaveholding community, and when the war broke out

---

1. C. Hugh Holman, *Three Modes of Modern Southern Fiction* (Athens, Ga., 1966), 6.
2. *Ibid.*, 55–57.

it was largely secessionist in sentiment. Its interests, tastes, and attitudes, if we are to believe Dixon Wecter and others who have studied its life, were notably southern—even to the extent that its bookshops offered for sale the *Southern Literary Messenger,* which the Hannibal *Journal* described in 1848 as being far superior to "the wishy washy concerns that issue from the Eastern cites."[3] Hannibal was certainly not part of the Tidewater or the Deep South; it was part of the westward migration from those places. But as DeLancey Ferguson reminds us, "Mark Twain was also a son of the South. To think of him in terms of the Nevada mining camps where he made his first literary reputation, to think of his youthful homes as they look to a New Yorker of today—as too many critics have done—is to miss the strongest forces of his life. Hannibal, Missouri, cannot be interpreted in terms of that rebellion against village and farm which began with Ed Howe in the 1880s and Hamlin Garland in the 1890s. The society Mark Twain lived in was not ours; it must be thought of in terms of its own dreams, not ours."[4]

Samuel Clemens' father, John Marshall Clemens, was a Virginian and a Whig, who before coming to Missouri lived in Kentucky and Tennessee, holding in the last-named state title to considerable land which to his dying day he expected would one day make his family rich. Jane Lampson Clemens, Sam Clemens' mother, was of Kentucky stock. Like her husband she believed in the rightness of slavery throughout her life. "She had never heard it assailed in any pulpit," her son tells us, "but she had heard it defended and sanctified in a thousand; her ears were familiar with Bible texts that approved it, but if there were any that disapproved it they had not been

3. Dixon Wecter, *Sam Clemens of Hannibal* (Boston, 1952), 209.
4. Delancy Ferguson, *Mark Twain: Man and Legend* (Indianapolis, 1943), 15.

quoted by her pastors; as far as her experience went, the wise and the good and the holy were unanimous in the conviction that slavery was right, righteous, sacred, the particular pet of the Deity, and a condition which the slave himself ought to be daily and nightly thankful for."[5]

In a notable passage in *The Flush Times of Alabama and Mississippi,* Joseph Glover Baldwin describes the difficulties that the Virginians had in the frontier South of the 1830s and 1840s, set down as they were, men of honor and pride, among the less scrupulous and less prideful plain folk. "Superior to many of the settlers in manners and general intelligence," Baldwin writes, "it was the weakness of the Virginian to imagine he was superior too in the essential art of being able to hold his hand and make his way in a new country, and especially *such* a country, and at *such* a time."[6] In many respects Baldwin might have been writing about John Marshall Clemens. Dignified, reserved, a man of probity and a high sense of civic role, conscious of his status and of his ancestry, he was respected by his fellow Missouri villagers; but he met financial ruin when he involved himself with a man of considerably humbler origins and stature who, however, was able to inveigle Clemens into a disastrous business transaction. Clemens had owned a few slaves; ultimately he was forced to sell them all. He wasted two hundred dollars of the family's money on a fruitless trip to Tennessee and Mississippi to collect a debt: he could not bear to foreclose on a man who owed him money (and who was apparently fairly well off), but he had no qualms about taking a slave along and disposing of him for ten barrels of tar.[7] When his wife reproached him

5. Mark Twain, *Mark Twain's Autobiography,* I, *Complete Works of Mark Twain: Authorized Edition* (New York, 1924), 123.
6. Joseph G. Baldwin, *The Flush Times of Alabama and Mississippi* (New York, 1957), 66.
7. Wecter, *Sam Clemens of Hannibal,* 74–76.

upon his return for his failure, he tried to justify himself and then, with a "hopeless expression" on his face, added, "I am not able to dig in the streets."[8] But his eldest son, Orion, was forced to go to work as apprentice in a print shop, and at first the comedown involved in having to perform manual labor chagrined the son. As for Sam Clemens, he was too young to go to work then, but when his father died in 1847 he found a job as helper in a print shop.

I have no intention of reciting Samuel L. Clemens' biography, but I would make the point that right here at the outset, in the boyhood of Sam Clemens' life, we have the situation that would become the hallmark of his humor: the awareness of status and the effort to maintain it. Here is the southern family of good standing, minor aristocracy fallen upon evil days, seeking to hold to status and *noblesse oblige* in a more crass and democratic society where aristocratic pose comes close to being quixotic gesture and high-minded scruples of honor become the vulnerability whereby the vernacular land speculator with no such scruples could bring the man of honor down to poverty and ruin. And here is the youth Sam Clemens, admiring and wanting to believe in the heroic gesture, the aristocratic pose, and yet observing its practical ineffectiveness and its weakness, and experiencing the deprivation and embarrassment that it brought to those dependent upon it. In Mark Twain's work the public pose, the claim of the gentleman's privileges to special treatment and respect, is always being contrasted with the leveling processes of a disrespectful vernacular society. In his writings, so much that happens in the fiction and the fact (and the "fact" is often fictionalized) revolves around the question of status, and more particularly the public recognition of

8. *Ibid.*, 77.

status. Colonel Sellers always maintains his role, at whatever cost to credibility. Tom Sawyer constantly strives to "be somebody" in the eyes of the community and stakes everything on the "theatrical gorgeousness" of his performance. "We can't let you into the gang if you ain't respectable, you know," he warns Huck. In *Life on the Mississippi* the town boys envy the deckhand his privileged status, and the cub pilot covets the rank and dignity of the estate of piloting. In *Huckleberry Finn* a poor white boy finds it difficult to humble himself before a black man; two rogues masquerade as visiting nobility; a colonel stares down a lynch mob and berates their commonness. In *A Connecticut Yankee* a master mechanic from Connecticut becomes The Boss and takes down the king and knights of England a step or two. In *The Prince and the Pauper* an urchin changes places with a king. In *Pudd'nhead Wilson* the York Leicester Driscolls, Percy Northumberland Driscolls, and Cecil Burleigh Essexes cling to their privileged roles as best as possible, while a slave woman brags to her mulatto son that he comes from the best blood of Virginia.[9]

Mark Twain constantly makes humor out of this consciousness of status. "Who *is* I? Who *is* I?" declares a black man at a New Orleans dance in *Life on the Mississippi*; "I let you know mighty quick who I is! I want you niggers to understan' dat I fires de middle do on de *Aleck Scott!*"[10] But it was no joke that led the noted humorist Samuel Clemens to reply, when Howells cautioned him not to write "up" to the prestigious *Atlantic Monthly* readership, that "it isn't the Atlantic audience that distresses me; for *it* is the only audience that I sit down to in perfect serenity (for the simple reason that it

9. Arlin Turner, "Mark Twain and the South: An Affair of Love and Anger," *Southern Review*, n.s., IV (1968), 439–519, has thoroughly discussed the relationship of *Pudd'nhead Wilson* to Mark Twain's southern origins.

10. Mark Twain, *Life on the Mississippi*, VII, *Complete Works of Mark Twain: Authorized Edition* (New York, 1924), 122.

don't require a 'humorist' to paint himself striped and stand on his head every fifteen minutes)."[11]

He was no coarse funny man; he was a writer of taste and refinement, he assured Howells. And there was the night when, having made an audience roar with delight all evening, he groaned to his tour campanion George W. Cable, "Oh, Cable, I am demeaning myself. I am allowing myself to be a mere buffoon. It's ghastly. I can't endure it any longer."[12]

To the end of his life he openly sought the limelight, the public recognition that he was something grand and special. Happily he recounted how the policeman in Vienna recognized him and ordered him past the barricade, saying "For God's sake let him pass. Don't you see it's Herr Mark Twain?"[13] When he received his honorary degree from Oxford he wore his scarlet doctoral robe proudly and thereafter displayed it on every possible occasion, remarking that he wished he could wear it around all the time. All through his life he required the external signs of privileged position to keep him convinced that his rank and dignity were real. "His favorite recreation in New York," Justin Kaplan tells us, "when he was not playing billiards was to stroll up and down Fifth Avenue in his white suit, chat with the police, and be stared at."[14] It was as if he never quite believed it, was never completely assured of his status. The doubt, and the need to prove his claim to importance, stayed with him to the finish. He confessed as much, albeit obliquely, in his speech at the farewell dinner tendered him in 1907 by the Lord Mayor of Liverpool when he quoted Richard Henry Dana's anecdote of the skipper of the little coaster sloop who had a

11. Quoted in Henry Nash Smith, *Mark Twain: The Development of a Writer* (Cambridge, Mass., 1962), 93.
12. Quoted in Guy A. Cardwell, *Twins of Genius* (London, 1962), 25.
13. Justin Kaplan, *Mr. Clemens and Mark Twain* (New York, 1966), 353.
14. *Ibid.*, 380.

habit of hailing all passing ships "just to hear himself talk and air his small grandeur," and who hailed an inbound Indiaman, only to hear its majestic identification of itself, "the *Begum,* of Bengal, one hundred and forty-two days out from Canton, homeward bound. What ship is that?" The skipper of the sloop could only squeak back humbly, "Only the *Mary Ann,* fourteen hours out from Boston, bound for Kittery Point—with nothing to speak of!" For an hour of each twenty-four, Mark Twain told his English well-wishers, he lay alone at night with the realization that he was only the *Mary Ann,* fourteen hours out, with vegetables and tinware, but "During all the twenty-three hours my vain self-complacency rides high on the white crest of your approval, and then I am a stately Indiaman, ploughing the great seas under a cloud of canvas and laden with the kindest words that have ever been vouchsafed to any wandering alien in this world, I think; then my twenty-six fortunate days on this old mother soil seem to be multiplied by six, and I *am* the Begum of Bengal, one hundred and forty-two days out from Canton, homeward bound!"[15] It is a beautiful conclusion, and the imagery is revealing, for Samuel Clemens sometimes saw himself very well.

It requires no Freudian psychologist to suggest how importantly the figure of John Marshall Clemens, the proud Virginia-born father unable "to dig in the streets," whose life ended with his family moved in over a friend's drugstore and the family furniture sold to pay debts, possesses his son's imagination. We see him repeatedly in Samuel Clemens' fiction: as the pathetic and amiable Colonel Sellers, as the masterful but blood-feuding figures of aristocracy in *Pudd'nhead Wilson,* and elsewhere. Tom Sawyer, of course, has no liv-

---

15. Mark Twain, "The Last Lotus Club Speech," in *Mark Twain's Speeches,* XXIV, *Complete Works of Mark Twain: Authorized Edition* (New York, 1923), 373–74.

ing father; his only competition for the limelight is with his brother Sid. Huck Finn's father is a vicious old poor-white reprobate who, however, is satisfactorily killed in midnovel, though Huck is spared the knowledge until the close. Of Sam Clemens' relationship with his own father we know that it was distant: "a sort of armed neutrality, so to speak," he described it. His father, he says, only whipped him twice, and then not heavily.[16] But Mark Twain's lifelong love-hate fascination with men of aristocratic bearing, especially southerners, surely grows out of that relationship. Of Judge Driscoll in *Pudd'nhead Wilson* he writes: "In Missouri a recognized superiority attached to any person who hailed from Old Virginia; and this person was exalted to supremacy when a person of such nativity could also prove descent from the First Families of the great commonwealth." The Virginian, he says, "must keep his honor spotless. . . . Honor stood first."[17] But honor was no protection against the willingness of one Ira Stout to use the bankruptcy law and ruin the Clemens family,[18] and honor did not prevent Orion and then Sam from going to work in a print shop, and honor caused a slave girl who had been in the Clemens family for years to be sold down the river. Honor, especially when viewed in retrospect, clearly had its limitations.

In *Huckleberry Finn* we encounter Colonel Grangerford: "His hands was long and thin, and every day of his life he put on a clean shirt and a full suit from head to foot made out of linen so white it hurt your eyes to look at it. . . . There warn't no frivolishness about him, not a bit, and he warn't ever loud. He was as kind as he could be—you could feel that, you know, and so you had

16. Quoted in Wecter, *Sam Clemens of Hannibal*, 67.
17. Mark Twain, *Pudd'nhead Wilson and Those Extraordinary Twins* (Facsimile of the first edition; San Francisco, 1968), 156.
18. Wecter, *Sam Clemens of Hannibal*, 67, reports that town records show no indication of such an incident, but he notes that various sources do indicate the likelihood that something of the sort occurred.

confidence. Sometimes he smiled, and it was good to see; but when he straightened himself up like a liberty-pole, and the lightning begun to flicker out from under his eyebrows, you wanted to climb a tree first, and find out what the matter was afterwards."[19] But this same Colonel Grangerford could take part in a stupid and bloody feud against the Shepherdsons, killing young men and boys, without concerning himself with the human consequences. John Marshall Clemens could serve as judge and justice of the peace, a pillar of rectitude, but he could sell a slave downriver and trade another for ten barrels of tar. It was, in short, splendid to be a Virginian and an aristocrat—if you had no conscience to plague you for your sins.

As for the son, *he* had a conscience, all right; he felt guilt constantly, tormenting himself with it even when no guilt actually existed. Guilt for having given matches to an old drunk in jail, who promptly set fire to the jail and was burned to death; guilt for burlesquing old Captain Isaiah Sellers' newspaper column in New Orleans and shaming the old man into stopping his harmless pontification; guilt for having allowed his badly burned younger brother Henry to be given too large a dose of morphine after the *Pennsylvania* explosion, so that he died; guilt for having violated the purity of Livy Langdon Clemens' Elmira existence with his rough, uncouth, ungenteel way of life; guilt for having taken his young son Langdon out driving, so that he contracted "diphtheria" and died; guilt for having squandered Livy's inheritance and his earnings so that he had to plead bankruptcy; guilt for having fathered Susy Clemens so that she could die a horrible death of meningitis and Jean Clemens so that she could die of epilepsy; guilt for having once believed in slavery; guilt for the insult to Emerson, Longfellow, and Holmes in the Whit-

19. Mark Twain, *The Adventures of Huckleberry Finn,* with an introduction by Lionel Trilling (New York, 1948), 105.

tier Birthday Dinner address; guilt for the loss of his literary powers; guilt for being a member of the "damned human race"—small wonder that Sam Clemens raged against his Presbyterian conscience, slew it in print so often, and in "The Mysterious Stranger" brought Little Satan to Hannibal (moved to Germany for the occasion) in order that the son of the Arch-fiend might teach Tom and Huck that the absurdity known as the "moral sense" was at the root of all men's suffering. "No one, I think," Bernard De Voto has written of Clemens' paper entitled *What Is Man?* "can read this wearisomely repeated argument without feeling the terrible force of an inner cry: Do not blame me, for it was not my fault."[20]

Literary psychologists have expended considerable effort attempting to trace down the sources of Samuel L. Clemens' lifelong affinity for feeling guilty. The official biographer, Albert Bigelow Paine, describes a scene at the time of John Marshall Clemens' death. His son, says Paine, was fairly broken down. "Remorse which always dealt with him unsparingly, laid a heavy hand on him now. Wildness, disobedience, indifference to his father's wishes, all were remembered; a hundred things, in themselves trifling, became ghastly and heartwringing in the knowledge that they could never be undone." Jane Clemens took her son up to the room where his father lay, told him that what had happened did not matter now, and asked him to promise her to be a faithful and industrious man, like his father. That night Jane Clemens and her daughter were awakened to find a form in white entering their room. "Presently a hand was laid on the coverlet, first at the foot, then at the head of the bed." It was Sam, sleepwalking. "He had risen and thrown a sheet around him in his dreams. He walked in his sleep several nights in succession after

20. Bernard De Voto, "Symbols of Despair," *Mark Twain at Work* (Cambridge, Mass., 1942), 116.

that."[21] What Paine does not say is that apparently young Sam Clemens, peeping through a keyhole, had watched a doctor perform a postmortem on his father. As Wecter notes, doubtless the shock of the death and the guilty secret of the postmortem had more to do with the "heavy hand" of remorse and the somnambulism than any deathbed promise to his mother to be a good boy.[22]

What I am attempting to establish is not the nature of the guilt[23] so much as the fact that evidently it had considerable to do with Samuel Clemens' ambivalent feelings toward John Marshall Clemens. The consciousness of his "wildness, disobedience, indifference to his father's wishes," the "hundred things, in themselves trifling," which could nevermore be undone, must indeed have made him aware of his inability to feel proper respect for his father's stoic dignity and to emulate it. He feared his father, he resented his father, and if he felt awe and admiration he also felt contempt. Sam Clemens could not muster, for the memory of John Marshall Clemens and what he stood for, the kind of unquestioning respect that he shows Colonel Grangerford receiving in *Huckleberry Finn.* He did not believe in it, or in any case believe in it enough to live by it. His father was not only the lordly Colonel Grangerford; he was also the impractical Squire Hawkins and the unworldly Colonel Sellers of *The Gilded Age;* and the judge of *Huckleberry Finn* whose sentimentality delivered Huck over to his father's sordid brutality; and the credulous King Arthur of *A Connecticut Yankee* who allowed Merlin to hoodwink him so thoroughly; and every other gen-

21. Albert Bigelow Paine, *Mark Twain: A Biography* (New York, 1912), I, 74–75.
22. Wecter, *Sam Clemens of Hannibal,* 117–18.
23. For a survey of the long history of critical dispute over the nature of Mark Twain's "wound," see Lewis Leary, "Mark Twain's Wound: Standing with Reluctant Feet," in his *Southern Excursions: Essays on Mark Twain and Others* (Baton Rouge, 1971), 42–74.

tleman of aristocratic pretensions who proved either culpable or vulnerable, or both, in a wicked world.

In Mark Twain's day there was a literary tradition, or more precisely a subliterary, journalistic tradition, which was based squarely on the humor implicit in the confrontation of gentlemanly refinement and breeding with the vernacular shrewdness and realism of the new country beyond the Appalachians. The tradition had moved westward with the southern frontier—from Longstreet's rural Georgia to Baldwin's flush times in Alabama and Mississippi to Thorpe's big bear of Arkansas. It was not the literature of the Old South and the Northeast; it did not draw on the plantation stereotype and the chivalry of Sir Walter Scott; its language convention was not that of the historical romance. But it was equally a part of the southern experience, and always had been. It was to this literary mode that Samuel Clemens instinctively turned, composing squibs in the print shop of Orion Clemens' newspaper and later scribbling tales while in various places West, East, and South, as well as in the pilothouse of steamboats on the river. He was always writing something, his teacher and crony Horace Bixby remembered. And had Clemens been only a journalist, only a southwestern funnyman, that is doubtless the vein he would have worked the rest of his life. But he was not merely a comic journalist. He was Samuel L. Clemens, for whom being funny was not enough. He went West for a few years, then East, and each of his books, as Henry Nash Smith shows so convincingly, steadily deepened their exposure to the values that lay beneath the comedy upon the surface.[24]

The little village of Hannibal became St. Petersburg, and then Dawson's Landing and Hadleyburg, and finally Eseldorf. The gap between the real and the ideal, at first merely humorous, grew into a chasm that laugh-

24. Smith, *Mark Twain: The Development of a Writer*, 93.

ter could no longer bridge, until the rage at its failure to do so turned into a desperate effort for transcendence, the attempt to convince oneself that "you perceive, *now,* that these things are all impossible, except in a dream. You perceive that they are pure and puerile insanities, the silly creations of an imagination that is not conscious of its freaks—in a word, that they are a dream, and you the maker of it."[25] At such times the best thing to do is to solace oneself with the thought that, for twenty-three hours a day at least, in the eyes of the world one is no small thing, but the *Begum,* of Bengal, one hundred and forty-two days out from Canton, homeward bound.

What has this vision to do with the South? Simply everything. For what we have is a situation in which the private experience of the writer matches so perfectly the public meaning of the time and place that the concerns of one serve to exemplify and embody the concerns of the other. Henry Nash Smith has shown how the art of Mark Twain involves a developing exploration of the potentialities of the vernacular democratic culture as a replacement for the Official Culture, and of how this exploration was embodied in language. In an early work such as *Innocents Abroad,* the vernacular values of the narrator clash with traditional cultural attitudes toward the art, history, and sacred institutions of the Old World. In *Tom Sawyer* the genteel narrator serves only as a frame, with the chief narrator focus placed on the direct description of Tom's experience in the village. In *Huckleberry Finn,* through using for persona the viewpoint of a youth whose relationship to polite society is peripheral and disaffiliated, Mark Twain moves into a critique of the professed values of the society. The contradictions between the idealistic pieties and inflated rhetoric and the realities of selfishness, repression, sen-

25. Mark Twain, "No. 44, The Mysterious Stranger," in William M. Gibson (ed.), *Mark Twain's Mysterious Stranger Manuscripts* (Berkeley and Los Angeles, 1966), 405.

timentality, and brutality are given ever more savage exposure, until the story threatens to turn into a tragedy, so that the author must yank it back into burlesque. Is not this process, with its developing tension between aristocratic and democratic, genteel and vernacular, romantic and realistic modes, exemplified on the personal level in the child Sam Clemens' mixed admiration and contempt for the Virginian John Marshall Clemens? And on the historical, political level in the movement of the border South away from the aristocratic ideal of the old Tidewater? And does not the progressive discovery of the possibilities of the plain style, the "language of truth," as Lionel Trilling will have it,[26] embody in language the dynamics of the breakthrough from the windblown metaphor and ornate literary diction of so much Old South writing?

Mark Twain did not have to invent his style out of nowhere. The model was at hand—but in the subliterature and journalism of the Old Southwest humor. What he did was to intensify and elevate that style into the full imaginative ordering of literature. This was his triumph, his great contribution to the development of American fiction. The midwestern realists of the 1890s and thereafter would adopt it for their purposes but would use it for deliberate understatement; they would turn its simplicity into a means of depicting innocence betrayed, which was never Mark Twain's approach and was not what *Huck Finn* was about at all. The twentieth-century southerners would use it to cut away the excesses of the old high style and give new sinew and strength to the sensuous documentation of experience. It is impossible to read a work such as "Spotted Horses" or "The Bear," or the better stories of Flannery O'Connor, for example, without seeing the example of the prose style of Mark Twain. With each step away from

26. Lionel Trilling, introduction to *The Adventures of Huckleberry Finn*, xviii.

the literary language of genteel society, Mark Twain moves away from the official pieties and values of the community toward a searching scrutiny of those values. To cite only one example of many such, the joyful community affirmation of the church service in *Tom Sawyer,* in which the congregation choruses "Old Hundred" when the supposedly drowned youths return in glory, becomes, when seen through Huck's eyes and Huck's language, the hypocrisy of Miss Watson at prayer and the orgiastic sentimentality of the King at the camp-meeting (a scene drawn directly from southwestern humor by way of Simon Suggs).

We might profitably compare the camp-meeting scene to William Faulkner's portrayal of the Reverend Hightower and his relationship with the congregation in *Light in August.* Hightower perceives, at the end of the novel, that "that which is destroying the Church is not the outward groping of those within it nor the inward groping of those without, but the professionals who control it and who have removed the bells from the steeples."[27] Faulkner criticizes the perversion and prostitution of the religious values by those entrusted with their affirmation, but Mark Twain suggests that religion and piety themselves are hypocrisy and selfishness; when Huck decides "All right, then, I'll go to hell!" it is organized religion itself that is found wanting. But here Holman's distinction is useful. Faulkner is of the Deep South, whose writers, like those of the Tidewater, "have found the standards to judge their societies in the ideals of their citizens, however little these ideals found firm expression" within the society itself, while Mark Twain is of the border South, where "the standard by which it is judged, whether it be that of social justice, of religious order, or of moral indignation, has always been an outer and different standard from that embraced by the local

---

27. William Faulkner, *Light in August* (New York, 1950), 426.

inhabitants."[28] The border South of which Sam Clemens was part was engaged, in Clemens' own time, in just such a breaking away from the aristocratic ideal of the Tidewater and the Deep South as characterized the Piedmont South of a later day, toward a more generally American frame of reference; and the movement of Sam Clemens away from Hannibal and onto the river and then to West and back East embodies the process of dislodgment. Not simply the values of the society being left behind, but the tensions of the breakaway itself, are part of the southern experience.

Yet one might well ask this: if what is important is the breaking away, the dislodgment, then at what point in the transaction does the original identity cease importantly to matter? Granted that Samuel Clemens was born into a southern community, does he not cease, fairly early in the development of his art, to be part of it?

The answer, I believe, is that the essence of the art *is* the breaking away and is constituted of the tension between the pull of the old community and that of the forces separating the individual from it. In the art the separation can never really be effected, since the comedy and the pathos alike of Mark Twain's work consist of the effort to separate and the effort to resist the separation, expressed not uncharacteristically in the humor of incongruity. Here we have to watch Sam Clemens very carefully, for he was a master of disguise and duplicity. Consider the famed castigation of the Old South, the diagnosis of Sir Walter Scott disease that caused fake medieval castles to be built in Baton Rouge and "created rank and caste down there, and also reverence for rank and caste, and pride and pleasure in them."[29] Huck Finn himself diagnosed the Sir Walter Scott disease in this fashion: "So then I judged that all that stuff was only just one of Tom Sawyer's lies. I

28. Holman, *Three Modes of Modern Southern Fiction*, 53.
29. Twain, *Life on the Mississippi*, 376.

reckoned he believed the A-rabs and the elephants, but as for me I think different. It had all the marks of a Sunday-school."[30]

Yet Mark Twain cannot end that novel without summoning back Tom Sawyer and his A-rabs and elephants, and in defiance of the laws of fictional probability must bring him back onto the scene for the Phelps Farm "evasion." And as for rank and caste, he has Colonel Sherburn step out into the squalor and mud of the main street of Bricksville and shoot an old drunk who abuses him and then stand off a lynch mob, for all the world the defiant aristocrat who has contemptuously refused to be soiled by the riffraff. Sherburn tells the mob, with what can only be considered the full approval of Mark Twain (who has even shifted his persona from Huck to Sherburn for the purpose of having the speech delivered):

I was born and raised in the South, and I've lived in the North; so I know the average all around. The average man's a coward. In the North he lets anybody walk over him that wants to, and goes home and prays for a humble spirit to bear it. In the South one man, all by himself, has stopped a stage full of men in the daytime, and robbed the lot. Your newspapers call you a brave people so much that you think you *are* braver than any other people—whereas you're just as brave, and no braver. Why don't your juries hang murderers? Because they are afraid the man's friends will shoot them in the back, in the dark—and it's just what they *would* do.[31]

The trouble with southern writing, Samuel Clemens tells us in *Life on the Mississippi,* is that it hangs onto its old, inflated style— "filled with wordy, windy, flowery 'eloquence,' romanticism, sentimentality"—while the North has now discarded it.[32] But here is a three-sentence description of sunrise on the Mississippi from the same book:

30. Twain, *Adventures of Huckleberry Finn,* 14.
31. *Ibid.,* 259.
32. Twain, *Life on the Mississippi,* 377.

You have the intense green of the massed and crowded foliage near by; you see it paling shade by shade in front of you; upon the next projecting cape, a mile off or more, the tint has lightened to the tender young green of spring; the cape beyond that one has almost lost color, and the furthest one, miles away under the horizon, sleeps on the water a mere dim vapor, and hardly separable from the sky above it and about it. And all this stretch of river is a mirror, and you have the shadowy reflections of the leafage and the curving shores and the receding capes pictured in it. Well, that is all beautiful: soft and rich and beautiful; and when the sun gets well up and distributes a pink flush here and a powder of gold yonder and a purple haze where it will yield the best effect, you grant that you have seen something that is worth remembering.[33]

It is not a bad passage at all, but is is a far cry from Huck Finn's way of putting things, though if Tom Sawyer had written the next book instead of Huck he would have said it pretty much like that. The point is that when Mark Twain sounds off about the South's reliance upon the rhetorical embellishment, he is also chastising an aspect of himself, and not something he has long since put permanently behind him. Tom Sawyer's way of building up his adventures so that they will provide "theatrical gorgeousness" is the way of Sir Walter Scott, and though Mark Twain pokes fun at it, the next minute he will turn around and do the same sort of thing himself. Let us not forget that the book that follows *Huckleberry Finn* is *A Connecticut Yankee*, which however it satirizes feudalism involves an exploit that Tom Sawyer would have been proud to bring off.

It has always seemed to me that in *A Connecticut Yankee* the whole ambivalent love-hate relationship of Sam Clemens with the South is dramatized and laid out plainly. That the Arthurian England that Hank Morgan, master mechanic from Connecticut, sets out to reform is in effect the South of Clemens' youth is clear from the very outset, as in the Yankee's description of

33. *Ibid.*, 259.

the first town he sees: "In the town were some substantial windowless houses of stone scattered among a wilderness of thatched cabins; the streets were mere crooked alleys, and unpaved; troops of dogs and nude children played in the sun and made life and noise; hogs roamed and rooted contentedly about, and one of them lay in a reeking wallow in the middle of the main thoroughfare and suckled her family."[34] Substitute a few details, and that could be Hannibal, St. Petersburg, Bricksville, or Dawson's Landing. Hank Morgan is appalled by the squalor and the torpor, and proceeds to show the king and the knights of the Round Table what Yankee know-how and democratic egalitarianism can do toward eradicating the feudal backwardness of Old England. It is not long before he has the knights going about on their errantry wearing advertising boards and with soap commercials on the trimmings of their noble steeds. At the crisis of his battle to eradicate feudalism, he challenges a horde of armed knights to a battle to the death, and pots eleven of them with his Colt revolvers, causing the others to break and flee. "Knight-errantry was a doomed institution," he exults. "The march of civilization was begun. How did I feel? Ah you never could imagine it." Thereupon he sets out to modernize Old England, and he does pretty well;

Now look around on England. A happy and prosperous country, and strangely altered. Schools everywhere, and several colleges; a number of pretty good newspapers. Even authorship was taking a start. . . . Slavery was dead and gone; all men were equal before the law; taxation had been equalized. The telegraph, the telephone, the phonograph, the type-writer, the sewing machine, and all the thousand willing and handy servants of steam and electricity were working their way into favor.

Even a stock market had been instituted:

34. Samuel Langhorne Clemens, *A Connecticut Yankee in King Arthur's Court* (Facsimile of the first edition; San Francisco, 1963), 28.

Sir Launcelot, in his richest armor, came striding along the great hall, now, on his way to the stock-board; he was president of the stock-board, and occupied the Siege Perilous, which he had bought of Sir Galahad; for the stock-board consisted of the Knights of the Round Table, and they used the Round Table for business purposes, now. Seats at it were worth—well, you would never believe the figure, so it is no use to state it. Sir Launcelot was a bear, and he had put up a corner in one of the new lines, and was just getting ready to squeeze the shorts to-day; but what of that?[35]

As we know, however, it does not succeed. The medieval Church, with its massive authority of superstition, pronounces an Interdict. The supposedly democratized and liberated freemen revert to their former state of cowed, timid slavery. Everything is shut down, and ultimately the massed chivalry of Arthurian England marches against Hank Morgan's fortress. With horrible savagery the Yankee and his few loyal followers blow up, electrocute, or otherwise annihilate the entire establishment, their own citadel included. At the end only the Yankee is left, to sleep for eleven centuries under Merlin's spell, awakening briefly in the nineteenth century to die at last, lonely and lost, dreaming of a simple love long ago.

Henry Nash Smith has convincingly interpreted the tale as Mark Twain's fable of progress, and he identifies the terrible demolition at the close as an expression of the author's despair at the moral implications of the vernacular culture of the capitalistic nineteenth century. Because he could not finally discover a meaning for the society that has replaced what he had known and had rejected, he blew the whole experiment to smithereens. "He had planned a fable illustrating how the advance of technology fosters the moral improvement of mankind. But when he put his belief to the test by attempting to realize it in fiction, the oracle of his imagination, his institution, the unconsciously formulated conclusions

35. *Ibid.*, 515–16.

based on his observation and reading, his childhood heritage of Calvinism, at any rate some force other than his conscious intention convinced him that his belief in progress and human perfectibility was groundless."[36]

What I find interesting is the striking appropriateness of the story and its outcome to the South that Sam Clemens knew—a relevance that Smith and also James M. Cox, in *Mark Twain: The Fate of Humor,* have recognized. In effect it is a fable of the New South, as I see it. Is not the picture of the "happy and prosperous country" that Hank Morgan, the Yankee, creates out of the feudalism of Old England very much akin to the vision of the New South as advanced by Henry W. Grady, Marse Henry Watterson, and many others during Samuel Clemens' time, and which would convert the former Confederacy into a replica of the industrial Northeast where the adult Samuel Clemens lived? Factories, schools, newspapers, commerce, all the modern inventions; slavery dead and gone, and the former knights-errant become stockbrokers who "used the Round Table for business purposes, now"—this is just how he described and praised the up-to-date aspects of commercial New Orleans in *Life on the Mississippi.* Every one of the improvements is cited, and praised, even down to the newspapers and the authorship. If only the entire South, he suggests in that book, would throw off its "Walter Scott Middle-Age sham civilization," its "silliness and emptiness, sham grandeurs, sham gauds, and sham chivalries of a brainless and worthless long-vanished society," then it, like New England, might amount to something in the world.[37]

At times in *A Connecticut Yankee* he is explicit about the South's similarity to feudal England. Describing the

---

36. Smith, *Mark Twain: The Development of a Writer,* 170. Smith's more extensive analysis of *A Connecticut Yankee* is *Mark Twain's Fable of Progress* (New Brunswick, N.J., 1964).

37. Twain, *Life on the Mississippi,* 375.

callousness with which a group of pilgrims watched slaves being driven along a road, Hank Morgan comments, "They were too much hardened by lifelong every-day familiarity with slavery to notice that there was anything else in the exhibition that invited comment. That was what slavery could do, in the way of ossifying what one may call the superior lobe of human feeling; for these pilgrims were kindhearted people, and they would not have allowed a man to treat a horse like that."[38] Again, when Hank Morgan becomes disgusted with the way that oppressed peasantry instinctively sides with its noble oppressors, it "reminded me of a time thirteen centuries away, when the 'poor whites' of our South who were always despised and frequently insulted, by the slave-lords all around them, and who owed their basic condition simply to the presence of slavery in the midst, were yet pusillanimously ready to side with slave-lords in all political moves for the perpetuating of slavery, and did also finally shoulder their muskets and pour out their lives in an effort to prevent the destruction of that very institution which degraded them."[39]

Yet when the railroads and the factories and the telephones come, and the Round Table becomes a stock market, and moneymaking replaces knight-errantry and chivalry, the outcome is not what is hoped. Not at all. So that the author's attitude toward Hank Morgan seems to change. Toward the end he becomes more callous, and when having slaughtered twenty-five thousand knights he issues congratulatory battle communiques that burlesque those of Napoleon and the generals of the Civil War, the Yankee has changed from being an emissary of progress and freedom into a smug, conceited, cold-blooded warlord himself. He has wiped out feudalism and slavery and backwardness, but at the

38. Twain, *A Connecticut Yankee*, 262.
39. *Ibid.*, 387.

cost of dehumanizing himself and becoming a symbol of the nineteenth century's much more efficient brand of military destruction. The arrival of industrial capitalism in the green fields of Old England had proved pretty much of a disaster.

One of the drawings that Dan Beard did for the original edition of *A Connecticut Yankee* is quite revealing in this respect. It illustrates an episode in which King Arthur, though he wishes to see how the common people live, refuses the Yankee's suggestion that he learn to refer to a peasant as friend or brother. "Brother!—to dirt like that?" he asks. Beard provides a three-part drawing. The first shows a fat, bloated king, before whom a peasant in chains bows his head. The second shows an equally fat, bloated southern planter, complete with wide-brimmed hat and whip, with a black slave before him wearing a halter. The third shows a smug, officious-looking nineteenth-century businessman, with a workingman standing before him. Beneath the picture of the king is a sword, beneath that of the planter is a law book, and beneath that of the industrialist is a group of money bags. Under each drawing appears the identical cutline, three times repeated: "Brother!—to dirt like that?"[40]

I am not suggesting that in *A Connecticut Yankee* Samuel L. Clemens sat down to compose an allegory of the New South. What I am saying is that he envisioned feudal England in terms of the South and set out to show how it could be made into a garden with the coming of progress, industrial development, and democracy, only to realize at the end that the nineteenth-century industrial capitalism of northeastern society was no valid alternative—whereupon he destroyed the whole thing in his rage and frustration and ended with a lonely old man dreaming of a simpler past, a man very

40. *Ibid.*, 363.

much out of place in the modern world. The confusion of the fable, I believe, comes directly out of Samuel Clemens' southern origins, and its roots go all the way back to the Hannibal days. We can observe the results all too clearly in the episode in which Hank Morgan tries to tutor King Arthur in the ways of imitating the manner and bearing of the peasantry. For such purposes, he says, "your soldierly stride, your lordly port—these will not do. You stand too straight, your looks are too high, too confident . . . shamble. . . . You see, the genuine spiritlessness is wanting; that's what's the trouble."[41] The intent of the passage, and of several others, is to show that the peasantry has been so beaten down by oppression that its members are cowed and defeated. But what goes wrong is Samuel Clemens' ambivalent attitude toward aristocracy; he admires King Arthur's dignity and manliness so much that it becomes a matter not of upbringing but of inherent kingly character. King Arthur is a *king*; it is inborn in him, and Samuel Clemens admires just that kingliness, even though the implications happen to be disastrous for his social theorizing. Arthur is a king *because* he is kingly, and thus he will not compromise. One is reminded of Clemens' description of his father, as "Judge Carpenter," in his unpublished "Villagers of 1840–43": "Silent, austere, of perfect probity and high principle; ungentle of manner toward his children, but always a gentleman in his phrasing—and never punished them—a look was enough, and more than enough."[42] This kind of figure appears constantly in Mark Twain's fiction.

One could go on in this fashion with *A Connecticut Yankee*, but there is no need for it. The southern experience of Samuel L. Clemens is so thoroughly and deeply imaged in his life and work that one may scarcely read a

41. *Ibid.*, 361–62.
42. Mark Twain, "Villagers of 1840–43," in Walter Blair (ed.), *Mark Twain's Hannibal: Huck and Tom* (Berkley and Los Angeles, 1969), 43.

chapter of any of his books without encountering it. It was, after all, no callow youth, but a twenty-four-year-old man, who quit the Marion Rangers and joined his brother Orion for the journey out to the silver fields. How much more important to Sam Clemens the issues and loyalties of the Civil War must have been than he pretends they were in "The Private History of a Campaign That Failed," in which the Confederate enlistment is depicted simply as a lark by unthinking boys. Surely it went deeper than that. Cox ascribes Clemens' later zeal to identify himself as a loyal Radical Republican to the zeal of a popular humorist to have the approval of his audience, and his fear that such approval would be withheld if his southern past were known. Until the "Private History" was published in 1885, Cox declares:

The Civil War had been the great unwritten experience in the tall tale of his past. Moreover, it had been not simply forgotten, but evaded—and evaded from the very beginning. The discovery of "Mark Twain" in the Nevada Territory in 1863, while it had been Samuel Clemens' discovery of his genius, had quite literally been a way of escaping the Civil War past which lay behind him in Missouri. In effect, the humorous identity and personality of "Mark Twain" was a grand evasion of the Civil War. His form, the tall tale, was a means of converting all the evasions and failures of Samuel Clemens into the invasions and excursions of Mark Twain. Thus, aspects of the innocent, the gullible, the foolish, and the incompetent "young" Mark Twain are rehearsed by the experienced and "old" Mark Twain. Omitted in this humorous strategy is the transition between youth and age, failure and success, innocence and knowledge.[43]

And this, I think, is largely true. For the greatest art of Mark Twain is an art of childhood—Tom Sawyer in St. Petersburg, the cub pilot learning his trade (but never practicing it), Huck Finn and Jim on the raft. "So endeth this chronicle," *Tom Sawyer* concludes. "It being

43. James M. Cox, *Mark Twain: The Fate of Humor* (Princeton, N. J., 1966), 196.

strictly the history of a *boy*, it must stop here; the story could not go on much further without becoming the history of a man."[44] But into that childhood the author thrust the concerns of his adult years. Tom Sawyer is a "hymn to boyhood," but it is a boyhood in which the nostalgic image of an innocent childhood in a drowsing little town is made the scene of a young boy's determined battle for recognition and fame within the community, culminating in heroism, success, the accolades of the leading citizens, and wealth—money let out at 6 percent. It *must* end, all right, for what else could Tom do to maintain the delusion that the A-rabs and the elephants were all about him, and not just the Sunday school? The riverboat cub pilot of *Life on the Mississippi*, significantly younger and more naive than Sam Clemens was when he learned his trade, masters his craft and becomes a pilot; but there the story ends, to be resumed one page and twenty-one years later when the former pilot turned author comes back to inspect the river again. Besides, now that the tugboats and barges have taken over, and the pilot's association has been outmaneuvered by the boat owners, "the association and the noble science of piloting were things of the dead and pathetic past!"[45] Huck Finn, who did not believe in A-rabs and elephants, flees from the conformity and hypocrisy of the village and sets out on the long voyage downriver, his companion a runaway slave. As the journey progresses, the exploration of the corruption of the society along the banks widens, culminating in Colonel Sherburn's denunciation of the mob and then the claustrophobic, suffocating presentation of ignorant cruelty and emotion-starved sentimentality that is the Wilkes family episode. After that, Jim is sold into captivity, and Huck makes his liberating decision: to disregard the

44. Mark Twain, *The Adventures of Tom Sawyer*, I, *Complete Works of Mark Twain: Authorized Edition* (New York, 1922), 292.
45. Twain, *Life on the Mississippi*, 142.

"conscience" that his society has given him to distinguish between right and wrong and free his friend. But when he arrives at Phelps Farm, it is not really a Deep South farm that he finds: it is that of Sam Clemens' uncle, John Quarles, in Florida, Missouri,[46] only viewed not as the child Sam Clemens knew it but as it would appear to Huck Finn. Using Huck for his persona, Clemens can see the country of his youth without the blinders of nostalgia. But Huck cannot *act*. So along comes Tom Sawyer and the great evasion and the terrible anticlimax at the close in which we learn that Tom has known all along that Jim was free.

Why that wretched undercutting? Why could not Mark Twain have let Tom help Huck to free the slave? Because Samuel Clemens knew only too well that the boy that Tom Sawyer symbolized could never have set a slave free. Such was the continuing hold of his southern childhood upon Samuel Clemens' imagination: Huck might assume Tom's name at the farm, but Huck, with what he knew, could never *be* Tom. Yet Mark Twain had to become Tom again in order to end the novel.

Artistically, all that follows *Huckleberry Finn* is a comedown. In *A Connecticut Yankee* the Old South, with its feudalism and pseudochivalric ideal, is changed into the postwar industrial society of the urban Northeast, but that does not work either and must be erased in explosion and rage. In *Pudd'nhead Wilson* the drowsing village becomes Dawson's Landing with its confused and hopeless nightmare of miscegenation, hypocrisy, and violence; black is white, white black; the upright Virginia-born judge is dishonored and murdered. It has not helped to change things around so that the enslaved man is white and the aristocrat is a Negro; for the slavewoman whose story it is, what matters in life has been destroyed: "Her hurts were too deep for money to

46. For a discussion of the imagery of the Quarles Farm in Clemens' fiction, see Smith, *Mark Twain: The Development of a Writer,* 129–32.

heal; the spirit in her eyes was quenched, her martial bearing departed with it, and the voice of her laughter ceased in the land. In her church and its affairs she found her only solace." Clemens is clearly unable to make any sense of the story; significantly, even the active persona of Mark Twain is missing from the scene, appearing only in the calender entries which serve as headnotes for the chapters. We are left with Pudd'nhead Wilson's cynical maxim for summation: "October 12, the *Discovery*. It was wonderful to find America, but it would have been more wonderful to miss it."[47]

Mark Twain was born in the border South, of a Virginian father and a Kentucky-born mother. He grew up in a little slaveholding village along the river, a village very much like others in the country beyond the Tidewater and the mountains, where in his own words, "there were grades of society; people of good family, people of unclassified family, people of no family. Everybody knew everybody, and was affable to everybody, and nobody put on any visible airs; yet the class lines were quite clearly drawn, and the familiar social life of each class was restricted to that class. It was a little democracy that was full of Liberty, Equality, and Fourth of July, and sincerely so, too; yet you perceive that the aristocratic taint was there."[48] *His* family, by birth and pretension at least, was of the aristocracy, and his father a lawyer and leading citizen of the village. But in that town and in that time and place, it was not enough to be an aristocrat; for this was not Virginia, but the border South, where the land was too cheap and people too much on the move to remain within the old patterns. Unable and unwilling to lower himself, as he must have seen it, to the requirements for prospering in that new country, John Marshall Clemens failed and left his son a

47. Twain, *Pudd'nhead Wilson*, 142.
48. Mark Twain, "Jane Lampson Clemens," in Blair (ed.), *Mark Twain's Hannibal*, 46.

legacy of decline and fall, the pride of honorable bearing and the knowledge of its pathos and its inadequacy.

Had Samuel Clemens been born in the Deep South and had things worked out there in the same way, the literary result might well have been the equivalent of the Quentin Compson of *The Sound and the Fury,* holding desperately to concepts of southern honor in a world of Snopses and change, and finding a resolution only in tragedy. But this was the border South, and he was Sam Clemens of Missouri, who perceived the absurdity equally with the pathos.

Or to speculate further—always a risky business, to be sure—had he lived further South, the war might have caught him up in its magnitude—and surely his father would have wanted it that way for him, once Virginia had been invaded—and left him trapped in the confusion and the shock of the defeated Confederacy. Instead he went West with his brother, became a humorist, and then came East, where he flung himself gleefully into the money-making frenzy of the Gilded Age, scheming to make millions with typesetting machines and kaolin compounds in much the same way that Tom Sawyer dreamed of pirate gold. But all the while the forces of his creative imagination held ferociously on, in resentment and in pride, to that faraway country of his youth. Again and again he sought in art to find in the play of his memory the order and meaning that would tell him who he was. In comedy he strove to articulate and resolve the tensions, incongruities, and contradictions that his restless self scrutiny kept turning up. His great weapon was laughter. When finally it failed, he was left high and dry, dictating rambling memories to a secretary, along with furious but ineffective tirades against a hostile universe.

When we come to assess the place of Samuel L. Clemens in the story of southern literature, this much seems obvious. Clemens, as no one else in southern literature before the twentieth century, brought to bear upon the southern experience a critical scrutiny that enabled him to search below the surface pieties and loyalties and get at the underlying conflicts and tensions within the society. It seems safe to say that he saw these things so well because they were to be found within his own heart as well as in the life around him. No other southern writer came close to the liberation he achieved. He was able to do it for two reasons. The first was that by accident of time and place he was jarred loose from the southern community in a way that none of the others were, with the social tensions involved therein present within his family and his society. The second reason, of course, was that he was Mark Twain.

He stands, with all his genius and his shortcomings, in a relationship to the society he knew which anticipates that of the generation of writers who came to literary maturity after the First World War. Not for decades after his time would there be other southern writers who would find themselves both tied to and dissociated from the southern community in something like the way he was. When that day came, the twentieth-century southern literary renascence would be underway.

In February of 1901 a gathering was held at Carnegie Hall in New York City to celebrate the ninety-second birthday of Abraham Lincoln. The purpose was to raise funds for the Lincoln Memorial University at Cumberland Gap, Tennessee. Colonel Henry Watterson, editor of the Louisville *Courier-Journal* and a leading propagandist for the New South of commerce and industry, was the featured speaker, and to introduce the noted Marse Henry the sponsors called upon a cousin of his, Samuel L. Clemens. Mark Twain opened with some humorous remarks, and then went on about how he and Henry Watterson, both of them former Rebels, were, like thousands of other southern boys who had fought bravely for the flag they loved, proud to pay homage to Abraham Lincoln, remembering only that "we are now indistinguishably fused together and nameable by one common great name—Americans."[49]

It was a fairly standard reconciliation speech, one of many such made by many southerners during those years. The curious thing, however, is the pose that Samuel L. Clemens was assuming for that occasion. "We of the South are not ashamed," he declared, of having fought against the Union, for "we did our bravest best, against despairing odds, for the cause that was precious to us and which our conscience approved; and we are proud—and you are proud—the kindred blood in your veins answers when I say it—you are proud of the record we made in those mighty collisions in the fields."[50]

Knowing what we do of the several weeks of active avoidance of all possible collisions in the fields of Missouri that marked the entire Civil War record of Lieutenant Samuel Clemens of the Marion Rangers, what are we to make of that performance? Was he being ironic? What would Huck Finn have thought of it? God only knows. I doubt very much that Mark Twain knew himself.

---

49. Mark Twain, "On Lincoln's Birthday," in *Mark Twain's Speeches,* 231.
50. *Ibid.,* 230.

Politics and the Novel:
George W. Cable
and the Genteel Tradition

My subject is the rather broad and, happily, permissive
one of the various ways in which works of literature can
be affected by, and also can affect, the politics of a time
and a place. Of course it is foolish to maintain (as I have,
however, heard it sometimes maintained) that there is
no political dimension to some works of literature—
that, let us say, *Alice in Wonderland* or "Dover Beach"
is nonpolitical. For if politics, as has been remarked, is
the way in which men strive to give order to their social
arrangements, then any novel be it *Alice in Wonderland*
or *The Old Man and the Sea* or *The Lord of the Rings* or *The
Charterhouse of Parma* or *All the King's Men* or *The Am-
bassadors*—must be political, in the sense that it attempts
to portray men as they exist in relation to other men: to
society.

However, this is not to say that since every work of
literature involves politics, then the way to read and
judge every work of literature is in accordance with its

This essay was prepared for a colloquium on "The Writer and the Politics of
His Age" at Temple University, Philadelphia, Pennsylvania, September 18,
1970.

overt or latent political implications. What I shall be concerned with, therefore, is not the crude judgment of novels and novelists in terms of their party politics, but some of the ways in which the imagination of the novelist is involved with the political milieu of his time and place.

I want to deal with a novel that has interested me for many years, ever since I first came upon it in a used-book sale in downtown Philadelphia back in the mid-1950s. The novelist who wrote it is not one of our foremost literary figures, and the novel is certainly not a major novel. But George W. Cable was a good novelist, and *John March, Southerner* is, though seriously flawed, an interesting novel, I think—and the time and place in which it was written, the United States of America in the late nineteenth century, are not without considerable relevance, and even considerable similarity to our own instance. For the topical problems with which the novelist sought to deal—race, privilege, democracy, the use and misuse of natural and human resources—still engage our attention today, and indeed we are what we are and where we are today in large part because of what was done and not done to solve those problems in the late nineteenth century. I want to try to show how this novelist had certain explicitly political and social objectives and made certain explicit political and social assumptions, and how, because his editor and his audience had certain political and social objectives and assumptions, he was forced to modify his own objectives and assumptions. But I also want to show how because author, editor, and audience also had certain *implicit, unexamined* assumptions, the novel was also strongly affected. These implicit and unexamined assumptions—which on the surface had little or nothing to do with the author's political and social beliefs—seriously affected the social impact and the political meaning of the novel. It is what it is and is not, for good and for bad, in large part because of these factors. In seeking to understand the novel and the novelist, and also the time and the place, we cannot neglect considering them.

In January of the year 1895, the firm of Charles Scribner's Sons published *John March, Southerner,* written by the Louisiana novelist George W. Cable. For more than a decade Cable had been busy waging a campaign, which became more and more a one-man campaign, to persuade the southern states of the American Union not to disfranchise their Negro voters and relegate them firmly and finally into second-class citizenship, as was being done all through the 1870s, 1880s, and 1890s. Cable had begun the campaign as a novelist back in 1880, with *The Grandissimes,* his most popular novel and the one that is most often read today. In that first novel, which he afterward said he had intended to make "as political a novel as has ever been written," Cable set his scene in New Orleans just after the Louisiana Purchase of 1803, but what he showed about Creole notions of race and caste was, as he admitted, more pertinent to the 1870s than to the 1800s. *The Grandissimes* had been a considerable success, critically and popularly, but its impact on southern racial attitudes had been quite slight. In the middle 1880s, however, Cable had left off fictional treatment of racial problems and had taken to the platform and to the magazine essay to get his ideas across. He succeeded in stirring up considerable controversy, though it is not recorded that any votes on the issues of disfranchisement or Jim Crow laws were changed as the result of his efforts. But by the 1890s his position had been so thoroughly repudiated by the South, and his erstwhile northern supporters in the journalistic and editorial world had so clearly wearied of the fracas, that he decided to give up his public platform campaign. Instead, he resolved to write a new novel—it would be his first in a decade—which he initially intended to call *Johnny Rebb*. He worked away at it whenever his heavy lecturing and public-reading schedule permitted, and he even carried his manuscript about with him on his tours and worked on it on trains, in hotel rooms, and in railroad depots.

Now Cable's earlier fiction, both at its best—in *Old Creole Days* and *The Grandissimes*—and at its worst—*Bonaventure, Dr. Sevier*—had all been set in Louisiana and involved the French-speaking Creoles and Cajuns of that onetime French province. It was mostly what is known as "local-color" fiction—stories that emphasized unusual or exotic settings, quaint characters, and colorful dialect. It is no distortion to say that the popular success of that fiction, which was considerable, was based primarily on just that dimension of local color. The American reading public of the post–Civil War period reveled in such material, for a variety of reasons, but especially because it constituted a kind of nostalgic pastorale, whereby the new leisure-class readers of a swiftly urbanizing and industrializing nation could be assured that the simpler individualistic, nonmaterialistic ideals of an earlier time were still cherished and practiced out there in the provinces beyond the metropolitan regions. The defeated South, being still very much a rural region and gifted, as well, with the glamour of a genuine Lost Cause—one that was so satisfyingly lost—proved to be an ideal locale for good local-color writing, and Cable had led the way. He had a marvelous ear for dialect, a fine sense of sensuous atmosphere and exotic setting, and, for all that he was a very pious and proper Presbyterian, a taste for the voluptuous that sometimes enticed his characters into odd situations. However much Cable may have intended to make *The Grandissimes* into a political novel, the politics was not what accounted for its popularity. Cable had sought in it to *use* his Creole local-color material to flavor and sweeten his political and social commentary. But the novel was read and enjoyed primarily for the sweetening.

In 1889, when Cable set to work to make *John March, Southerner* into what he wished it to be, he made a crucial—and for his popular literary reputation, a most unfortunate—decision. He wanted his novel to be about the South and to embody directly the most pressing political and social problems that the South was facing, and so he decided to put aside the Louisiana scene and to set his story five hundred miles away from the Creoles, in the hill country of southeastern Tennessee and northwestern Georgia. His fictional southerners could thus be more representative—of Anglo-Saxon rather than Latin descent and Protestant rather than Roman Catholic. He wanted his novel to involve not only Negro suffrage and civil rights, but the problems of the development of natural resources that the post-Reconstruction South faced, with their attendant social implications—the cherished notion of the New South of commerce and industry, in other words. He wanted to ask—and to answer—the question of, What is the Good Life for the South? For such a purpose, he decided, the Creoles, with their bantering ways, their Latin attitudes, the languor of the *dolce far' niente* under semitropical Gulf skies, the piquant flavor of their French accents, would get in the way. They would distort the impact of his "fable of the New South" and force him to work too much by indirection. He wanted, to repeat, to get directly and realistically at the South of his own time. He would forego completely his best known and most marketable fictional commodity.

What he did, therefore, was to make several trips to the Etowah Mountains country of northern Georgia and southeastern Tennessee, visiting Marietta, Monteagle, Kennesaw Mountain, and Cartersville, where he made notes, interviewed residents, drew up lists of questions to be researched, and compiled statistical data. By

1890 he was ready to send a sizable portion of his new novel to his longtime editor, Richard Watson Gilder of the *Century,* for inspection. A poet of reputation, Gilder was the country's best known and most respected editor and the very epitome of the genteel tradition of polite ideality that in the 1880s and early 1890s so dominated American magazine literature. Under Gilder's editorship the *Century* was the largest and most prestigious magazine in the country. Gilder admired and liked Cable, and Cable was the *Century* magazine's most famous discovery, though of course it published all the best known writers of the period.

Because it is central to the argument of this essay, I want to cite at some length Gilder's response to the portion of the novel that Cable had sent him. Gilder wrote sadly that he "could weep for disappointment. Here are gleams of the delightful old art—but . . . a tract, not a story,—to my mind. Instead of a return to literature; an attempt to fetch everything into literature save & except literature itself." He complained that the new novel, in short, was on a par with the novels in which Judge Albion Tourgée had attempted, with relatively little literary skill, to fictionalize his experiences as a Reconstruction judge in North Carolina. Gilder clearly did not like the idea of Cable using fiction for purposes of political and social commentary. "If it needs must be that all this *must* go into an (allegory) story—a pill with the sugar on the inside & the quinine on the outside—so it must be. I fear you have hoped to put too much of your own serious thought on public, political & humanitarian questions into just this form; and that it must be worked off this way & not merely in essays and addresses." And Gilder concluded, "I can't tell whether the story could, with your conscientious consent, ever be what I hoped for. *Beware of the fate of Tolstoi.* A greater user of language—and a more conscientious man never lived."

I want now to examine some of the assumptions, implicit as well as explicit, about that response. What Gilder said he most objected to was Cable's didacticism—his attempt to use his novel as a tract, to air his "serious thought on public, political & humanitarian questions." The material, Gilder says, is not being used fictionally —there are "a series of political conversations between which scarcely an incident is interjected." Cable has written an allegory, which Gilder likens to a malaria pill—only the sweetness is all on the inside, while the medicine is on the outside. What he wanted was just the reverse—he wanted Cable to palliate the impact of his political and social concerns by hiding them in a story that would be pleasant and enjoyable and inoffensive. To make his point, Gilder invoked the spectre of Leo Tolstoi, the great artist of *War and Peace* and *Anna Karenina,* who had in the 1880s and 1890s turned aside from fiction to preach morality. Cable, Gilder was warning, was in danger of doing precisely the same thing, and, like Tolstoi, for motives that in themselves were quite praiseworthy. Now of course Gilder's dislike of didacticism in fiction was sound doctrine—his reference to Albion Tourgée was not without relevance, since much of Cable's concern and attitude was close to Tourgée's. Gilder was telling Cable that though he was far more accomplished a literary craftsman than Tourgée, in his new novel he was so neglecting his craft in order to communicate his political and social ideas that the result was literarily as poor a product as *Bricks Without Straw* and *A Fool's Errand.*

This might seem sound enough advice. But notice what it is that Gilder specifically objects to. The novel "opens with a corpse, then goes into a brutal thrashing," he complains. Now the earliest draft of *John March, Southerner,* the one that Gilder first saw, does not exist, but those that do, as well as the novel as published, all have a scene, early in the story, in which two Confederate officers, returning home after the surrender, pause at the scene of a battlefield and catch a glimpse of a college in the distance. One surmises that in the earliest version the corpse must have been discovered on the battlefield.

Apparently in response to Gilder's objections, Cable deleted the battlefield corpse in his next draft. In so doing, he eliminated what if properly handled could have been a very moving and important symbol indeed. For since the novel is about the South that could and did develop after the Civil War, it would appear to have been quite appropriate for the two homeward-bound veterans of the war, headed back to pick up the fabric of their lives, to have come upon a dead soldier, until then left undiscovered and unburied upon a battlefield of the war, and thus a summation of the terrible human cost the war had exacted. For them first to have come upon the corpse, and then to have caught sight of the college in the distance, would have posed the problem of the novel very appropriately. Having paid this cost, the two returning soldiers must perforce meditate, how shall we southerners build a new Southland that will be worthy of so costly a sacrifice, and how shall we avoid another calamity for our society such as has just occurred, and which is exemplified by this dead soldier? The distant college represents the hope of a better, more enlightened future; the corpse represents the price of the failure of the past. As for the "brutal thrashing," which does remain in the published novel, it is administered by one of the two Confederate officers, Major Garnet, who is also a minister and the founder and president of Rosemont College, to a Negro slave who has been the major's body servant during the war but now dares to inform his former master that the results of the war have made them equals. Thus, following after the battlefield scene, the beating of the former slave for declaring himself the white southerner's equal would have signified that the tragic flaw in the South's character, the sin that had brought about its downfall and defeat, was still alive, and that, unless conquered and transcended, it would jeopardize all the hopes of the future as well. Since this is precisely what Cable felt about southern racial attitudes, and since much of what takes place in *John March, Southerner* is directed to just this point, it seems regrettable that by objecting to the discovery of the battlefield corpse that would set up the symbolism, Cable's New York editor would gravely weaken so dramatic a demonstration of what the book would be about.

What Gilder objected to, it is clear, was the unpleasantness. Anything so gory as the discovery of a battlefield corpse, followed by the brutal beating of a Negro, was in Richard Watson Gilder's eyes a betrayal of the "delightful old art" that Cable was capable of producing. For Gilder, then, ugliness and violence were inartistic. In Gilder's eyes, too, the ugliness was fully as objectionable as the didacticism; they seemed to him part of the same tractarian impulse. This of course was the genteel tradition speaking; unpleasant subject matter was to be avoided because it was inartistic. One remembers something that Gilder wrote to Cable earlier in his career. "Write something intensely interesting—," he declared, "but without the terrible suggestion you so often make use of." (This was the same Gilder who, in editing *Huckleberry Finn* for the magazine serialization in the *Century*, excised the Duke's remark, "There, if that line don't fetch them, I don't know Arkansaw!" after the Duke had placed the words "Ladies and children not admitted" under the poster advertising "The Royal Nonesuch.")

It should be obvious that Gilder's assumption that unpleasant material was inartistic, and that its presence in a novel in effect constituted preaching, carried important political consequences. In public life Gilder was a reformer, interested in good government and opposed to vice, corruption, graft, predatory business practices, victimization of the poor, and intolerance. But his prudishness, his belief that unpleasant subject matter was undesirable in a work of fiction, necessarily worked to deprive those who would oppose the political and economic victimization of the lower orders, whether former slaves or urban proletariat, by depicting graphically and realistically the brutalization of their daily lives.

In the United States of the 1880s and 1890s, there was widespread misery, both rural and urban, and the cause, we have long since realized, was the inability of the accepted forms and concepts of government and law to deal with the realities of an industrial society. The older notions of the role of government, the relationship of employer and employee, the attitude of government toward individual enterprise, the limitations of individual freedom of profit-making in an industrial society were inadequate for a different kind of society. Finance capitalism, monopoly, trust, mass transportation and communication, a large urban proletariat made up of new immigrant groups not of the old northern European stock, whose barriers of language and culture made them less able to fend for themselves and move into secure places in a middle-class economy, an illiterate, uneducated, moneyless black proletariat in the South—all imposed impossible strains upon the notions of government and society that had been adequate to an earlier and simpler society. To adapt the old notions to the new conditions, to change and expand the role of government in accordance with the needs of an urbanized, industralized society, was (and still is) a pressing task, and to accomplish the task it would first of all be necessary to make the American electorate realize the urgent need for such reform. Clearly one way to achieve this realization was to show the misery, deprivation, and squalor that human beings were being forced to endure in city and countryside of the land of the free and home of the brave. But if the unflinching depiction of misery, deprivation, and squalor in fiction was to be held inartistic and didactic, then a powerful advantage was being denied those who would accomplish such reform, and an equally powerful advantage was being tendered those who opposed such reform. The anesthetics of the genteel tradition, therefore, with the emphasis on sweetness and light, constituted a political weapon in the hands of the defenders of the political and economic status quo. Malnutrition, slums, disease, graft, brutality, race hatred, intimidation by force, these *were* unpleasant and ugly things. To show them at work was to force people to become aware of their existence. To forbid their depiction was to inhibit such awareness. Thus if the subject matter of fiction could not be unpleasant and ugly, but must be the "delightful old art" of local-color quaintness, it was clear that fiction was being placed on the side of the economic, social, and political status quo.

Of course Gilder was correct; Cable *was* in effect delivering a political and social message when he depicted battlefield corpse and then a Confederate major beating a former slave. For to show the corpse was to remind the reader of the heavy cost in human lives of the war. To follow it with a depiction of the major beating the slave for asserting his equality was to suggest to southern audiences that by refusing to accept the results of the war they were dooming their children to the same kind of useless sacrifice that a previous generation had been forced to pay, while to northern audiences the implicit suggestion was that all the human sacrifice of the war was being negated by the nation's unwillingness to see that the black man was given his freedom in fact as well as in law.

But Gilder's objection to the opening scene was not

based on such grounds as that. He didn't *mind* the moral so much as the ugliness; the administering of a medicinal dosage was all right, provided that the sweetness was on the outside and in adequate quantity, and the medicine was concealed within and not made obtrusive. But clearly there was little room in Gilder's aesthetic physiology for the catharsis of genuine tragedy, since the experience of tragedy is not customarily composed of very much sugarcoating. Now Cable's way of beginning his novel, it seems to me, was essentially that of tragic action; it was incipiently tragic, a way of looking at the matter at hand that seems hardly inappropriate for a former Confederate soldier who saw his beloved Southland failing to rid itself of the selfsame racial attitudes that had caused its recent defeat and devastation. Though we do not have that first draft that Cable sent to Gilder to read and so do not know what it was to be, I doubt that Cable intended a tragedy or was capable of writing one even if he had so intended. But even so, it seems very likely to me that Gilder's response, his demand for "the delightful old art," must have had a positive as well as a negative effect upon the manuscript as finally completed. It is true that Gilder never finally accepted the manuscript even when it was revised, and *John March, Southerner* was serialized in Scribner's *New Monthly Magazine,* not in the *Century;* but it was submitted to Gilder and his associates twice again before its author accepted the fact that it was not destined to win Gilder's approval. What Cable wrote and revised after that first installment, then, was written and revised with the thought that it must pass Gilder's scrutiny.

To what extent did this affect Cable's writing? We know that he dropped the battlefield corpse episode. What did he *put into* the novel to please Gilder? How much of the long and insipid love plot, about which I shall comment later, was designed as "delightful old art" to please Gilder and what he represented? There is no way of knowing. One can only speculate.

So much for Gilder. Let us now consider the matters from Cable's standpoint. What did the genteel tradition mean from his point of view? There is in *John March, Southerner* a character named Cornelius Leggett. Leggett is the former slave who is beaten by Garnet, the Confederate major, for daring to suggest that the war has made them equal. Thereafter what happens to Leggett is curious business. We find that, in response to Garnet's beating, he in turn cruelly flays a little boy, John March, with whose care he had been entrusted. Later we find Leggett a power in Reconstruction politics. He is ignorant, pompous, lustful, vain; at one point the adult John March rescues him from certain lynching. He is made the butt of several practical jokes by John March. His way of talking is made by Cable into something heavy-handedly comic, with the misuse of big words and the like, in the style later popularized by Amos and Andy. He is guilty of graft. Late in the novel he simply drops out of the picture. Now this is Cable's prototype of the black politician of the Reconstruction, and though it is a very effective characterization, it is not very complimentary. What Cable must have wanted Leggett to show, however, is that, even if every cliché used by the white South to excoriate the black man— ignorance, concupiscence, gullibility, rascality, pomposity—were true, it was still in the black man's interest to support good government and better education and the white southern politician who would stand for good government and increased expenditures for education could count on the support of the blacks. Furthermore, what Cable wanted to suggest, too, was that the kind of petty graft and dishonesty that the black Reconstruction politician might have managed was of slight importance

compared with the large-scale graft and financial buc-
caneering that supposedly respectable white men were
doing within the law, under the guise of economic development. Leggett himself points this out to a lobbyist,
comparing his public role and that of Major Garnet:
"'Thass the diffunce' twixt me and Gyarnit. Nobody re-
putes him to steal, an' I don't say he do. I ain't ready to
say it yet, you un'stan'; but his politics—his politics, seh,
they does the stealin'! An' which it's the low-downdest
kind o' stealin', for it's stealin' fum niggers. But thass the
diff'ence; niggers steals with they claws, white men with
they laws. The claws steal by the pound; the laws steal by
the boatload!'"

In the course of the story, it is shown that Leggett's
analysis is quite accurate: Major Garnet, supposedly a
picture of respectability, a college president, minister,
Confederate hero, leading citizen, turns out at the end
to have been a swindler and a profligate and a mur-
derer, who had used his position and his political con-
nections to enrich himself at the expense of the common good.

This was Cable's intention, and his characterizations
of Leggett and Garnet were both designed to make the
point. But why, one wonders, did Cable, who had battled so bravely and eloquently against the white South's
treatment of the black man, and who had denounced
the affront to dignity that Jim Crow laws constituted for
respectable Negro citizens, feel it appropriate to give
Cornelius Leggett, his Negro politician, so many of the
attributes of a minstrel-show darky? Surely he of all
people knew better than to stereotype his leading black
character in this fashion.

Part of the reason, of course, was to make his point,
which I have already suggested, that a black man even
when at his most venial and contemptible was automatically an ally of anyone who would support fair government and better education, and also that those who

concentrated their indignation upon such a man were being blinded to the presence of the real enemy of the common good, the "respectable" white profiteer. And doubtless, too, Cable wanted to show, in his book about the problems of the South, that it was not true, as his southern critics had contended so often, that he idealized the Negro and refused to accept his shortcomings. But what I wonder is whether the knowledge that his new novel was going to have to please Richard Watson Gilder is not also partly to blame? Telling as he was trying to do a serious, sometimes even sombre story, anxious to have his heartfelt analysis of the nature and problems of the South of his time read and understood, to what extent did he find it necessary to seize upon every possible opportunity to amuse and please along the way? Deprived of the previous possibilities of colorful Creole characterization in this novel, since he had deliberately not set it in New Orleans, he felt obliged to use whatever was available in the way of potential local-color material. Since Cornelius Leggett, despite his key role in the meaning of the novel, seemed a possibility for local-color darky humor, Cable used him for that purpose, hoping that the comedy would so please Gilder that the political statement would be accepted. If so, in this instance it worked: for after Gilder had seen the revised manuscript, which he rejected too, he did concede that Leggett was Cable's "best & most original character" and that "the reader does get some fun out of him!"

Here again, we see how the political implications arise out of the supposedly aesthetic criteria of the form of fiction and, conversely, how the political implications affect the supposedly nonpolitical material. Because the local-color genre encouraged authors to think in terms of character types and because character types were supposed to be picturesque, Cable strove, in a novel that essentially is not given over to local-color stereotyping, to produce "delightful old art" whenever possible, and that meant placing Cornelius Leggett into the minstrel stereotype. It has been said that by the 1890s Cable had become tired of his campaign for civil rights and increasingly out of sympathy with the cause of reform, so that Leggett's less than admirable characterization represents Cable's disenchantment with the black man. I do not believe this is so; otherwise why write the novel *John March, Southerner* at all? What is it, thematically, if not an attempt to rally the conscience of the best instincts of the South? I don't think Cable ever lost his conviction about the injustice of southern treatment of the black man; I do think that during the 1890s and 1900s he despaired of its ever being remedied. I ascribe the characterization of Cornelius Leggett to the author's feeling that he must sweeten his political commentary with pleasing comedy, and I think Gilder's response to Leggett shows why he thought so. But what it meant, alas, is that the black man as adult political creature is cruelly satirized, and this is not really rectified by the eventual realization that the supposedly respectable white politician is more dangerous to the public welfare than the corrupt Negro politician.

The inescapable fact is that Cable, in his portrayal of the post-Reconstruction South, showed the black man to very poor advantage and thus gave some aid and some comfort to those who wanted him kept out of political power. This was certainly not what Cable intended; the culprit is the local-color genre and the insistence by his editor (which is to say, by the genteel tradition that dominated American magazine fiction at the time) that social criticism in fiction must be sugarcoated. For the fact is that almost alone of the major characters of the novel, so far as the political and social theme is involved, Cornelius Leggett is stereotyped. He comes out of the local-color genre of comic darky, and he appears thus in a novel that is not essentially local color but a work of realism. Without the Creoles with their lilting accents to furnish his comedy this time, as they had in *The Grandissimes* and *Dr. Sevier,* Cable used what he could find along that line: he seized upon the Negro for amusing language and comic fallibility because his editor, his time and place, his literary training, all told him that he needed such caricature. So we get the terribly ironic spectacle of the South's leading and most courageous advocate of civil rights and recognition of the black man's humanity producing, in his most realistic southern novel, a local-color darky sterotype that contradicted his whole campaign! For the literary genre, and the editors who presided over it, demanded "delightful old art," and that meant local-color stereotyping.

The political implications of the local-color genre as practiced in and on the South during the 1870s, 1880s, and 1890s have long been noted. One might well agree with the statement that it was the local-color genre, as practiced by such writers as Joel Chandler Harris and Thomas Nelson Page, that was most responsible for changing the nation's image of the black man and his place in the South from that of Uncle Tom to Uncle Remus. Harriet Beecher Stowe's gentle old uncle was treated cruelly by his white superior; Uncle Remus is likewise a gentle old uncle, but his white folks indulge him and love him. Thus it is not the characterization that is different, but the meaning of the characterization; and the political implications of that change in meaning are obvious. The Negro seen as Uncle Tom carried the demand that he be saved from the southern white man's cruelty; seen as Uncle Remus, the implication was that he could best be left to the southern white man's understanding benevolence. Now Cable believed no such thing; and in *The Grandissimes,* his first novel, he sought to show the reality of helpless indignity, suffering, and victimization that lay behind the stereotype of "happy darky." But in that novel he had the Creoles to furnish the local-color quaintness and comedy. In *John March, Southerner* he did not. He thought he had to have such material if his novel was to succeed; he used what was available. Thus Cornelius Leggett as we have him.

The supposedly nonpolitical, aesthetically based factors of literary genre, we see, turn out to have important political implications. But the reverse is true, too. That is, political considerations can be seen as affecting the formal, aesthetic considerations. We have seen how Cable may have portrayed the faults of Cornelius Leggett so glaringly in order to forestall criticism that he idealized the black man and could not recognize his shortcomings. But it goes much deeper than that. The very creation of the book itself—that is, the desire to write a story of the South that would present the real problems and prospects of southern society, honestly and without the usual trappings of costume romance— surely grows out of social as well as artistic motivations. The decision to write, not of New Orleans and Creoles, but of northern Georgia and Protestant southerners of Anglo-Saxon stock, was political and social at least as much as literary and aesthetic. The impulse to create a genuine fictional world, to tell a story and make the people in it believable and real, is likewise the impulse to give or discover order and meaning in experience. Dissatisfaction with the way the South had hitherto been presented in fiction, the desire to get down in words what it really was, went hand in hand with the desire to say something about the political and social conditions of the South. The urge to write realistic fiction and the urge to make his fellow southerners realize the actualities of the region's political, social, and economic problems were so linked in Cable's mind that it would be quite impossible to say which was dominant. It was unfortunate for Cable that Gilder, and the genteel tradition that he exemplified, could not envision these two impulses as complementary, but could only deal with them in terms of static, mutually exclusive elements. All that Gilder could suggest to Cable was that he ought to do a better job of sugarcoating the pill. His only solution to the problem of didacticism was to urge Cable to leave his social and political concerns out of his fiction entirely. Not once in the lengthy correspondence between Cable and Gilder does the editor ever try to show the writer how to *use* his social and political concerns artistically. He complains because the long political discussions are given without incidents being interspersed between them. He does not suggest, because he cannot envision, how the political material might be *used* artistically. The manuscript, he tells Cable, is an attempt to "fetch everything into literature save & except literature itself"—as if political, economic, and social concerns could not be literary concerns as well. As Edmund Wilson says, "The influence of the Northern editors was to prove in the long run as lethal to Cable's career as the South's hostility to his views on race," and "the slow strangulation of Cable as an artist and a serious writer is surely one of the most gruesome episodes in American literary history."

As finally published by Scribner's in 1895, *John March, Southerner* was a badly flawed novel. On the one hand, it is the story of a young southerner who wants to do the right thing and who must learn to act and think for himself. To do what is right, he must understand what is going on in the society around him. Tradition, prejudice, loyalty, piety—all conspire to make it extremely difficult for him to achieve that understanding, and the long, painful struggle whereby he comes to such knowledge is very much the structural development of the novel. Grafted onto this, however, clumsily and insipidly, is the romantic plot—John March's tediously detailed romance with Barbara Garnet. As a flesh-and-blood character in the drama of the New South, young John March is believable and real; but as earnest young lover, he is tiresome and fatuous. The hearts-and-flowers note on which the novel ends is cloyingly saccharine. And the only way that Cable can manage to join his love story and his drama of the New South together is by a hackneyed, unconvincing, melodramatic plot device involving switched land titles and dark secrets continually hinted at. Apparently he never realized the incongruity. I have been highly critical of Richard Watson Gilder, not because he was uniquely a prude, but because he exemplifies the genteel tradition. But it is George W. Cable's name which appears on the title page, not Gilder's. The fault, in the final analysis, must be laid at Cable's door, for it was he who *let* Gilder's views prevail. The ultimate responsibility is the writer's. For the truth is that however much he may have wanted to write realistically about his time and place, Cable himself was part of the genteel tradition, too. His most successful art—the stories of *Old Creole Days, The Grandissimes*—draws its impulse and texture squarely out of the local-color genre. It contains elements of realism; at its best it transcends the genre; but local-color fiction it is nonetheless. Cable's trouble, in *John March, Southerner,* is that he wanted to break away from genteel local color, but he did not quite know how. He had to provide a happy ending. The romantic love story that so spoils the form of the novel was not, for Cable, mere window dressing. He believed in that, too—equally with the political and social realism. That they were in fact antithetical—that the insight one brings to the depiction of men engaged in politics and economics and the insight into their engagement in love and sex cannot be separated, since a novel is not about politics and economics or about love, but about people—this Cable never realized. This was his limitation as an artist. It is the limitaiton inherent in the genteel tradition, and it required more than a Cable to transcend it. It took a Clemens, or a James. But that is another story.

Suffice it to say, then, that *John March, Southerner,* by George W. Cable, is a flawed work. A banal, wearisome romantic love plot is joined with the most searching, realistic, honest depiction of southern society during the late nineteenth century ever penned. I cannot emphasize the latter too strongly. Not until the coming of Faulkner and his contemporaries do we get the fabric of southern society delineated with such clarity and insight. You will not find the South that Cable shows in other southern fiction of the period. Rather, you will find it in works of political and economic history. Cable's South is the South of C. Vann Woodward, Francis B. Simkins, W. J. Cash, T. Harry Williams, Dewey Grantham, George Tindall—and the South of William Faulkner, Robert Penn Warren, Thomas Wolfe, Ralph Ellison, William Styron, Richard Wright. But for his romantic leads, the place to look for their prototypes, alas, is in the fiction of William Gilmore Simms, Mary Johnston, and the author of *When Knighthood Was in Flower.*

Cable's novel stands, it seems to me, both in its strengths and weaknesses, as testimony that there cannot be something known as the good political novel, or the economic novel, or the novel of race or of class or yet a good novel of "delightful old art" devoid of such concerns as those. There can only be the good novel—a total vision, an entire ordering of life through the image of fiction.

Uncle Remus
and the Ubiquitous Rabbit

In late August of 1876, an epidemic of yellow fever struck the city of Savannah, Georgia. By the first of September, twenty-three persons had died, and physicians were advising all who could leave to do so at once. Among those departing was a twenty-seven-year-old newspaperman who feared for the health of his family and decided to seek safety in the higher elevation of Atlanta; it was not long before the editor of the Atlanta *Constitution,* Evan P. Howell, and his new associate editor Henry W. Grady arranged to have this man join the staff on a temporary basis. On November 21 the *Constitution* was able to announce that Joel Chandler Harris had accepted a permanent position.

Grady and Harris were old friends; each admired the other's work immensely. Thus it came about, as C. Vann Woodward points out, that during the 1880s there were at work across the desk from each other in the *Constitution* office the author of the Uncle Remus stories, which

This essay was originally published in *Southern Review,* n.s., X (Autumn, 1974), 787–804.

made of an animal-tale-telling plantation Negro a household symbol of the good old days, throughout the United States and overseas, and the ardent, exuberant promoter of a New South of commerce and industry that would supposedly break away from the outworn southern past and inaugurate a new era of progress and prosperity.

The alliance of Joel Chandler Harris and Henry Woodfin Grady was not as incongruous as it might seem. For both Harris and Grady were marketing the same product—reunion. The gentle old darky telling amusing tales of the days when the creatures could talk was one form of packaging; the image of a bustling, go-getting New South bent upon business and dedicated to the American way of thrift and enterprise was another. Both men were utterly sincere in their endeavors. There were depths to Harris' view of the Negro, which I suspect he secretly realized, that carried implications ultimately contradictory to the way that his stories were received during the years of their greatest popularity. Similarly, Grady's ideological approach to the good life contained contradictions that in the future would work directly against the promulgation of the racial and social assumptions that he was making. But in their time and place, what these two newspapermen accomplished was to help give the former slaveholding Confederate South a legitimate and accepted place in the American Union—a place in which southern racial and social attitudes would not serve to bar participation.

The impact of Harris' work, and the example he gave to subsequent southern writers, can be seen if we consider the following depiction of an old black retainer: "He was a large, broad-chested, powerfully made man, of a full glossy black, and a face whose truly African features were characterized by an expression of grave and steady good sense, united with much kindliness and benevolence. There was something about his whole air self-respecting and dignified, yet united with a confiding and humble self-sufficiency." And again, "Nothing could exceed the touching simplicity, the child-like earnestness of his prayer, enriched with its language of Scripture, which seemed so entirely to have wrought itself into his being as to have become a part of himself, and to drop from his lips unconsciously; in the language of a pious old negro, he 'prayed right up.'"

Now we may consider another such old black man: "The figure of the old man, as he stood smiling upon the crowd of Negroes, was picturesque in the extreme. He seemed to be taller than all the rest; and, notwithstanding his venerable appearance, he moved and spoke with all the vigor of youth. He had always exercised authority over his fellow-servants. He had been the captain of the cornpile, the stoutest at the log-rolling, the swiftest with the hoe, the neatest with the plough, and the plantation hands still looked upon him as their leader. . . . His voice was strong, and powerful, and sweet, and its range was as astonishing as its volume. More than this, the melody to which he tuned it, and which was caught up by a hundred voices almost as sweet and as powerful as his own, was charged with a mysterious and pathetic tenderness."

The second black man being portrayed is Uncle Remus; the first is Harriet Beecher Stowe's Uncle Tom. The similarity of the portraits is obvious, for the characterizations are very much alike. There are individual differences, to be sure: Uncle Remus is not so religious in his common utterance as Uncle Tom, and Uncle Tom is not given to reciting animal tales. But both uncles are "happy darkies": simple, gentle, unlettered but wise in human nature, tolerant of the foibles of mankind, kind to children, mellowed by time, unspoiled by the artificialities of too much civilization.

The enormous disparity between the reception of Mrs. Stowe's novel by the American reading public, and that public's response, less than thirty years afterward, to the Uncle Remus tales, did not lie, therefore, in the depictions of the black protagonists. Rather, it was the relationship of the black men to the resident whites that made the difference. Mrs. Stowe showed Uncle Tom as mocked, beaten, starved, his humanity denied, his virtue unrewarded. Harris showed Uncle Remus as honored, pampered, respected, his simplicity and gentleness cherished by his grateful and indulgent white patrons. Thus, if the northern reading public could feel that it was not Mrs. Stowe's version of black-white relationships, but Joel Chandler Harris', that typified life in the South, then the proper response was not to send armies southward to trample out the vintage where the grapes of wrath were stored, but to let the underlying amicability and mutual trust of black-white relationships down there exist free of the meddling of northern politicians and the blunders of misguided reformers. And this, all in all, was what the stories of Joel Chandler Harris and his imitators helped to accomplish. As Paul M. Gaston wrote in *The New South Creed,* "By convincing Northern readers that relations between the races were kindly and mutually beneficial, a principal obstacle in the way of sectional harmony was removed. The North had doubted this point, but on the authority of Harris and others it came to accept the Southern point of view." Such "acquiescence by the North in the Southern scheme of race relations permitted the South to deal with (or to fail to deal with) its race problems unmolested."[1]

Joel Chandler Harris was a complex, reticent man, who must secretly have pondered the contradictions and compromises in his own life, but if ever he revealed them to anyone, there is no record of it. The nearest he came to hinting of the agonies and doubts that espe-

1. Paul M. Gaston, *The New South Creed: A Study in Southern Mythmaking* (New York, 1970), 181–82.

cially in his earlier years must have plagued him was in some letters he wrote to a friend in Forsyth, Georgia, shortly after he left there to write editorial paragraphs for the Savannah *Morning News* in the early 1870s. To Mrs. Georgia Starke, he wrote letters full of loneliness and pain. He was in his early twenties, and no doubt the full implications of his illegitimate birth and lack of social position were sinking into his consciousness for the first time. "My history is a peculiarly sad and unfortunate one," he wrote to her, "—and those three years in Forsyth are the brightest of my life. They are a precious memorial of what would otherwise be as bleak and as desolate as winter." And again, "The truth is, I am morbidly sensitive. With some people the quality of sensitiveness adds to their refinement and is quite a charm. With me it is an affliction—a disease—that has cost me more mortification and grief than anything in the world—or everything put together. The least hint—a word—a gesture—is enough to put me in a frenzy almost. . . . You cannot conceive to what an extent this feeling goes with me. It is *worse* than *death* itself. It is horrible. My dearest friends have no idea how often they have crucified me."[2] Not too long after that Harris was married, and things improved for him, but to the end of his life the shyness and the melancholy remained. One senses it in the determined effort made in his later writings to have everything turn out happily, to gentle whatever was harsh or unpleasant, to insist, in spite of all, that people were basically good and kind, and everyone friendly and happy. In such assertions he goes too far, leaves out too much, makes too many disclaimers in the face of evidence to the contrary, for his idyllic portraits of simple life among the plain folk of middle Georgia to be accepted at face value.

2. Joel Chandler Harris to Mrs. Georgia Starke, September 9, 1870, and December 18, 1870, quoted in Julia Collier Harris, *The Life and Letters of Joel Chandler Harris* (Boston, 1918), 78, 83–84.

He was an ambitious man. He was driven by the wish
to succeed, to win renown as an author, and at the same
time he was afraid of his ambition and constantly asserted his disinterest in fame and minimized his own
abilities. He liked to pretend that he wrote without
artifice or art and that he had done little more than
transcribe the Negro folk tales that won him worldwide
acclaim. Yet he once showed Ray Stannard Baker the
drafts of sixteen introductory passages to a single story.
He was tongue-tied and terribly embarrassed among
strangers; never would he allow himself to speak in
public. If he saw an unknown caller coming to his house
he would sneak out the rear door. Yet among friends
that he trusted, he was often the soul of mirth; when he
came in for work at the *Constitution* office in the morning, if things appeared to be too serious, he would break
into a little jig and shuffle in the center of the floor, so as
to get everyone laughing. He wrote to his publisher on
one occasion that his big mistake had been ever to allow
his name to appear on his books: "There was no need
for such a display and it has created for me a world of
discomfort." Yet one of his last requests was that after
his death the magazine that he was editing in his final
years bear on it the legend "Founded by Joel Chandler
Harris."

Just what manner of man Joel Chandler Harris was
we shall never know, but one thing seems clear: he was
certainly not the simple, gentle, easygoing soul pictured
by his earlier biographers. Given the artistic sensitivity
that made him into the writer he became, the very facts
of his origins and early experience alone would render
that unlikely. Harris was born in Eatonton, Georgia, on
December 9, 1848. His mother's people were of pioneer
Georgia stock. Apparently (for we actually know nothing definite about it) his mother fell in love with an
Irish railway worker, and when her parents would not
consent to their marriage, she ran away and lived with

the man in Eatonton. Little is known about him; he seems to have departed shortly after his son's birth and was never afterward heard from. The mother retained her own family name, Harris, and gave it to the child. She was befriended by local citizens, reconciled with her mother, and earned her living as a seamstress in Eatonton. In later life Harris was always full of praise for the friendly, democratic society of the little town of Eatonton and repeatedly expressed his gratitude to the townsfolk for their kindness toward him and, by implication, their failure in any way to look down upon him when he was a boy or make him ashamed of his illegitimate origins. Yet it is obvious that, as he grew somewhat older, the clouded circumstance of his birth worried Harris very much. That it is not unrelated to his morbid shyness, his fear of new situations, his stammering and social unease, seems evident. Several of his novels, set in communities like Eatonton, involve orphaned, illegitimate children who later turn out to be the lost heirs of aristocratic families. Indeed, one has the suspicion that Harris was not always completely convinced that an itinerant Irish day laborer had been his real father at all.

There lived on Turnwold plantation, not far from Eatonton, a remarkable man named Joseph Addison Turner. He sometimes called at the Harris home with sewing work, and to judge from what happens in the novels, Harris would appear at times to have fantasized that Turner was his father. A planter, Turner had great literary ambitions. He published poetry and essays, started several magazines with the object of giving the South a literary outlet, and during the Civil War procured a Washington hand press and type and began issuing from his plantation a weekly literary paper, *The Countryman,* modeled on *The Spectator* and *The Tatler.*

Harris, who was a redheaded, freckled, homely lad, very small for his age, liked to hang around the Eatonton post office, reading the newspapers, and when in

1862 he found in the first issue of *The Countryman* an advertisement for "an active, intelligent white boy, 14 or 15 years of age to learn the printer's trade," he applied at once. Turner called for him, took him out to Turnwold, and Joel Harris began work as an apprentice printer. Quickly he learned to set type and was given the run of Turner's substantial library. Soon he began composing little items for *The Countryman,* some of which Turner was happy to print.

Harris described his days at Turnwold in a fictionalized autobiography, *On the Plantation* (1892), dedicated to Turner's memory. This book, which except for the Uncle Remus stories is by far his most readable work, shows young Joe Maxwell hunting, reading, working, and listening to plantation slaves tell stories. Between the boy and the blacks there was immediate rapport and trust. On one occasion the boy discovered a runaway slave from a nearby plantation and, instead of turning him in brought him food and looked out for him. After that the plantation slaves were assiduous in their attention to him. He also accompanied a search party using dogs to follow the scent of the fugitive, and while Harris will not exactly say so, it seems likely that Joe Maxwell went along with a view toward looking after the runaway slave's interests. At one point he observed a bateau drifting past along a stream, sitting low in the water, and surmised that it contained the runaway slave. Later another slave confirmed the suspicion.

Did this happen? Harris declined to identify what was fact and what was fiction in *On the Plantation.* What is interesting is the extent to which Joe Maxwell's situation is reminiscent of that in *Huckleberry Finn.* That child of uncertain parentage also befriended a runaway slave and helped throw hunters off his trail, and the incident with the bateau is not without its precedent in Mark Twain's novel. There are also numerous other similarities, both to *Huckleberry Finn* and *Tom Sawyer.* Harris was a great admirer of *Huckleberry Finn,* declaring in the *Critic* in 1885 that it was a genuinely great work of serious literature—a status that most critics were unwilling to accord the book at the time. But whether the episode with the runaway slave came from literature or life—my own feeling, based on the difference between the tone of the material and that of the other, clearly fictional episodes in the book, is that something like it must indeed have taken place—what is important about it is the relationship it sets up with the slaves. There was a sympathy, amounting to an identification of interests, that is unmistakable. As Jay B. Hubbell notes in *The South in American Literature,* "It is almost as though he were one of them. . . . His illegitimate birth seemed not to matter. It would have been different if he had been the son of a great slaveholder like Turner or perhaps if he had lived in Turner's house." This instinctive identification, so different from anything else in southern local-color fiction except for Clemens', was to be of absolute importance to the dynamics of the Uncle Remus stories Harris would later write and would remain valid in spite of Harris' conscious adherence to the official southern position on the subject.

While at Turnwold, too, as Hubbell points out, Harris first read *Uncle Tom's Cabin,* a book which he later said "made a more vivid impression on my mind than anything I have ever read since." Union troops came through Turnwold during Sherman's march to the sea, but did no damage except for some pillaging. It was in the wake of their departure that Harris witnessed an incident that he described in *On the Plantation* and elsewhere. He came upon an old Negro woman shivering and moaning. An old Negro man lay nearby, his shoulders covered with a ragged shawl:

"Who is that lying there?" asked Joe.
"It my ole man, suh."

"What is the matter with him?"
"He dead, suh! But, bless God, he died free!"

After postwar conditions ended publication of *The Countryman,* Harris worked as a printer on the Macon *Telegraph.* He also began reviewing books and writing poetry. Offered a job as private secretary to the publisher of a New Orleans literary magazine, he went there, but this did not work out well, so he returned home and was hired as assistant on a weekly, the Monroe *Advertiser,* setting type, printing the newspaper, and contributing humorous paragraphs. This led to a position, at the handsome salary of forty dollars a week, on the Savannah *Morning News,* edited by William Tappan Thompson, whose earlier *Major Jones' Courtship,* humorous sketches of middle Georgia life, had won him widespread notice.

It was while he was employed in Savannah that Harris met and in 1873 was married to Esther LaRose, the daughter of a French Canadian ship captain. In 1876 came the family flight to Atlanta to escape the yellow fever epidemic, and there Harris began the job on the *Constitution.* For that paper he wrote editorials and continued his comic paragraphing.

Harris' discovery of the Uncle Remus material came over the course of several years. The *Constitution* had been publishing some Negro dialect sketches by a member of its staff, Sam W. Small, in which one Old Si was used to make political comments and local observations. Upon Evan P. Howell's purchase of the paper in 1876, Small left the staff. Looking around for someone to continue the feature, Howell asked Harris to try his hand at it. Harris wrote two sketches, one of them involving a Negro character named Uncle Remus, who related a story about another Negro's ill-fated attempt to ride a recalcitrant mule. These were well received, and Harris tried some more, some of them also involving Uncle Remus. These earliest sketches, which were later included in Harris' first book, were not animal tales, but conventional anecdotes of the minstrel variety, poking fun at the vagaries of uneducated blacks, along with political sermons to promote the *Constitution*'s policies. What chiefly distinguished them from numerous such pieces by other journalists was their richness of idiom and their attention to the nuances of dialect. Gradually Harris began evolving the characterization of Uncle Remus, and though at this stage he was made to exhibit many of the attributes of the comic darky stereotype, Remus was coming to possess a dignity and a pride that transcended his merely comic role.

Later that year Sam Small rejoined the *Constitution,* and Harris gave up his Negro sketches and began writing essays for the Sunday edition. He could not, however, stay away from Remus. After some months Harris reintroduced Remus as the hero of a story describing how during the war the old Negro had been left in charge of the plantation and had spied a Federal sharpshooter in a tree, taking aim at a Confederate on horseback whom the slave recognized as his own master, whereupon he had raised his own rifle and killed the sharpshooter. In many ways the story was a conventional local-color yarn, designed to exhibit the slave's fidelity to his white owner. When Harris published his first Uncle Remus book several years afterward, he revised the tale so that the Yankee sharpshooter, instead of being killed, was merely wounded and was subsequently nursed back to health by his intended victim's family and ultimately wed to the daughter.

Such a plot, of course, could as well have been produced by a thoroughgoing plantation apologist such as Thomas Nelson Page. There is, however, one difference. When, in the book version, the northern woman to whom he is telling the story asks Remus, "Do you mean to say that you shot the Union soldier, when you

knew he was fighting for your freedom?" Harris has
Remus reply, "Co'se I know all about dat, en it sorter
made cole chills run up my back; but w'en I see dat man
take aim, en Mars Jeems gwine home ter Ole Miss en
Miss Sally, I des disremembered all 'bout freedom en
lammed aloose." Page would never have included this;
he would not have had his Negro feel any such debt to a
Yankee, or allowed any hint of conflicting loyalties. The
difference here is not vital, so far as the overall meaning
of the story itself is concerned, but it is indicative of a
quality in Harris that Page did not possess: that of being
able to recognize the existence of a difference between
the interests of the slave and those of his white owner.
Harris was not always consistent in this perception; in a
later volume such as *The Chronicles of Miss Minervy Ann* it
is singularly absent. But it is precisely this awareness,
however consciously played down in much of the non-
Remus fiction, that made the Uncle Remus animal
stories possible.

In the December issue for 1877, *Lippincott's Magazine*
published an article, "Folklore of the Southern Negroes," by William Owens. Harris commented on it in the
Constitution for November 21, 1877, and remarked on
the author's lack of expertise in translating dialect. But
the article made Harris realize that literary value existed
in the animal stories and myths that he had once heard
from slaves in Eatonton and at Turnwold. So he moved
Uncle Remus from Atlanta back to "Putmon County,"
where he had been a slave for "Mars Jeems," and set
him to telling the six-year-old white boy of the plantation a story of how Mr. Rabbit outwitted Mr. Fox. The
account appeared in the *Constitution* for July 20, 1879.
He waited four months before publishing a second
animal story, which appeared on September 17. Mr.
Rabbit and Mr. Fox now became Brer Rabbit and Brer
Fox, and the story was about how Brer Fox fooled Brer
Rabbit by constructing a tar baby. Harris had found his

subject. More than that, he had found a way to tell what he knew in print.

The format of the Uncle Remus animal stories, developed at the start and maintained with little change through eight books, has the little white boy—in later volumes, the first little boy's son—visiting Uncle Remus in his cabin on the plantation and listening, with occasional comments, while Remus tells about the days when the creatures could talk.

Clearly it is not the folktale subject matter as such that provides the chief appeal of the Uncle Remus stories, though when he began publishing them Harris discovered to his surprise that he was indeed contributing to the literature of folklore and that the same stories of rabbit, fox, wolf, terrapin, raccoon, and opossum that plantation Negroes in Georgia had told to him were known to ethnologists the world over, with their counterparts existing among the Indians of North and South America, the bushmen of Australia, and the Moro tribesmen of the Philippines. The appeal lies in the way that they are told and in the dynamics of the relationship between Uncle Remus, the successive little white boys who listen, and the animal protagonists of the tales themselves, notably Brer Rabbit. The animal legends were necessary to Harris for the basis of his stories; when he exhausted his stock of recollections he advertised for more, and his readers supplied him with new materials. But Mark Twain was quite right when he told Harris that "in reality the stories are only alligator pears—one merely eats them for the sake of the salad dressing." The importance of the stories is that, because of their content and the associations they had for Harris, they enabled him to tap wellsprings of creativity hitherto unknown and fully available to him in no other form. When he tried to do it through other guises, it was never the same. In the Uncle Remus stories Harris was indeed able to *see* the world as a black man did, and also to sense *why* the black man looked at it in that fashion.

The important thing to remember about the Uncle Remus stories is that not merely the old Negro telling the stories, but the animal protagonists themselves, are southern rural blacks. What they do is inseparable from the idiom used to describe their actions. It is Brer Rabbit, and occasionally Brer Terrapin, whose antics provide the plot of the stories. The various tricks that Brer Rabbit plays on the fox, the wolf, the bear, the cow, and sometimes even Mr. Man himself, all exhibit his cunning and his resourcefulness, and it is this that Uncle Remus most admires as he relates them. Sometimes Brer Rabbit acts in order to procure food, sometimes to protect himself from being eaten, sometimes to avoid work while enjoying its benefits. At times his chief motivation is that of gaining revenge for attempted attacks on himself or his family. His dignity is also very important to him; he is quick to avenge any insult or slight. Sometimes, too, he will go to work on his fellow creatures merely in order to keep them mindful of his identity. Occasionally he is prompted by sheer mischievousness; in company with Brer Terrapin he will suddenly decide to have some fun with the others.

Harris knew very well that the rabbit was a Negro. In the preface to the second published volume, *Nights with Uncle Remus,* he declared of the black man's preference for the rabbit as hero of his folklore that "it needs no scientific investigation to show why he selects as his hero the weakest and most harmless of all animals, and brings him out victorious in contests with the bear, the wolf, and the fox. It is not *virtue* that triumphs, but *helplessness;* it is not *malice,* but *mischievousness.*" Several critics have pointed out, however, that strictly speaking, this last is not true of the Uncle Remus stories, for usually Brer Rabbit is more than merely mischievous: he can be quite malicious at times, and he is very much set on maintaining his prestige and reputation. Often his triumphs are based on the instinct for sheer survival rather than on any taste for prank playing. But it is something of a mistake to allegorize these stories, as some have done, merely as showing the Negro rabbit using his helplessness and his apparently insignificant status as weapons against the white power structure in the guise of the fox, bear, and wolf. The matter is a trifle more complex than that. What the rabbit exemplifies is the capacity to survive and flourish in a world in which society can be and often is predatory. The rabbit confronts life; the realism with which his situation is depicted, as Louise Dauner shows, "precludes any sentimentality. . . . Both life and death must be fatalistically accepted."[3] The power is in the hands of the strong; the weak cannot trust to any supposed belief in benevolence or fair play, for the real rules are those of power. That this had profound implications for the situation of the black man in rural southern society is obvious; yet what makes the stories work so well is not any such direct political and social allegory, but the realism with which Harris can view the life he is depicting.

It is not that Harris was, consciously or unconsciously, trying to allegorize the plight of the black man; these are not parables of protest, and their success comes because they are not thus shaped. If they are moral, they are so as all great art is moral: through depicting the actualities of the human situation and by implication contrasting them with what we hold to be ideal. Through his instinctive identification with the black man, Harris was able to depict society as it confronted the underdog (or under-rabbit, perhaps). Writing about animals, he could describe humans, and with a realism that was not subject to verification by the rules of poetic justice. A slave—or a sharecropper—must accept things as he finds them, not as he might like for them to be.

3. Louise Dauner, "Myth and Humor in the Uncle Remus Fables," *American Literature*, XX (May, 1948), 135.

"De creeturs dunno nothin' 'tall 'bot dat dat's good en dat dat ain't good," Uncle Remus tells the little white boy. "Dey dunno right fum wrong. Dey see what dey want, en dey git it if dey kin, by hook er by crook. Dey don't ax who it b'longs ter, ner wharbouts it come fum. Dey dunno de diffunce 'twix what's dern en what ain't dern." In telling about the animals, Harris did not have to shape the morality and motivations of his characters in accordance with what the ideality of his time and place decreed ought to be; he could view their actions and responses in terms of what truly *was*. Uncle Remus could accept harsh actualities in a way that a white narrator might not have been able to do, because the experience that was Remus'—the experience of the plantation slave, as Harris had been privileged to perceive it—was all too elemental and devoid of merely sentimental gestures. "In dem days," Remus tells the little boy on another occasion, "de creeturs bleedzd ter look out fer deyse'f, mo' speshually dem w'at ain't got hawn en huff. Brer Rabbit ain't got no hawn en huff, en he bleedzd ter be his own lawyer." Harris knew this, but it was only when writing of Negro life in the guise of the animals that he could, as a writer, tell what he knew.

Writing about black experience in the form of animal stories, therefore, served to liberate Joel Chandler Harris' imagination. It provided him with a technique whereby a writer who had once been a shy, stammering, redheaded, illegitimate youth and faced social realities in a way that was direct and unprotected, could draw upon what he knew and create stories that depicted reality as few other writers of his time and place were able to do. He could make use of his humor, his awareness of the savageness and the remorseless nature of human circumstance, his sense of fatality, without the inhibitions of the genteel literary tradition, social respectability, or southern racial imperatives.

The Uncle Remus animal stories are not tragic; they

are comic. But the comedy is decidedly not that of foolish, childlike darkies, the standard fare of local color. It is not comedy sweetened by sentiment. When, for example, in the story entitled "Why Mr. Possum Has No Hair on His Tail," the rabbit and possum decide to raid the bear's persimmon orchard, and the rabbit decides to have some fun and informs the bear that Brer Possum is up in his persimmon trees, it is not Brer Rabbit who gets punished, either for his collaboration in theft or his betrayal of his accomplice. The possum is the one who suffers; he is shaken down from the tree, flees, and just as he escapes through the fence the bear grabs his tail in his jaws and rakes it forever clean of fur. The rabbit enjoys the spectacle thoroughly. The aggression, the pleasure taken in the possum's discomfiture, the cleverness of the rabbit, are amusing, but only because the characters are animals; one cannot imagine Harris or any other such writer suggesting a similar outcome to a story involving people. Yet the characters *are* people —black people. Thus was Harris enabled, however obliquely, to deal with reality, whether white or black.

As for the narrator, Uncle Remus, he enjoys the whole account. *He,* of course, wouldn't do such things; for he is the kindly, noble local-color retainer. But he tells the little white boy about a world in which such things do happen, and then, when the little white boy occasionally becomes disturbed by the indifference of the creatures to conventional ethics, Uncle Remus reminds him that rabbits, foxes, bears, possums, terrapins, and the like cannot be judged by human standards. As Louise Dauner says, "In Uncle Remus we have the symbol of the wisdom of Things-As-They-Are, a realistic acceptance and humorous transmission of the strenuous conditions and paradoxes of life. In Brer Rabbit we have the inescapable irony of the Irrational, coupled with man's own terribly humorous struggle for survival." Truly, the implications of the Uncle Remus stories are ferocious—as ferocious as those of the Mother Goose poems.

Only in the animal stories can Harris offer such an unsentimental version of reality. Those Uncle Remus stories which are not centered on animal fables achieve no such directness, nor did they enjoy any such popularity as the animal tales. In those Atlanta sketches, Uncle Remus is all but indistinguishable from a hundred other literary plantation uncles.

Harris wrote a large quantity of fiction. Several of the early stories, notably that entitled "Free Joe and the Rest of the World," are among the better local-color fiction. Harris does, in that story, come closer to imaging the black man's situation than does most local-color fiction. The story describes a freed Negro during slavery times and tells of how, because he has no economic value to the white community, he is separated from his wife, who is still a slave, and left to starve. Some critics—Darwin Turner, for one—have read the story as an example of white racism, declaring that it exemplifies Harris' habit of thinking of Negroes who are not protected by white men as pathetic creatures. There is truth to this. Turner criticizes the depiction of Mom Bi, in "Mom Bi: Her Friends and Enemies," as so selflessly devoted to her white family that she resents less her aristocratic master's selling her daughter than his sending his son off to fight side by side with low-caste whites in the Confederate army, where he is killed.[4] Such devotion, Turner remarks, is rather farfetched. Harris' insistence in print that white southern fear of the black man is without rational basis is explained by Turner as being due to his view of blacks as harmless, comical children: "One does not hate or fear a child or a pet, even when he misbehaves."

Again, there is justice to what Turner says. But the

4. Darwin Turner, "Daddy Joel Harris and His Old Time Darkies," *Southern Literary Journal*, I (1968), 36.

difficulty with such criticism is that it is ahistorical and thus cannot recognize and acknowledge what was quite clear to Harris' own contemporaries: that, viewed not by the standards of the 1960s and 1970s but in the historical context of white-black relationships in the South and of the depiction of blacks in fiction, Harris' black characters represent an important advance in the literary representation of the black man's humanity. Harris was not writing his stories at a time when that humanity was generally acknowledged, whether in the South or the North. He was showing black characters as suffering because mistreated, misjudged, misunderstood—during an era when the very depiction of the fact that, for example, a Free Joe could be deprived of all human dignity and joy by cruel or thoughtless whites merely because he was black constituted something of a rebuke to contemporary attitudes. In stressing the loyalty of his blacks to the whites, he was advancing the hypothesis that a people capable of such loyalty were worthy of help and trust and fair treatment, and such was decidedly not what a great many southerners were interested in giving them at the time, or willing to concede that they merited. It is quite true that portraiture along such lines, no matter how well intended, is ultimately demeaning; but that was not the issue in the years of the 1880s when Harris was writing those stories. The issue was much more stark and elemental. It was whether, as a recipient of the policies and attitudes of the white majority, the black man was worthy of the treatment accorded to a human being. In story after story, Harris said he was, and that was a great deal more than many of his fellow southerners were prepared to admit, if the political and social developments of the late nineteenth century are any indication. If the attitudes of today seem far removed from those of the 1880s and 1890s, it might be proper to suggest that writers such as Joel Chandler Harris had something to do with that.

A large portion of Harris' writings, from the early novel *The Romance of Rockville* onward, is focused not upon the black but the plain folk. He considered the area of middle Georgia where he grew up the most democratic region in the country: and in many of his stories, as well as his two later novels, *Sister Jane* (1896) and *Gabriel Tolliver* (1902), he sought to recreate that democratic village environment in fiction. This was in line with Harris' own origins and his views; as one of a relatively few important southern writers after 1865 who did not come from the gentry, he did not envision everyday southern experience as primarily an affair of plantations, but of small towns and villages. Uncle Remus, it is true, lives on a plantation; but the stories he tells are of the days when the creatures could talk, of the rural farming community, and have little to do with plantation life. Even the autobiographical *On the Plantation* is the account of a youth employed on a plantation, associating not with the planter and his family so much as with the slaves, the Irish journeyman printer, nearby middle-class whites, and villagers. In a story, "Ananias," Harris dealt rather sarcastically with one Colonel Flewellyn, who is clearly modeled on Joseph Addison Turner, emphasizing his impracticality and foolishness. In *Sister Jane* the local squire turns out to be the seducer of a farm girl. Indeed, it might be said that in the long run Joel Chandler Harris worked importantly to undercut the plantation literary tradition. He not only shifted the center of attention from the lordly master and lovely lady to the black slave, but he made the plain folk of the village the focus of his non-Negro stories, thereby opening the way for much realistic southern fiction of a later day.

Yet it must be said that except perhaps for one or two stories such as "Free Joe and the Rest of the World," the only work of Harris that has importantly survived its day are the animal stories. To some extent this may be ascribed to the format of the Uncle Remus stories; Harris was able to handle such episodes of 1,500 to 2,500 words with a formal expertness that he was not able to bring to longer, more complicated stories, and when he sought to work at the novel length he was out of his depth. In this respect his journalistic limitations stayed with him always; once he exceeded the length of the newspaper format he got into trouble. Yet this by itself will not suffice as an explanation; for when he tried the same thing later on, with his Billy Sanders sketches, with the spokesman-protagonist a sage, humorous middle Georgia white farmer, the results are not impressive.

The real difficulty would seem to be that except when he was writing about life as experienced by southern Negroes in the guise of rabbits, terrapins, and other animal creatures, he became too much the sentimentalist and all too unwilling or unable to look at life without making everything come out right. There *had* to be happy endings; village life had to be shown as sweet, tolerant, without prejudice; slaves had to be treated with kindness; seducers had to have hearts of gold; blacks during the Reconstruction and afterward had to be loyal to the white folks. Only in the tales told by Uncle Remus do people steal, lie, and triumph even so; only in them do people live by their wits and enjoy it; only in them are deception and trickiness portrayed as virtues and economic necessities as more binding than moral imperatives. Harris never read any of the animal tales to his own children. "I was just thinking," the little boy remarks to Uncle Remus after an episode in which Brer Rabbit cleverly steals Brer Fox's provender, "that when Brother Rabbit got the chickens from Brother Fox, he was really stealing them." To which Remus replies, "Dey ain't no two ways 'bout dat. But what wuz Brer Fox doin' when *he* got um? Pullets an' puddle ducks don't grow on trees, an' it's been a mighty long time sence dey been runnin' wil'. No, honey! Dey's a heap er idees dat you got ter shake off if you gwine ter put de creeters 'longside de folks; you'll hatter shake um, an' shuck um. . . . Folks got der laws, an' de creeturs got der'n, an' it bleeze ter be dat away." Life in the world of Uncle Remus is no picnic; as he remarks upon another occasion, "ef deze yer tales wuz des fun, fun, fun, en giggle, giggle, giggle, I let you know I'd a-done drapt um long ago. Yasser, w'em it come down ter gigglin' you kin des count ole Remus out."

Was Harris fully aware of what he was doing in those stories? Such remarks as that just quoted seem to leap out of the page with startling clarity. What are they doing there at all? We know that Harris was quite aware that he was writing about black people. It seems inevitable that, having heard the stories under the circumstances that he did, he would have known that they were not, in their symbolic action, without relevance to the daily lives of the blacks. Yet before we go too far in crediting Harris with any secret racial subversiveness—and for a modern reader the temptation is all too real—we must remember that very little in his nonanimal stories involving black people in the South will validate any such theorizing, while there is considerable evidence to show that Harris was of his time and place and that, however benevolent his attitude, he did not transcend his circumstance. Furthermore, whatever it may have been that Harris intended, and whether consciously or unconsciously, his audience surely did not read the stories as subversive. In their time the stories seemed only to confirm the stereotype of the contented darky. They told readers that the black man was happy. They seemed to glorify life on the old plantation.

He was a curious man—not at all the simple sage of Snap-Bean Farm that he is made out to be, but a very private and complex person. It is as if there were two Joel Chandler Harrises—the journalist, citizen of Georgia, and man of letters who wrote pleasant, optimistic, moral tales in which right triumphed and the plain folk were good and kind; and the fiercely creative artist, his uncompromising realism masked to the world and to the other Harris as well by the animal-tales format, one who saw life devoid of sentiment and unclouded by wishful thinking. He himself sensed this. Here is what he once wrote to his two daughters:

You know all of us have two entities, or personalities. That is the reason you see and hear persons "talking to themselves." They are talking to the "other fellow." I have often asked my "other fellow" where he gets all his information, and how he can remember, in the nick of time, things that I have forgotten long ago; but he never satisfies my curiosity. He is simply a spectator of my folly until I seize a pen, and then he comes forward and takes charge. . . . Now, I'll admit that I write the editorials for the paper. The "other fellow" has nothing to do with them, and, so far as I am able to get his views on the subject, he regards them with scorn and contempt; though there are rare occasions when he helps me out on a Sunday editorial. He is a creature hard to understand, but, so far as I can understand him, he's a very sour, surly fellow until I give him an opportunity to guide my pen in subjects congenial to him; whereas, I am, as you know, jolly, good-natured, and entirely harmless.

Now, my "other fellow," I am convinced, would do some damage if I didn't give him an opportunity to work off his energy in the way he delights. I say to him, "Now, here's an editor who says he will pay well for a short story. He wants it at once." Then I forget all about the matter, and go on writing editorials and taking Celery Compound and presently my "other fellow" says sourly: "What about that story?" Then when night comes, I take up my pen, surrender unconditionally to my "other fellow," and out comes the story, and if it is a good story I am as much surprised as the people who read it. Now, my dear gals will think I am writing nonsense; but I am telling them the truth as near as I can get at the facts—for the "other fellow" is secretive. Well! so much for that. You can take a long breath now and rest yourselves.[5]

5. Joel Chandler Harris to Lillian and Mildred Harris, March 10, 1898, quoted in Julia Collier Harris, *Life and Letters*, 385–86.

In his later years, Harris grew increasingly out of sympathy with the booming, bustling progressive spirit that continued to exemplify Atlanta commercial and civic life, the heritage of his friend Grady. He did not like the new ways and did not share in the latter-day enshrinement, as he saw it, of the almighty dollar. There was too much materialism in the air; more and more he looked back at the village life of his childhood as having embodied a simplicity and a spiritual cleanliness that he thought was disappearing now from Georgia and the South. He never repudiated or even criticized what his friend Grady had meant for the South, and yet he must have realized that it was Grady's program that was more than a little responsible for the emphasis on money-making that was building huge skyscrapers along Peachtree Street and mansions in Druid Hills, even while the slums grew more dilapidated along Rusty Row and Decatur Street. "We hear a good deal about Progress," we find him writing in 1907; "it is held over the head of the conservative in the semblance of a big stick, but there is nothing crueler or more sinister, for progress is nothing more than the multiplication of the machinery and methods by which certain classes and people increase their material gains. The necessity of trade and barter has always existed . . . but modern business is the result of a partnership between greed and gain, and it consists in nothing but an abnormal cleverness in assembling and dispersing pieces of paper that stand for nothing, and in massing the details of large and unnecessary transactions." It was a long way from Henry W. Grady that he had traveled, toward the end.

On July 3, 1908, at the age of fifty-nine, Joel Chandler Harris died of uremic poisoning, the result of cirrhosis of the liver. Two weeks before his death he sent for a Catholic priest, Father O. N. Jackson, and asked to be baptized in his wife's faith. "I have put off this impor-

tant matter too long," he told the priest, "but procrasti-
nation has been the bugbear of my life; and I feel that
the Lord will make allowance for this weakness, for I
have believed the teachings of the Catholic Church for
many years." Father Jackson reported that when he
asked whether fear of criticism by others had helped
cause Harris' delay in joining the Church, he was told,
"No; I should say shyness had more to do with it."

The Passion of Sidney Lanier

If one had to characterize the personality of Sidney Lanier, the word that would probably come to mind is *intensity*. To judge by his letters and by the reminiscences of his friends, from his early years onward he seems to have vibrated with feeling. Had he been a New Englander rather than a Georgian and grown up in the orbit of transcendentalism, he would have led them all in the intensity of his response to life. As it was, he went from Macon, where he was born in 1842, to Oglethorpe University, where the controversial Professor James Woodrow introduced him to philosophical and theological speculation. During his college years Lanier also discovered Thomas Carlyle, and through him the German romantics and the intoxication of their transcendentalism. For the rest of his life he remained drunk on ideas—or, more specifically, on intellectualized emotion.

His continuing love for music—he was a skilled flutist—both fed and was fed by his philosophizing; he is said to have declared that during his college years the playing of violin music "would sometimes so exalt him in rapture, that presently he would sink from his solitary music-worship into a deep trance, thence to awake, alone, on the floor of his room, sorely shaken in nerve."[1] But for Lanier it seemed necessary that everything about life be exalted to the utmost degree; he wrote, played music, studied, and loved with a degree of emotional intensity that, when not held rigorously in check by the discipline of a form, was often embarrassing. The famous concluding line of his later poem "The Symphony"— "Music is Love in search of a word"—however vague its poetic meaning, is almost a paradigm of his own mental attitude: all his life he seemed to be seeking a way to transcend the boundaries of human life and the material world and attain a unified, visionary celebration of pure essence, without knowing exactly how to go about it. In later years he is described as having a kind of luminous look to his features, a look that impressed all who came in contact with him. Daniel Coit Gilman relates the way in which various persons attempted to describe Lanier's appearance, as captured in a bust. One said, "He looks like Moses"; another said, "He looks like Christ." A German physiologist simply said, "Tuberculosis."[2] But the same kind of intellectual intensity characterized Lanier long before he contracted the lung disease that was eventually to kill him. His college roommate recalled that when he played music "it would seem as if his soul were in a trance, and could only find existence, expression, in the ecstacy of tone, that would catch our souls with him into the very seventh heaven of harmony. . . . I have never seen one who enjoyed nature more than he. And his love for her was so intense that I have sometimes imag-

1. William Hayes Ward, "Memorial," in [Mary Day Lanier, ed.] *Poems of Sidney Lanier, Edited by His Wife* (New York, 1913), xii.
2. Daniel Coit Gilman, "Sidney Lanier: Reminiscences and Letters," *South Atlantic Quarterly,* IV (April, 1905), repr. in William Baskerville Hamilton (ed.), *Fifty Years of the South Atlantic Quarterly, 1902–1952* (Durham, N.C., 1952), 99.

ined he could hear the murmur, the music, that springs from the growing of grass."[3]

Even four years of often-arduous wartime service did not serve to tone down his spiritual and emotional intensity very much. With his beloved brother Clifford—Lanier habitually addressed him as "My darling Cliff" in his correspondence—he enlisted in 1861 in the Confederate service. The two Laniers saw duty in coastal Virginia and North Carolinia, fought in the Seven Days battles around Richmond, then transferred to the Signal Corps where they served in Virginia until sent to Wilmington, North Carolina, for sea duty aboard Confederate blockade runners. Sidney's ship was captured in the Gulf Stream on November 3, 1864, and he was sent to various Federal prisons, ending up at Point Lookout, where he underwent four months of deprivation that caused permanent damage to his lungs. By the time he was exchanged, in early 1865, he was in wretched physical condition; and when he finally got back home to Macon, after walking most of the way, he was gravely ill for months afterward. Yet during the war he had managed to keep his beloved flute with him, even in prison, and had begun a novel, *Tiger-Lilies*, which his completed in 1865–1866.

Tiger-Lilies is a bizarre novel, a preposterous combination of German transcendentalist philosophizing, after the manner of Novalis and Jean Paul Richter. The opening sections take place in a Tennessee mountain retreat named Thalberg, inhabited by heroes, villains, philosophers, and musicians from several continents; there is also a melodramatic revenge plot and some Civil War scenes, including several interesting army episodes. It is largely the last-named that elevate the novel above the level of Augusta Evans Wilson's *St. Elmo* and

3. T. F. Newell, quoted in William Malone Baskervill, "Sidney Lanier," *Southern Writers: Biographical and Critical Sketches*, I (Nashville, Tenn., 1897), 150–51.

Macaria, which otherwise it resembles in technique. On the other hand, there is an element of exuberance in *Tiger-Lilies,* a ferocity of expressiveness that gives the work, in its very failure, a dignity of sorts. One has the feeling about it, for all its clumsiness, its amateurish handling of plot and characterization, its undigested (and in the form presented, undigestible) pudding of ideas, that the person who wrote it was no mere hack, no journeyman romancer, but an intellect of potentially formidable powers. Perhaps this is what prompted the critic of the *Round-Table* to remark that "his errors seem to us to be entirely errors of youth and in the right direction. . . . We hope to have from his pen a better novel than *Tiger-Lilies*—a better one, in fact, than any Southern writer has hitherto blest us with."[4]

What would have been needed for Lanier to write a good novel was never to happen: a much more sophisticated and intelligent tutelage in the form of fiction than he was ever to receive. He had no idea at all of what it was possible to achieve in fiction, or how to achieve it; when his father and uncle, having read the early sections of *Tiger-Lilies,* objected to the author's habit of philosophizing about what was going on, Lanier replied, "I think perhaps you have failed to appreciate the distinctive feature of the *Novel,* as contrasted with the Drama. The difference between these two great methods of delineating events is, simply and only, that the Novel permits its Author to explain, by his *own mouth,* the 'situation': whereas, in the drama, this must be done by the characters. . . . A novel is nothing more than a *Drama with the stage-directions infinitely amplified and extended.*"[5] *Tiger-Lilies* exemplifies this naïve

4. Review, *Round-Table,* December 14, 1867, quoted in Garland Greever (ed.), "Introduction" to Sidney Lanier, *Tiger-Lilies and Southern Prose,* Vol. V of *Centennial Edition of the Works of Sidney Lanier* (Baltimore, 1945), xii.

5. Sidney Lanier to Robert S. Lanier, July 13, 1866, in Sidney Lanier, *Letters, 1869–1873,* ed. Charles R. Anderson and Aubrey Starke, Vol. VIII of *Centennial Edition,* 212.

concept of narrative form: Lanier uses his authorial role to expound exuberantly upon all manner of things; his commentary is a bewildering assortment of ideas and emotions, and the plot, instead of serving to develop and embody the meanings he wants it to have, moves capriciously from one melodramatic episode to another.

Lanier's ideal for the novel would have been a work of which there is no evidence that he ever heard: Melville's *Moby-Dick.* But so disorganized, so undisciplined, and so romantic was Sidney Lanier's intellect that he could never have managed the profound exploration into motive and meaning that Melville offers. Lanier was really not, as Edmund Wilson declares, "sometimes a little stupid."[6] Instead, he was very poorly educated—it is most unfortunate that he was prevented by the war from pursuing the doctoral studies he planned in Germany—and also *mis*educated, in that the sentimental romanticism that passed for intellectual currents in western society of the mid-nineteenth century prevented him from examining and coming to terms with the life around him and his own relationship to it. Nothing could be further separated than the occasional realistic dialogue and humorous satire in *Tiger-Lilies* and the overriding romanticism, sentimentality, and empty ideality of the novel. Lanier had no notion of how to bring them together; for his puritan theology prevented him from making any exploration into psychology. The result was that he attempted to etherealize everything; in particular the strong sexual element in his makeup went completely unrecognized—for he had been taught to ignore the body—and instead was diffused in wild, ungrounded, latently pantheistic ideality.

During this period Lanier was writing and publishing some poetry. None of it is noteworthy, for the idiom in which he wrote and the conventions that he knew were

6. Edmund Wilson, *Patriotic Gore: Studies in the Literature of the American Civil War* (New York, 1962), 461.

most unsuitable to his talents and alien to his temperament. He was trying to write the abstract, bloodless, formally regular poetry of ideality, as practiced by his friend Paul Hamilton Hayne, by Longfellow, and by the other poets of the genteel school. What Lanier needed was a poetic convention that would permit him to develop and combine images, not arrange them separately in isolated units; and he needed an approach to language that would bring him closer to the representation of the things of his experience, not one that drew him away from a saving grounding in actuality and toward abstract summary. These were not to be found in the magazine verse of the period, with its equation of beauty with ideality and of emotional intensity with self-conscious, "Literary" diction.

He did not confine his tumultuous emotional response to ideas or to literature. He was also, during the years just after the war, constantly falling in and out of love and composing mawkishly passionate letters to his enamored—often to more than one young lady in swift succession. Thus on October 6, 1866, we find him writing to Mary Day, "Let me say that I *do* desire to meet you, again. At such a time, perhaps a momentary flash of Heaven-light out of those old brilliant *first*-days might dazzle my eyes which have been all unused to such light, since then; but I should recover, and the succeeding Earth-light, displaying you as my faithful friend and me as yours, would still be delightful and not too strong for me."[7] On October 14, he writes to Ginna Hankins, "Today I would see your face and eyes and hands. It is the very passion of hunger that comes over me,—of hunger for you in the sweet body. Today I am not content to know, as I *do* know, that your Spirit is here, but I yearn ceaselessly with heartswelling and sighing that I might walk the fair solemn fall-fields with you, as we walked

7. Sidney Lanier to Mary Day, October 6, 1866, in *Letters, 1857–68,* ed. Anderson and Starke, Vol. VI of *Centennial Edition,* 243.

them once."[8] On November 5, he writes to her that "it utterly breaks my heart that I cannot fold You up, now, from all this grief, from all this dead drudgery which fits you no more than a body fits a soul."[9] December sees him writing to Mary Day, "I was replying to your letters when your last one came. See what I wrote! I, too, was crazy:—but, Child, your words were too much; some of them were even *cold*, to *me*! Well—Away with all that—it is Night-talk, it is dank and terrible:—here is the Morning, let us talk in the light: here are flowers about us, with dew and odors, let us enjoy them; we are tired wandering in the Dark, here is Nature, a rock covered with moss. Sit with me and rest: our ears are full of Night-sounds, let us sit in Music like Michael to chase these Devils out of our Heaven. . . . Your dainty letters breathe and stagger with beautiful things like a Spring with more flowers in her lap than her jaunty apron would hold!"[10] To judge from the available letters, his lady friends apparently replied in kind. Mary Day finally emerged winner, and on December 19, 1867, they were married.

In these years Lanier's lungs were giving him much trouble, as they would do for the remainder of his life. He spent periods of time in New York City where a specialist treated them and pronounced them cured, but the trouble continued. Earning a living was a constant problem; sustained work proved impossible. For a while he clerked in a hotel, then studied law, was admitted to the bar, and sought to practice for a time in his father's firm, but his health deteriorated rapidly and he was forced to give that up. His aversion to trade, given expression in *Tiger-Lilies* and thereafter a constant refrain in his writings, did not prevent him from coming up with several speculative schemes, one of them involv-

8. Lanier to Virginia Hankins, October 14, 1866, *ibid.*, 249.
9. Lanier to Virginia Hankins, November 5, 1866, *ibid.*, 254.
10. Lanier to Mary Day, December 9–15 [?], 1866, *ibid.*, 255.

ing going to New York in an effort to sell some of the
family land for iron mining, and another for producing
charcoal and furnishing it to an iron mill in northern
Georgia and elsewhere in the state. He also taught
school and sought to secure a position at the University
of Alabama. Meanwhile he continued writing poetry,
primarily a long poem he called "The Jacquerie" which
he was never to finish, and spent long periods away
from his wife and children looking for a place with a
climate favorable to his lungs, where he might settle
permanently. It was while he was in Texas to sample the
climate there that he resumed seriously playing the flute
and decided to attempt to find a vocation at that, in New
York and then in Baltimore; typically he immediately
borrowed $240 to buy a sterling silver Boehm flute. His
father and his brother Clifford, and his wife's father as
well, did their best to sustain him and his ever-growing
family. Lanier himself did all he could to earn money,
but whenever matters began showing any signs of improving financially for him, his lungs would give way
and it would be necessary for him to give up work. Had
he only been able to practice law in the family office on a
continuing basis, much of his financial woe would have
been alleviated.

Lanier's entrance into the musical life of Baltimore
was a stirring experience for him. That he was an excellent flutist he did not doubt—Lanier never lacked
confidence in his abilities, in whatever he decided to
do—but he was largely untrained and without experience in playing in orchestral groups. Though the Peabody Conservatory Orchestra was not notably large—
approximately thirty-five musicians—in its complexity it was quite beyond anything he had previously
known. To his wife he wrote a glowing description of
the first rehearsal: "O my Heart, O my Twin, if thou
cdst. but be by me in this sublime glory of music! All

through it I yearned for thee, with heart-breaking eagerness. The beauty of it maketh me catch my breath,—to write it. I will not attempt to describe it."[11] To Ginna Hankins, with whom he still corresponded, he wrote, "We have a magnificent Orchestra: the delights, the ecstasies, the manifold Heavens, through which I pass in playing with them,—are not to be described."[12] There is no doubt that Lanier was distinctly a success in his debut with an orchestra; he was repeatedly praised in reviews of the orchestra's performances, and the conductor, Hamerick, was delighted with him.

He seems, however, to have found his new role of playing as one musician in a large group very demanding. To his brother Clifford he wrote that "suddenly saddled with the duty of interpreting a responsible part in works which I had never even heard before, in company, too, with old musicians most of whom have been playing ever since they were children and doing nothing else—, all this nearly made my spirit give way many times."[13] A remark to his wife in early 1874 is indicative of what was involved:

My greatest trouble in playing has been to keep in tune with the Oboe: the tone of that instrument is so strange, so strident, and so indecisive when one is close to the player, (he sitteth immediately behind me) that I have infinite difficulty in accommodating my pitch to his. Some of the notes on his instrument, too, are incorrect; and, inasmuch as he *cannot* change his tones, and as my music is often written in octaves above his, I have to use the utmost caution and skill in turning the embouchure in and out, so as to be in perfect accord with him. For some weeks I did not succeed in this, and suffered untold agonies thereanent: but I believe I have now discovered all his quips and his quirks, and tonight we were in

11. Lanier to Mary Day Lanier, December 2, 1873, in *Letters, 1869–1873*, p. 426.
12. Lanier to Virginia Hankins, December 23, 1873, *ibid.*, 443.
13. Lanier to Clifford A. Lanier, January 4, 1874, in Sidney Lanier, *Letters, 1874–1877*, ed. Anderson and Starke, Vol. IX of *Centennial Edition*, 8.

lovely harmony with each other. I read far better than at first: and am greatly improved in the matter of keeping time with the Orchestra. How much I have learned in the last two months!"[14]

As we shall see, it may indeed be that Lanier had learned more than he realized.

He went back home to Georgia after the musical season; and after a stay in Brunswick he worked at law in Macon for a while, then installed his family at a farm at Sunnyside, near Griffin, Georgia. He now had several months of comparative freedom. For the past two years he had written little verse, and it was his intention to resume work on his long poem "The Jacquerie," but now another theme began interesting him. The farmland about Sunnyside was thickly planted with corn, and the crop was unusually beautiful. In former years the locale had been given over to cotton cultivation. Lanier began thinking of how the change to corn-growing was symbolic of the prosperity of a new South, no longer mortgaged to the demands of the old cash staple crop. He began writing a poem. When the summer was over, he carried the unfinished manuscript northward with him for further extensive revision.

What was significant about the new poem was its changing attitude to language. While in Baltimore Lanier had been reading Chaucer and Shakespeare; he had been playing music in an orchestra, in which he had had to learn how to discipline his virtuosity in order to achieve an orchestral harmony, to accommodate his own skill to the demands of others. At the same time, as he wrote again and again in his letters, he had been caught up in the enveloping, flowing progression of the music, with its ongoing, complex, rhythmic variations on melodic themes. (He had written, for example, of playing Berlioz' *Symphonie Fantastique,* in which "every movement centreth about a lovely melody, repeated in

14. Lanier to Mary Day Lanier, February 7, 1874, *ibid.,* 27.

all manner of times and guises."[15]) Now he produced a poem in which, for the first time, instead of using language merely to fill out conventional stanzaic forms, he began to shape metrical patterns toward an overall tonal effect, with words chosen toward that goal.

The most notable feature of "Corn" is the way in which, using the model of the Cowleyan ode with its lines of irregular lengths and its diverse patterning, Lanier begins to break away from the singsong repetition of conventional lyric verse. He had already written to his wife of his unhappiness with the *"forms* of today" which "require a certain trim smugness and clean-shaven propriety in the face and dress of a poem."[16] Now he allowed himself to interpolate dactyls and trochees into the dominant iambic meter, and the resulting freedom made it possible for him to choose words that could provide tonal effects of alliteration and consonance. He began, for almost the first time, to place the premium on language texture, and the result was that he found himself doing what so much of the poetry of his time did not manage: selecting words for their sensuous associations as much as for their denotative use in the thought content of the poem. Poe, whose work Lanier's sometimes resembled, had placed a similar importance upon the sound effect of language, but had done so crudely and mechanically, achieving for the most part only a vulgar, repetitive excess that often clashed with the content. Lanier, however, was able, in certain lines and stanzas of his new poem, to create rhythms and images that genuinely blended sound with meaning and achieved subtle formal effects:

> Dreaming of gods, men, nuns and brides, between
> Old companies of oaks that inward lean

15. Lanier to Mary Day Lanier, December 21, 1873, in *Letters, 1869–1873*, p. 427.
16. Lanier to Mary Day Lanier, March 15, 1874, in *Letters, 1874–1877*, pp. 39–40.

> To join their radiant amplitudes of green
> I slowly move, with ranging looks that pass
> Up from the matted miracles of grass
> Into yon veined complex of space
> Where sky and leafage interlace
> So close, the heaven of blue is seen
> Inwoven with a heaven of green.

This is better than anything Lanier had ever previously managed. There is an attentiveness to overall pattern— a marshaling of rhyme, sound, texture, and sense, with each line given a distinctive role in its own right as well as in the total development of the poem—that is not only new for Lanier but otherwise largely missing from the American poetry being written during his time. The movement is *orchestral:* it is as if, at last, Lanier was not merely concentrating his entire effort on a single theme, but was adapting the idea he was developing in the poem to the total performance, seeing to it that the texture of the language, the weight of the individual words, images, and lines, the advancing rhythm of the whole—all functioned in unison.

Musical analogy is a tricky business and all too easy to make: but one has the feeling that somehow the experience of playing as first flutist in the Peabody Orchestra was more than incidentally involved in the new development in poetry. We know that by this juncture in his career Lanier was seriously attempting to fuse the two arts; there is a notable letter that he wrote to his wife, describing the music of an overture entitled "Hunt of Henry IV," by Étienne Nicholas Mehul, and producing a detailed scenario of an actual hunt in Tennessee. And his next poem, "The Symphony," would make the specific analogy of music and poem. Be that as it may, it seems evident that the experience of having had to discipline his flute so that it became part of a larger and more complex musical utterance was making itself felt in the richness and massed complexity of the new poetic technique. Until then, Lanier had never as a poet been able to harness and control the intense, lavish exuberance of emotion and idea that dominated his consciousness; now, by moving to give his poetry an orchestral tone rather than to perform as a solo instrument, he was beginning to find the formal control he needed to express himself.

This is not to say, however, that "Corn" is a successful poem, or even, all in all, a particularly good one. Not only is there still far too much abstract ideality and poeticizing, but the overall thought content of the poem is hackneyed and trite. The personification of the corn as "the poet-soul sublime" is all too farfetched:

> Soul calm, like thee, yet fain, like thee, to grow
> By double increment, above, below . . .
> . . . .
>
> Yea, standing smiling in thy future grave,
>   Serene and brave,
> With unremitting breath
> Inhaling life from death,
> Thine epitaph writ fair in fruitage eloquent,
>   Thyself thy monument.

This is a bit much to make even of a very Wordsworthian stalk of corn. And when Lanier gets to the comparison of corn farmer with cotton farmer, he loses control of the overall movement and imagery of his poem in the interests of delivering his economic message. The result at that point resembles nothing so much as third-rate eighteenth-century programmatic verse, or perhaps Wordsworth at his more simplistic, as when the poor cotton farmer–speculator "mourned his fate unkind":

> In dust, in rain, with might and main,
> He nursed his cotton, cursed his grain,
> Fretted for news that made him fret again,
> Snatched at each telegram of Future Sale,
> And thrilled with Bulls' or Bears' alternate wail—

It is difficult to conceive of either a bull or a bear wailing, much less in alternation; and the use of capital letters to signify that the stock exchange is meant, rather than the stockyard, especially when appearing in a poem about rural life, only makes the figure more artificial. "Corn" is, finally, withered by its message; the ideological argument, so simplistic and so tendentious, comes as an appalling anticlimax to the description of the natural scene, and even the dignity and music of the final stanza, which is one of Lanier's best, cannot salvage it.

Yet if it is a failure, it is of a different order than his earlier work, and one that augured well for the future. The scope of the poem, the massed effects of language and imagery, the imaginative conception of the whole labeled it the work of no ordinary, vegetable-garden variety artist. "Corn" also represented Lanier's first notable popular success. After being rejected by the *Atlantic Monthly* and *Scribner's,* it was accepted by *Lippincott's Magazine.* As Charles Anderson notes, this proved fortunate, for *Lippincott's* was eager to make a reputation through discovering new talent. In the three years that followed, the magazine bought fifteen of Lanier's poems, commissioned prose pieces, and through its publisher issued his first volume of poems. When "Corn" appeared in February, 1875, Gibson Peacock, editor of the Philadelphia *Bulletin,* praised the poem highly, as better than anything produced by the New England poets for decades, and helped launch Lanier's literary reputation.

Meanwhile Lanier had begun a new and even more ambitious poem, "The Symphony." Here was a conscious attempt to fuse music and poetry, in theme as well as technique. The poem concerns itself with Lanier's favorite villian, the spirit of trade, posing against it the beauty of art, as sung by the instruments in the orchestra. Lanier personifies violins, string section, flute, clarinet, horn, oboe, and bassoons, each inveighing against moneygrubbing, and he attempts to give each instrument the language and meters that personify its unique voice. The lines, rhymes, and rhythms of the poem are designed to exemplify the effect of musical statement, with appropriate solo passages, harmonies, choral motifs, and the like. Thus the violins' mode of statement is intricate and highly patterned, while the full string section is more massive. As might be expected, the flute, the voice of nature, is the clearest and most lyric spokesman of all and is assigned the longest solo:

> "Yea, all fair forms, and sounds, and lights,
> And warmths, and mysteries, and mights,
> Of Nature's utmost depths and heights,
> —These doth my timid tongue present,
> Their mouthpiece and their instrument
> And servant, all love-eloquent."

Then comes the "melting clarionet," depicted as a lady who "sings while yet/Her eyes with salty tears are wet," followed by the "bold straightforward horn," whose melody is plainer and more staccato in form. Then the oboe, and finally the wise old bassoons,

> "Like weird
> Gray-beard
> Old harpers sitting on the high sea-dunes,
> Chanted runes"

And the ultimate agreement that

> ". . . yet shall Love himself be heard,
> Though long deferred, though long deferred:
> O'er the modern waste a dove hath whirred:
> Music is Love in search of a word."

The poem is just about as contrived as it sounds from this brief description. Not only is the personification of the instruments as singers inveighing against trade a very strained device, but the theme of the poem, as

developed by Lanier, is sentimental and insubstantial.
Charles Anderson declares that the poem is "the first
important American poem protesting against economic
tyranny and its enslavement of the spirit by commer-
cialism"[17] (which, unless one counts such poems as
Emerson's "Hamatreya" and "Ode to Channing," is
true); but in the form that Lanier voices his protest it is
not very effective. If "The Symphony" is compared with
a work such as Thoreau's *Walden,* its sentimentality is all
too obvious. For Thoreau utilized the rhythms of the
seasons and developed the exploration of nature and
consciousness as both rebuke and counterforce to industrialism and the accumulative instinct, and posited
the organic vitality and simplicity of life and growth
against the sterility and specialization of modern urban
society. Lanier has no such counterforce and no such
vital, explorative metaphor to oppose to trade; the best
he can manage is all-too-repetitiously to inveigh against
it, in the name of "love," without any metaphoric embodiment of a way that love is to go about overcoming
its enemy. He has his flute propose the spirit of nature
as alternative, but does not offer any hint of a method
whereby the opposition is to be mounted. All he can do
is declare,

> ". . . Thou Trade! thou king of the modern days!
>   Change thy ways,
>   Change thy ways . . ."

Thus the protest remains abstract and unspecific, dis-
embodied and, because without any grounding in the
actual conditions of human needs and possibilities, sentimental.

Lanier's distaste for trade crops up in his writings
almost from the beginning. The long poem "The Jacquerie," which occupied him for years and was never

---

17. Charles R. Anderson (ed.), "Introduction" to Sidney Lanier, *Poems
and Poem Outlines,* Vol. I of *Centennial Edition,* xliii.

completed, was concerned with a peasant revolt against usurious nobles in medieval France. In part, Lanier's attitude is a protest against the rapidity with which industrialization was transforming life in the Republic; as such it is obviously not unrelated to his southern origins and upbringing. The notion that the chivalrous South was threatened by the materialistic, money-worshiping North was a commonly held view before the war, and the North's victory seemed to many southerners to be the triumph of the commercial ethos over knightly honor and courtesy. Lanier shared this assumption. We find him, for example, writing to his fellow Georgian Logan E. Bleckley that "it is *now* the *gentleman* who must arise to overthrow Trade."[18] Lanier's often-voiced yearning for the lost days of chivalry is a familiar one among postwar southern writers. With Lanier, however, other factors are involved. His romanticism was thoroughgoing and complete, temperamental as well as ideological. His fondness for Carlyle and for the German romantic idealists is, like a similar fondness on the part of the New England transcendentalists, the manifestation of a disinclination to accept the idea of a materialistic, utilitarian universe. For Lanier, trade was the emblem of just such a soulless world. He would have thoroughly approved of Emerson's lament that "things are in the saddle/and ride mankind." The practical men of business and finance, who view life as commodity and property, are without spirituality; trade is of the head, the rational intellect, while love and art are of the heart. Though at various times he came up with moneymaking schemes of his own, none of which ever worked, Lanier resented the social order that forced him to concern himself with material things and that made money-grubbing so important in his own life. "I have not a solitary trouble which does not come from the need of

18. Lanier to Logan E. Bleckley, November 15, 1874, in *Letters, 1874–1877*, p. 122.

money,—twelve hundred dollars would make me the happiest king on earth!" he once wrote to his wife from New York.[19] He was constantly forced to borrow money, propose publication and lecturing schemes, and depend on the generosity of his father and brother to buy the necessities of life for himself and his family. "Perhaps you know," he wrote to the poet Bayard Taylor, "that with us of the younger generation in the South since the War, pretty much the whole of life has been merely not-dying."[20] Lanier's hostility to commercial society of his time, therefore, came from deep personal feeling as well as a philosophical distaste for the kind of life that concerned itself with materialistic values.

Unfortunately, however, it never really becomes anything beyond an emotion: strongly held, constantly felt, but not ever critically examined or made the occasion for a searching analysis of the underlying premises of the society. In the 1930s the publication of Aubrey Starke's excellent biography of Lanier, with its depiction of Lanier as a stern and farseeing critic of industrial capitalism, touched off a dispute in which several of the Nashville Agrarians, who had recently published in *I'll Take My Stand* an indictment of an industrially oriented society, insisted that Lanier's hostility to trade was sentimental and superficial.[21] Starke responded that in discounting Lanier, the Agrarians were denying a prophet and leader. Certainly the Agrarians—Robert Penn Warren, Allen Tate, and John Crowe Ransom—were quite correct when they pointed out that in paradoxi-

19. Lanier to Mary Day Lanier, October 10, 1873, in *Letters 1869—1873*, p. 399.
20. Lanier to Bayard Taylor, August 7, 1875, *ibid.*, 230.
21. For the dispute between Starke and the Agrarians, see Starke's *Sidney Lanier: A Biographical and Critical Study* (Chapel Hill, 1933), *passim;* Robert Penn Warren, "The Blind Poet: Sidney Lanier," *American Review*, II (1935), 27–45; Allen Tate, "A Southern Romantic," *New Republic*, LXXVI (August 30,1933), 67–70; Starke, "The Agrarians Deny a Leader," *American Review*, II (1934), 534–53; and John Crowe Ransom, "Hearts and Heads," *American Review*, II (1934), 554–71.

cally championing an expansive American nationalism
while decrying the commercial spirit that sinewed it,
Lanier was failing to realize that the two were mutually
interdependent and that the theme of a burgeoning,
developing America that Lanier was praising in his
"Psalm of the West" and "Centennial Cantata" was in
reality a manifestation of the economic spirit that he so
despised. Lanier's oft-recited "Song of the Chatta-
hoochee," for another example, was a hymn to the
New South of commercial exploitation championed by
Henry W. Grady and other propagandists for a
business-oriented South.

The Agrarians were just a little unfair. Lanier's views
on industrialism and the commercial ethos, and their
incompatibility with the artistic impulse, were closer to
those of the Agrarians than they cared to admit, and
Lanier's attitudes were like theirs, importantly an out-
growth of southern origins. What the Agrarians really
objected to about Lanier, it seems more probable, was
his Victorian optimism, his belief in ideality, and also his
poetics, which they rightly associated with the kind of
sentimental, high-minded, genteel progressivism of the
pre–World War I era (as exemplified in the approach to
literature and society of Edwin Mims, longtime chairman of the English department at Vanderbilt University
and author of *The Advancing South* and, significantly, of
a biography of Lanier). It was not Lanier's economic
views, but the superficial, emotional form in which he
advanced them, as in "The Symphony," that offended
the Agrarians. They seem to have reacted to Lanier and
his work much as they did to a southern contemporary
of their own, the novelist Thomas Wolfe—and with
good reason, for Lanier and Wolfe were very similar in
their intellectual makeup. They shared a taste for cas-
cading rhetoric, romantic storm and stress, and largely
undiscriminating yea-saying, along with an attitude toward society and thought processes that was basically

emotional and subjective rather than rational and disciplined.

Be that as it may, when the Agrarians objected, as they did, to the didacticism and the crude, emotional, polemical statement of theme in "The Symphony," they were on firm ground. Edd Winfield Parks's verdict on the poem— "a clever experiment in technique by a dexterous artificer, which concentrates attention on the superficial form"—is the best that can be said for it.[22] Yet though as a poem it is a failure, once again the failure is of a different order and scale than what most of Lanier's contemporaries were managing. Though the poem sinks under the burden of its polemics, Lanier does develop and maintain a controlling metaphor throughout, and this gives unity and coherence to the language, so that it does not depend entirely on its social message. However awkwardly, Lanier is using language for its connotative properties as well as for its idea content. The poem lacks the richness and concrete texture of the rural descriptions in "Corn," but Lanier does develop the specific metaphor of the orchestra throughout. Thus "The Symphony," for all its vagueness of argument and its contrived form, does to an extent create its own context rather than merely refer to one based on ideas, as the general run of poetry of the period is wont to do, and it possesses a clumsy and rather diffused but genuine vigor.

Publication of the poem, following that of "Corn," gave Lanier a distinct reputation in the literary circles of the period. His success brought him into touch with such leading men of letters as Bayard Taylor, E. C. Stedman, and Longfellow, and led to Lippincott's decision to publish his first verse collection, *Poems,* in 1876. On the strength of "Corn" Lanier was also offered a welcome commission by the Atlantic Coast Line Railroad to visit Florida and write a guidebook.

Even more desirable was an invitation, through the good offices of Bayard Taylor, to write a cantata to be sung at the opening of the Philadelphia centennial celebration in May, 1776. Lanier also produced a long, commissioned centennial poem, "The Psalm of the West," for publication in *Lippincott's*. He designed it in the shape of a symphony, to express, in epic form, the theme of sectional reconciliation and devotion to national ideals. Charles Anderson proclaims it, "in spite of its obvious defects, a forceful national poem,"[23] but it seems to me to be little more than a rather painfully and determinedly versified idea, an oratorical set piece, without even the enforced unity and coherence of the orchestral metaphor of "The Symphony" to give it life in language. Unlike either "The Symphony" or "Corn," it differs in no important way from the standard rhymed platitudes and rhetorical exercises in abstract pieties that constitute most of the magazine verse of the time. A sample of its level of technique will suffice:

> Now haste thee while the way is clear,
> Paul Revere!
> Haste, Dawes! but haste thou not, O sun!
> To Lexington.

The several years that followed should have been favorable for the long-delayed arrival of at least some financial security for the hard-working poet, but this was not to be. The magazine assignment to write on Florida sapped his energy, and in the winter of 1876 he suffered a severe setback in health. From this point on, the condition of his tubercular, hemorrhaging lungs was desperate; he was seldom without illness. He resumed playing for the orchestra, wrote some magazine

23. Anderson (ed.), "Introduction" to Lanier, *Poems and Poem Outlines*, xlix.

articles, produced a few new poems, and otherwise scavenged as best he could for money to support his family. He had come up with a new idea for financial rescue. Daniel Coit Gilman had arrived in Baltimore and was creating the new Johns Hopkins University. Lanier first attempted to secure a fellowship to study the physics of musical tone, general science, and language, and then to get a professorship. Gilman liked Lanier, admired his work, and wanted to employ him, but was unable to do so until 1879, when he invited the poet to become a lecturer in English literature at a salary of one thousand dollars a year. Lanier had already begun lecturing for a women's group in Baltimore and for the Peabody Library. Meanwhile he had moved his family to Baltimore for the season of 1877, and thenceforth they would stay with him.

It was partly in order to prepare his lectures and partly to demonstrate his qualifications for appointment as professor of English at Johns Hopkins that Lanier began in the late 1870s to study literature and poetics on a much more sustained and thoroughgoing basis than ever before. His friend William Hand Browne had introduced him to the older English poetry, notably that of Chaucer, to which he had responded at once. He now began reading extensively in both Anglo-Saxon and Middle English poets, and his imagination was kindled by their power of language, their reliance upon quantitative stress rather than standard iambic rhythm, and their use of techniques such as alliteration and lift. The possibilities of such verse fascinated Lanier, for it seemed to him a direct avenue of access to the goal he had so long contemplated: the fusion of poetry and music. As we have noted, the rather dubious last line of "The Symphony"— "Music is Love in search of a word" —is by no means so obscure in meaning if we read it as a way of expressing the poet's own passionate quest to write poetry that could have the emotional and (as he saw it) spiritual impact of music. Lanier wanted very much to compose verse that would create the ravishing *effect* that music had on his own sensibility. But as long as he attempted to do this through so-called noble and beautiful ideas, which was the only way he had hitherto known, the result was abstraction—*i.e.*, the content of the line "Music is Love in search of a word," with the emotion dissolving into sentimental excess.

But when he read "The Battle of Maldon" and *Beowulf* and Caedmon and "The Wanderer," he came upon poems originally meant to be chanted rhythmically, not recited, and with a prosody designed to guide the response to the chant. Such poetry seemed to him to possess, in its mechanics, precisely the virtues and techniques of music-making: a measure based on time intervals and not metric feet, with duration as the guide to syllabic stress, and sound combinations used for emotional coloring. To be sure, the same was true of later poetry, but the dominance of the iambic foot in the verse of his own time had impeded, for him, the perception of the nature of that relationship. When he thought of poetry in terms of iambic meter, he had thought in terms of its idea content, so automatic was the conventional iambic rhythm. Reading the older poetry broke up the usual expectations and made him conscious of what it was possible to do with language in terms of duration, stress, combinations of sound, and pitch. His discipline in adjusting his flute playing to the larger melodic sound of the orchestra had been guiding him in that direction; now he thought he had discovered a model in language itself.

The immediate result of Lanier's studies was a series of lectures delivered on the physics of poetry at Johns Hopkins. To solidify his academic status and to provide a programmatic textbook to reform prosodic theory in

English, Lanier spent six weeks in 1879 writing *The Science of English Verse,* which with a subsidy by the author was published the next year. This work, which Karl Shapiro has described as "justly the most famous and influential in the field of temporal poetry" and one that "remains one of the best expositions of its theory in the literature of metrics,"[24] has its flaws, yet is altogether a distinguished production. It represents what Lanier was capable of as an analytical thinker when his subject was precisely defined and his terms of reference were specific and limited. The method he proposes is not really a "science": Lanier was basing his insistence upon the musical nature of poetry by a method of defining it as the duration and pitch of sound waves, but the physics is the least of it. What he does is to deal with English poetry from its beginnings to the nineteenth century. He shows that the relative duration of time units is the basis of rhythm in verse and that the unit of sound, like the musical bar, is best understood not through its syllabic regularity but as the rise and fall of pitch, with the time units in the bar, and not the traditional metric foot count, providing the rhythm. In a demonstration based on abundant examples from Old English and later poetry, Lanier illustrated and interpreted his theory. Deficient though some of the examples are, there can be no doubt that he provided a method of accounting for the way that verse is structured that helped notably toward freeing the theory of prosody in English from the straitjacket of an outmoded, too mechanical system of metrical form.

Where he went wrong was in his disinclination to recognize the essential difference between the rhythm of verse and that of music. It is not only, as Paul Elmer More has pointed out, that poetry involves a creative

---

24. Karl Shapiro, *A Bibliography of Modern Poetry* (Baltimore, 1948), 16.

tension between the normal, unrhythmical enunciation of the language itself and the instinct to force a controlling rhythmic pattern upon the poem.[25] More importantly, the rhythm of poetry is achieved in language and serves the purpose, along with the connotative associations of words, of fusing emotion and idea into a larger unit of meaning. The words of a poem both *denote* experience and also, along with sound, rhythm, rhyme, and imagery, *connote* it; and the total meaning of the poem cannot be perceived through musical relationships alone, any more than through a prose paraphrase of the ideas denoted therein. Music, by contrast, does not serve to represent ideas; it develops, sustains, and explores emotional states, and its rhythms and patterns are not subject to any such denotative function. Thus when Lanier says that "the term 'verse' denotes a set of specially related sounds,"[26] and builds his theory upon determining the relationships between sounds, he views the rhythmic and tonal relationships of verse as a mathematical absolute, rather than as one very important functional device of a more complex overall objective.

For Lanier's future as a poet, it was not so much the actual writing of *The Science of English Verse* as his thinking about the subject and his involvement in the older, noniambic forms of English poetry that were significant. One immediate and observable result was a ballad entitled "The Revenge of Hamish," which Lanier apparently wrote in 1878 as an experiment in the use of logaoedic dactyls. In *The Science of English Verse* Lanier pointed out that the classical dactylic foot, in which a stressed syllable is followed by two without stress, has a different time valuation from that of the dactylic verse written by Longfellow in *Evangeline* or Tennyson in

25. Quoted in Starke, *Sidney Lanier: A Biographical and Critical Study,* 342–43.

26. Sidney Lanier, *The Science of English Verse* (New York, 1903), 22.

"The Charge of the Light Brigade." The classical dactyl was a stately measure in 4/8 time, with the first, accented syllable equal in rhythmic importance to the two unstressed syllables. Longfellow and Tennyson, by contrast, were using the dactyl in 3/8 rhythm, the basic rhythm of English verse, with the rhythmic interval equally distributed among all three syllables, producing a much more rapid beat. To illustrate this logaoedic— *i.e.,* prose-poetic—dactyl, Lanier chose to versify an episode from a contemporary novel by William Black, *Macleod of Dare.* He produced a narrative describing how a serf, unjustly flogged, caught up his master's child by the edge of a cliff, forced the laird to undergo ten lashes on pain of having his child dropped into the sea, then sprang over the cliff with the child in his hands, shouting his revenge.

The poem is not only one of the very few successful American narrative poems, but, as Edmund Wilson interprets it in his book *Patriotic Gore,* very much an emblem of the defeated South. "The arrogant suicide of Hamish," Wilson says, "leaping with the child in his arms, is a parable of the action of the South in recklessly destroying the Union. Like George Harris, the creator of Sut Lovingood, tall Hamish the henchman dies poisoned—by hatred, by the lust for revenge. Sidney Lanier in this piece is a dramatic poet, and that spirit has spoken through him."[27] (Something might also be done with the lashed Hamish as "son of Ham"—an association with which Lanier would have been all too familiar.)

What is equally interesting, I think, is what the writing of the poem shows about Lanier as poet. By deliberately selecting an incident presumably out of Scottish history, and setting it as a narrative in order to illustrate the use of an ancient poetic rhythm, Lanier was subjecting his muse to an arbitrary formal discipline not only of

27. Wilson, *Patriotic Gore,* 528.

rhythm and pattern but of content as well. He was all but eliminating his usual didactic stance; there could be little or no philosophizing about love versus trade, the beauty of truth, and the unity of love, music, and language, in a narrative poem designed to accomplish so precise an objective. The result is, as poetry, quite satisfying:

> And sprang with the child in his arms from the horrible
> height in the sea,
> Shrill screeching, "Revenge!" in the wind-rush; and pallid
> Maclean,
> Age-feeble with anger and impotent pain,
> Crawled up on the crag, and lay flat, and locked hold of dead
> roots of a tree—
>
> And gazed hungrily o'er, and the blood from his back drip-
> dropped in the brine,
> And a sea-hawk flung down a skeleton fish as he flew,
> And a mother stared white on the waste of blue,
> And the wind drove a cloud to seaward, and the sun began
> to shine.

Thus the poem constitutes an indication of the direction in which Lanier still must travel if his poetry was to become what he wished it to be. He needed distancing, the discipline of a formal pattern and also of a concrete, externalized content, if he was to break loose from the idealized abstractions of the poetry of his time and create in language. By using the dactylic lines and the narrative pattern he had achieved a sense of power and sonorousness of language that came closer to what he wanted to get into poetry. But in "The Revenge of Hamish" the pattern and content were ultimately *too* formal, *too* external; he was unable to get his own passionate concerns into it at all; the first-person utterance of lyric poetry would be required for that.

In December of 1876, with his lungs in very bad shape, Lanier was told by a physician to go down to Florida at once. An anonymous five-hundred-dollar gift—probably from Gibson Peacock—made it possible for him to do so. While his children stayed with the Peacocks in Philadelphia, Lanier and his wife traveled to Tampa. Soon Lanier's health began improving, and he began writing verse. More important, he began, for the first time, to read extensively in the poems and essays of Ralph Waldo Emerson.

The resulting impact on Lanier was profound. He had encountered the ideality of German transcendentalism and of Carlyle many years earlier; but that had been abstract, philosophical, an unanchored, emotional ideality based on categories of thought. Emerson's version was more concrete, metaphoric: nature was the divine *other*, of which the soul was the idea; and Emerson's nature, sprung as equally from the old Calvinistic sense of the immanence of God as from the concept of the oversoul, bristled with personification and precise observation. Here was a metaphor, then, for Lanier's sense of the divine presence as passion and feeling, one that offered a sensuous texture that could absorb and contain all the ideality with which he might wish to imbue it, yet retain its tangible, palpable concreteness. Lanier had discovered his poetic image and, as Anderson rightly remarks, "in discovering Emerson, he found himself as a poet. His true vein lay, not in social protest or in celebrating the national spirit or even, except subconsciously, in the marriage of music to words—it lay in his religious interpretation of nature."[28]

And there was still another important discovery that he made during those years, one that would finally complete his literary apprenticeship. Visiting Bayard Taylor in New York early in 1878, he had borrowed a copy of Walt Whitman's *Leaves of Grass*. Until then, he knew little of Whitman except that he was a poet who had altogether too much to say about the physicality of the body and who tended toward a coarseness of lan-

28. Anderson (ed.), "Introduction," to Lanier, *Poems and Poem Outlines*. lvii.

guage and subject that was, he had heard, rather too cheap and sensational. Now he found Whitman's verse, he wrote to Taylor, "a real refreshment to me—like rude salt spray in your face—in spite of its enormous fundamental error that a thing is good because it is natural, and in spite of the world-wide difference between my own conceptions of art and its author's."[29] A few months later we find him writing directly to Whitman, to order a copy of *Leaves of Grass*. "I cannot resist the temptation to tender you also my grateful thanks," he wrote, "for such large and substantial thoughts uttered in a time when there are, as you say in another connection, so many 'little plentiful manikins skipping about in collars and tailed coats.'" Lanier feels it incumbent to set forth his disagreements, but finds them "a very insignificant consideration in the presence of that unbounded delight which I take in the bigness and bravery of all your ways and thoughts. It is not known to me where I can find another modern song at once so large and so naive: and the time needs to be told few things so much as the absolute personality of the person, the sufficiency of the man's manhood *to* the man, which you have propounded in such strong and beautiful rhythms."[30]

Lanier's reservations about Whitman's physicality and his belief in the excellence of the common man were very real. He was far too much the southern gentleman to be able to abandon himself to either idea. Passionate and sensuous though his emotional attitudes were, they were never overtly manifested in physicality; one always has the feeling, when reading the tumultuous fervor of his letters to his wife and Ginna Hankins, that a great deal of physical passion is somehow being sublimated into clouds of sentiment and poetic thoughts. Like

29. Lanier to Bayard Taylor, February 3, 1878, in *Letters, 1878–1891*, ed. Anderson and Starke, Vol. X of *Centennial Edition,* 18.
30. Lanier to Walt Whitman, May 5, 1878, *ibid.*, 40.

Emerson, Lanier cannot go along with Whitman's singing the body electric; it offends him. Nor can he do without the class structure; he must believe in chivalric leadership; and the notion that the average man is, in his very ordinariness, good goes too radically against the southern cavalier myth to win his acceptance. All the same, he absorbed the lesson of Whitman, however imperfectly. He recognized the freedom that Whitman gained through his long lines and his irregular stanzas (even though he thought "Captain, My Captain!" his best poem). He saw in Whitman the same use of the dactylic and spondaic verse rhythms as in early British poets, the same expressiveness of alliteration and vowel tones, and without the archaism of *Beowulf* and "The Battle of Maldon." Above all, he recognized the way that Whitman's prosody permitted the enunciation of the sensuousness and passion that seemed so much a part of the philosophy, but not the prosody, of Emerson. So when, in April of 1878, he was invited by George P. Lathrop to contribute a poem to an anthology in the "No Name" Series being published by Roberts Brothers, entitled *A Masque of Poets,* he wrote a poem which he called "The Marshes of Glynn."

"The Marshes of Glynn" is by no means a perfect poem—nothing that Sidney Lanier wrote ever approached that status. He is, as always, too willing to settle for sound at the price of appropriateness, as in his too precious rhyming, "emerald twilights" with "virginal shy lights." In his famous strophe to the marsh hen:

As the marsh-hen secretly builds on the watery sod,
Behold I will build me a nest on the greatness of God:
I will fly in the greatness of God as the marsh-hen flies
In the freedom that fills all the space 'twixt the marsh and
    the skies . . .

there remains, alas, a slight taint of the ludicrous, the marsh hen not being a notably religious fowl in its nest-building activities. On the other hand there is a

distinct gain in the fact that he *is* writing about marsh
hens, marsh grass, watery sod, live oaks, and other items
of his experience of coastal Georgia—not about the
ravens, doves, moors, coverts, nymphs, and fauns of
English romantic poetry. For "The Marshes of Glynn" is
the poem in which, emboldened by the emphasis upon
nature he learned from Emerson and the language-use
he learned from Whitman and the older English poets,
Lanier for the first time draws deeply and amply on the
specificalities of his own locale, without trying to trans-
late them into terms of a more abstract, literary reference. The poem is *about* the coast of Georgia, and the
language is bent to the purpose of describing it, as is
apparent from the outset:

Glooms of the live-oaks, beautiful-braided and woven
With intricate shades of the vines that myriad-woven
Clamber the forks of the multiform boughs . . .

It is his intention to imbue the natural scene with religious meaning, and he does it with and through the
imagery of nature:

But now when the noon is no more, and the riot is rest,
And the slant yellow beam down the wood-Aisle doth seem
Like a lane into heaven that leads from a dream. . . .

The language, in syntax and word-tone, is full of
movement, allowing Lanier to make his point by ac-
cumulation, with the long sentences and the linking
constructions designed to lead the reader's attention
onward rather than to fragment the experience into
separate parts. This is what Whitman had shown him,
and this is what he needed if he were going to communicate his own view of the world. For as we have
seen, what he had always wanted to do was to release
passion into affective language, to find words to express
and give form to the emotion that he experienced in
playing and listening to music. His art and his temperament were not suited for analytical discrimination or

working out of complex relationships; what he had to offer was expansiveness of feeling, the passionate fullness of an affirmative, romantic response to a multiplicity and variety of experience. Long lines, alliteration and assonance that built one association upon another, internal rhymes that joined the images within a line together, end-rhymes that brought the long strings of images and associations into cumulative relationship, and an irregular pattern of verse that did not strive to force a too fixed, too intricate form upon the experience but only kept it controlled and moving forward—this was the proper prosody for Lanier.

His youthful Calvinism had become pantheism now— or rather, a kind of enthusiastic yea-saying, a delighted affirmation of God, whose kingdom was nature, and who, however theologically undiscriminated, was worshipped in passionate praise for His creation. Lanier does not quite go the route of New England transcendentalism: God is not *in* nature, but nature is His emblem:

> By so many roots as the marsh-grass sends in the sod
> I will heartily lay me a-hold on the greatness of God

The poem ends, as is proper for a poem in which the religious experience of nature and the day and night are fused into a kind of emotional, sexual fulfillment, with an image of release into mystery, in which the themes of marsh, sea, night, and God are joined into one final statement, the marshland in darkness:

> And now from the Vast of the Lord will the waters of sleep
>   Roll on in the souls of men,
>   But who will reveal to our waking ken
>   The forms that swim and the shapes that creep
>   Under the waters of sleep?
> And I would I could know what swimmeth below when the
>   tide
>   comes in
> On the length and the breadth of the marvellous marshes
>   of Glynn.

Thus concludes Sidney Lanier's best poem and, I think, one of the two or three most distinguished of all poems written by nineteenth-century southern poets. It comes as culmination of a long process of education, in which Lanier had not only to learn much, but also to unlearn even more. The poem is very much in the long tradition of southern poetry, in that it emphasizes formal texture, sound, rhetorical ornament, rather than direct personal statement, content, meter-making argument. In actuality "The Marshes of Glynn" reveals very little of the biographical Lanier; for all the intensity that went into its making, it is formal, essentially impersonal, public. It is characteristically southern, too, in its strong emphasis on place. No one would ever mistake "a league and a league of marsh-grass, waist-high, broad in the blade,/ Green, and all of a height, and unflecked with a light or a shade," for Cape Cod or even the Jersey meadows.

But there is one element of the poem that represents a distinct break with Lanier's southern origins. If one compares "The Marshes of Glynn" with such poems as Simms's "The Edge of the Swamp" or Timrod's "Spring" or, for that matter, with a twentieth-century poem such as Robert Penn Warren's "Bearded Oaks," it becomes obvious that Lanier is doing what the others cannot or will not do: he is directly identifying his situation with nature, and declaring not only that man may learn *in* nature but that his true image of himself is *as* natural rather than social being. The other southern poets will not proceed that far; however beautiful they may find nature, they tend always to see it as separate from man and finally aloof from him. But Lanier, tutored by Emerson, ventures beyond that. Viewing the edge of the marsh and the sea, he declares,

Somehow my soul seems suddenly free
From the weighing of fate and the sad discussion of sin,
By the length and the breadth and the sweep of the marshes
    of Glynn . . .

which is farther into nature by a crucial step than the southern writer has usually been willing to go. Lanier in his best poem has joined Emerson, Thoreau, Bryant, Whittier, and, intermittently, Emily Dickinson in a transcendent view of nature that erases the barrier between it and man and places man at home in nature as refuge from society.

What is involved, I think, is the distance that Lanier has traveled away from the southern community. It is not simply a matter of having left Macon for Baltimore. One feels, rather, that even as a youth and a young man Lanier had felt out of place, and, without realizing it, constrained by the southern community role and the attitude toward literature and ideas that were his birthright. The personal extravagance of feeling, the early absorption in the ideas of German romanticism, the Carlylean notion of "the great man" that remained a constant in his thinking, indicate a basic incompatibility with his cultural and intellectual situation. One thinks of Poe in Richmond. As Allen Tate says of Poe, he meant business; literature was no pleasant, gentlemanly diversion for him. And neither was it for Lanier. What he got in Baltimore and the Northeast, finally, was a tardy exposure to and education in the dominant creative and intellectual currents of the middle-nineteenth century. For a poet, this was no small thing; attention to the language convention was of absolute importance. What Lanier required was precisely the kind of literary milieu that, briefly, had seemed to be developing in Charleston in the years just before the Civil War and that was otherwise unavailable in the South during the nineteenth century: a community of professional writers, working together.

It seems clear that Lanier had the talent, and the professional motivation, to become an important writer; even so uneven a work as *Tiger-Lilies* was in that respect quite promising. But as Jay B. Hubbell says, "Few artists ever lived at a time or in a region more unfavorable to the artistic life than the South of the late sixties and early seventies";[31] and these were precisely the years when Lanier should have been developing his talent, expanding his intellectual horizons, coming to terms with the formal problems of his chosen art. For the prose writers of the period a more active literary climate was not quite as vital to their development, perhaps because fiction is by nature less of an art of language convention and formal technique and more closely dependent upon social documentation. But for a poet like Lanier, there was almost nothing on the local scene that could help him develop and explore new modes of creativity in language. He needed Emerson and Whitman; all he got was Paul Hamilton Hayne. He would have been far better off and would perhaps have developed into a more important writer had he been able to leave for Baltimore and the Northeast a decade earlier than he did.

For Sidney Lanier, I think, was potentially a major poet; and the tragedy is that it was only in the final years of his short life that he was exposed to the conditions that could enable him to develop his abilities. Lanier required what Mark Twain, by reason of circumstance of birth and upbringing, possessed: the experience of distancing from his origins that could give him the perspective and the contrast of social attitudes and values that in Mark Twain's instance resulted in several great works of fiction. Historically, socially, Lanier was closely bound to the South; temperamentally, emotionally, he was at odds with many of its attitudes and qualities. Thus his ways of thinking about conduct, decorum, the social ideal prevented him from following the lead which his temperament and his intellect suggested, which was along the same paths as an Emerson, a Whitman, or an Emily Dickinson. Temperamentally, emotionally, he was a pantheist, a naturalist; but as

31. Jay B. Hubbell, *The South in American Literature, 1607—1900* (Durham, N.C., 1954), 760.

a product of the southern social and cultural community he drew back. From the evidence of his several major poems of the late 1870s and 1880s, it seems obvious that he was breaking away from what for him were frustrating restraints. Had he been able to begin the process sooner, the break would have become more crucial for him, and the creative tension between the two antithetical modes of thought and feeling might well have produced just the kind of dialectic of head and heart that, embodied in language, could result in major poetic achievement. All the elements for such a struggle, and its potential artistic resolution, were there, but they came into focus too tardily and too briefly.

It might have been that with "The Marshes of Glynn," as Lanier began to enter the full range of his poetic development, he would have gone on to create a body of poetry that would have firmly established his reputation. But by then his own physical body was giving out. Continuing to work desperately on such moneymaking projects as a boy's version of the King Arthur stories and of the Percy ballads, preparing his Johns Hopkins lectures, he could work at his verse only fitfully. He found time for only a few poems, mostly of indifferent merit, though he did produce the brief "Ballad of Trees and the Master," which is one of his better, if limited, efforts. He also wrote an essay, "The New South," which was published in *Scribner's Monthly* for October, 1880. In it he expressed his satisfaction with the rise of the small farm in the South as a counterbalance to what he thought was a dangerous development of large, commercial farming in the Midwest and predicted that the race problem would find its solution in the growing identity of interests among small farmers both black and white. What he did not realize was that while there were indeed many more small farms in the South than in antebellum days, the share-cropping and tenant-farming system was also expanding, so that his vision of the sturdy southern yeoman tilling his own land was hardly accurate. Lanier was now in the final stages of tuberculosis. With a temperature of 104 degrees he worked on a new poem, "Sunrise," which was to make up part of a sequence to be known as "Hymns to the Marshes." The poem was in spirit and in technique closely allied to "The Marshes of Glynn." Again the Marshland, at dawn now, affords the knowledge of God, blending body and soul, matter and spirit, the primal heat of life:

> Old chemist, rapt in alchemy,
>   Distilling silence,—lo,
> That which our father-age had died to know—
> The menstruum that dissolves all matter—thou
> Hast found it: for this silence, filling now
> The globed clarity of receiving space,
> This solves us all: man, matter, doubt, disgrace,
>   Death, love, sin, sanity,
> Must in yon silence's clear solution lie.

The sun rises in a stirring dawn that is at once artistic and life-giving, bringing the lordly heat that creates:

O Artisan born in the purple,—Workman Heat,—
Parter of passionate atoms that travail to meet
And be mixed in the death-cold oneness—innermost Guest
At the marriage of elements,—fellow of publicans,—blest
King in the blouse of flame, that loiterest o'er
The idle skies yet laborest fast evermore—

The sun is the greatest artist, the emblem of God. The final lines propose a transcendental union of the soul, in death, with the sources of solar creativity, until

> . . . yonder beside thee
> My soul shall float, friend Sun,
> The day being done.

In the winter and early spring of 1880–1881 Lanier struggled through his lectures, then departed with his wife and infant son for a trip in the North Carolina mountains, hoping to stave off his growing weakness.

For a while things looked better. He read proof, worked on ideas for new poems, went riding every day. Then at the end of August came a relapse. He died on September 7, 1881, near Lynn, North Carolina, at the age of thirty-nine. The body of Lanier's poetic work is small, and of that, very little is of first importance. Indeed, the total quantity of Lanier's poetry that merits the attention of later generations might be safely contained in several dozen printed pages. But in a poem such as "The Marshes of Glynn" we can see what he might have been as poet. At his best he was quite original, and full of a kind of powerful, passionate sincerity that breaks out of the morass of contrived pieties and warmed-over ideality in language and attitude that characterizes the poetry of his time. Certainly he wrote a handful of poems that are better by far than anything written by the so-called leaders of American poetry of the period: nothing by Stedman, Taylor, Boker, Stoddard, or Aldrich is of the order of "The Marshes of Glynn," "Sunrise," or even "Corn." Emily Dickinson and Whitman are another matter; but in Lanier's time the one was utterly unknown and the other considered neither respectable nor poetic. Lanier's achievement, desperately won, is that even while paying his respects to the outward forms of the poetry of the dominant genteel tradition, he stretched them to new limits and actually managed to force new vigor and life into them. It could not endure; and a new literary generation would find it necessary to break with them entirely. When that day came, however, it could finally be recognized what this former Confederate soldier, adherent to the attitudes and values of his time and forced by dint of his origins and circumstance to contend against appalling odds, came close to doing. Not for half a century after his death would there be another southern poet worthy to stand alongside him.

Fugitives as Agrarians:
The Impulse Behind
I'll Take My Stand

There has always been some confusion over the relationship of the Nashville Fugitive poets to the group known after 1930 as the Nashville Agrarians, who produced the symposium *I'll Take My Stand: The South and the Agrarian Tradition* in 1930. Some have insisted upon a complete and utter distinction, as if there were no real relationship at all. The facts are that only four of the Fugitives—Allen Tate, John Crowe Ransom, Donald Davidson, and Robert Penn Warren—were involved in *I'll Take My Stand*. (Andrew Nelson Lytle was technically one of the Fugitives, but he played no part in their deliberations as a working group of poets.) Other Fugitives, such as Merrill Moore, William Yandell Elliott, Sidney Mttron Hirsch, were not only *not* involved in *I'll Take My Stand*, they were to varying degrees hostile to it. And conversely, even if Lytle is counted as a Fugitive,

This essay was originally published in J. Howard Woolmer, *A Catalogue of the Fugitive Poets* (Andes, N.Y., 1972), 9–26. Much of the material also appears in Louis D. Rubin, Jr., *The Writer in the South: Studies in a Literary Community,* Mercer University Lamar Memorial Lectures, No. 15 (Athens, Ga., 1972).

145

seven others of the Twelve Southerners involved in *I'll Take My Stand* were not Fugitives at all. So it won't do to telescope the two groups into one. Yet neither will it do to pretend that there is no important tie between the one and the other. For the four Fugitives who *did* go on into Agrarianism are also precisely the four who became professional writers and whose literary careers are responsible for the continuing reputation of the Fugitive group. Were it not for the presence of those four in the ranks of the Fugitives, the Nashville poetry group would be almost completely forgotten today. The only really important Fugitive poets thus became Agrarians, and not only that, they provided the impetus and leadership for *I'll Take My Stand.* They were joined by John Donald Wade, Frank Owsley, and others, but it was Ransom, Tate, and Davidson— and Andrew Lytle—who were the nucleus for the Agrarian group (Warren was out of the country most of the time, but contributed an essay). So there *is* a relationship, and an important one. It is not a one-for-one relationship, but it was decidedly no accident that the leading Fugitive poets also became Nashville Agrarians.

It is on *I'll Take My Stand* that I want to comment now. I want to try to show what I think the impulse behind this book was, in part at least, and why it has remained a book to be reckoned with for more than four decades since it appeared. For the Agrarians were talking about the kind of community that would keep the artist in what they considered an organic relationship with his society. It was because they saw at least the rudiments of such a community in the nonindustrial (or preindustrial) life of the South into which they were all born, and because they saw that community disintegrating around them as the South began its belated reentry into the mainstream of American society after 1900, that they wrote their book.

What was involved in all this can be illustrated by an

anecdote. It happened to me about sixteen years ago, and I have thought about it often since. The Southeastern American Studies Association was holding its biennial meeting in Macon, Georgia, and I was one of the participants, along with a friend of mine who was and still is a distinguished scholar of American literature. During the course of the meeting he and I each received a note from the late John Donald Wade, asking us to come down after the meeting concluded and have dinner with him in Marshallville. I had had some correspondence with John Donald Wade through the offices of a good friend to us both, the late Donald Davidson; and of course I knew both his distinguished biography of Augustus Baldwin Longstreet and his essay, "The Life and Death of Cousin Lucius," which I still think the most beautifully written of the twelve essays in the Agrarian symposium, *I'll Take My Stand*. As for my friend, though he was an avowed Yankee from Upstate New York, he was more than ordinarily interested in the South and was in fact at work on what proved to be an excellent anthology of southern writing. So when the meeting broke up early Saturday afternoon, we got in my car and drove down through the peach orchards to Marshallville.

When we got there, Mr. Wade had company—two of his colleagues from the University of Georgia, one of them a noted southern historian and the other an economist distinguished in his field far beyond the boundaries of his campus. The three of them were sitting around in Mr. Wade's living room, sipping Jack Daniels from silver cups and swapping stories. We joined them for a while, and then John Wade took the two of us off in his automobile for a tour of his place. What we were shown was an arboretum and, executed on a scale dozens of acres wide, a Garden of the World, with trees and shrubs trained on wire scaffolding to form Stonehenge, a Druid temple, the Eiffel Tower, a huge cross, and so on. My northern friend was astounded; he could not imagine anyone working on a scale like this, and to such long-range purpose. It was an eighteenth-century sort of enterprise, he kept whispering to me. Afterward we returned to the house and rejoined the two Georgia friends of John Donald Wade, who had been improving the hour in our absence, and we spent the next four hours helping them in their endeavors toward further improvement, with time out for dinner. Mr. Wade and his friends obviously fascinated my friend, for they were good raconteurs. They kept telling stories to each other, one after the other, and laughing uproariously at every opportunity, slapping their sides at each quip and sally. Their stories, and the way they told them, were stories about people around home. They told these stories in good southern fashion, with lots of drawling and contracting of syllables—and if you hadn't known that the storytellers consisted of a distinguished literary scholar and editor, a distinguished historian, and a distinguished economist, you might have thought that they were members of the local farming community thereabouts. In any event, it was a most amusing evening, concluding about 9 P.M. or so with a ceremonial tribute to the camellias just off the front porch, and then my friend and I said goodbye and we climbed back into my automobile and were soon on the way to Atlanta.

No sooner had we gotten out of the driveway and driven down the street than my northern friend began expressing his astonishment. "Why, did you *hear* them? Going on like that, talking like *countrymen?* And there he was with that *garden,* that obviously could not possibly be *completed* for another fifty years. . . . Why, you would never have *guessed* who they *were!* It was absolutely *incredible!*" and so on.

He was amazed, for he had never encountered anything remotely like it before. But I was not amazed.

What dear old John Wade and his two distinguished academic colleagues were doing was demonstrating to each other, but most of all to themselves, that they were still southern boys. They were, to put a more formal construction upon it, asserting their community identity. For there they were: three southerners who had grown up in much the same way as other southerners of their time, but who had then gone off to college and to graduate school and had become scholars in universities. They had composed their books and taken part not only in the intellectual enterprises of their own campuses but in those of the American and even worldwide scholarly community as a whole, and yet they all felt just a little uneasy in their allegiance to such a community; and for all their achievement and renown, they wore their academic robes a trifle uncomfortably. Ideas and theories and researches did not seem quite real to them, for they still had a vivid memory of another kind of reality, a different kind of community identity, in which individual people were considered more real than ideas and in which the participants were not set off into academic disciplines and professions and economic brackets, but were part of a society made up of various kinds of men and women with all kinds of jobs and interests and levels of education. It was a society to which they too had once belonged, and they still remembered that society and the kind of real-life identity it had afforded its members; and no matter how absorbing their intellectual careers and how important a part of the scholarly world they were, they missed that kind of identity, still, and felt a bit strange and unworldly without it. So now that they could get together over a drink with old friends whom they trusted, each was doing his best to reassert that earlier identity, to show the other and, most of all, himself that he was still part of it and it was still part of him.

As I say, my northern friend was baffled by this. He

felt no such inclinations himself. He was quite satisfied with being a scholar and a university professor: that was all the real life he craved. He could not understand why it was that three such noted scholars would want to seem anything other than noted scholars, or why they might find stories about what ole Bill Smith said and what ole Charlie Jones did "real" in a way that ideas and intellectual concerns were not.

I do not want to make too much out of this incident, except that the more I think of it the more it seems to me that what it offers is an insight into one of the central dimensions of the literature of the modern South. It is emblematic, I think, of a relationship of the southern man of letters to his society, and out of this relationship have come important qualities for the literature he has composed.

I think not only of "The Life and Death of Cousin Lucius," but of another of John Donald Wade's essays, that on southern humor, which he contributed to a volume entitled *Culture in the South,* published in 1934. In this essay Wade was discussing the lineage and the prevalence of humor in southern literature, and he portrays an imaginary Christmas dinner in the year 1932, to show how the spirit of the old frontier humor of Judge Longstreet and others survived as a form of social life. He describes a gathering of several generations of a family and friends, and he details their occupations. There are a farmer, a small-town merchant, a lawyer, a doctor, a mail carrier, a teacher, a knitter of bedspreads, a cousin who is curator of an art gallery in Chicago, a Sorbonne-trained teacher of French at Vassar, and so on. He describes their conversation. "Would it do, here," he asks, "for Cousin Julius to talk of Proust's analyses, for Cousin Mary to tell of Epstein, for Uncle Tom to make Bergson clear, for someone else to echo Swift's mordancy, Wilde's glitter? I ask this question unabashedly as rhetorical. It would never, never do." He proceeds to show them telling stories "that mail-carrying Uncle Jack and Proust-teaching Cousin Julius will both think pointed." And he gives the participants in this imaginary Christmas dinner names that doubtless belong to members of his family, but he gives some of them the names of persons whom I recognize as fellow Nashville Agrarian and other Vanderbilt associates of John Wade. I notice a John, a Caroline, a Red, an Andrew, and doubtless there are others that someone more knowledgeable than I could readily identify.

The moral that John Wade drew from this imaginary Christmas feast is that southern humor historically was and is yet based on the sense of individuality of the participants, and much of the joy arises not from the story being told as such (which all the others have often heard before) but from the effect of the story on the teller himself. This in turn, he says, is based on the existence of a social tradition "which insists that human beings must quite inescapably remain humorous if they are to remain human, and one may well believe that it will reassert itself."

What the story means to me, while it may not exclude that, is something else again. What I find most interesting about the passage is its self-consciousness. It seems to me that what John Wade was attempting to do was to demonstrate that though, to choose one example of several such, Red Warren was just back from being an Oxford student, his truest kinship did not lie in his intellectual Oxford identity but in that which he shared with the farmer and mail carrier. What a southern man did on his own as an intellectual—whether studying Proust or whatever—was one thing, but what joined him with the other people who mattered was not the Proust but the story about the plain folk.

Now of course there is considerable truth to this, but not all the truth. The world in which Cousin Julius, the

Proust scholar of the anecdote, lives is not nearly as populous with Proust scholars as it is with mail carriers and farmers, and the social and political units in which we participate and by which we govern our relationship with the society we live in are not so specialized that Proust scholars consort only with other Proust scholars, or even only with other scholars, of whatever sort. This is so even in the vast universities which so many of us inhabit today, and which, as John Barth has delightfully shown in *Giles Goat-Boy*, tend to become inclusively metaphorical of the world beyond the campus. Universities exist within larger societies, are functioning parts of larger societies; and what happens in universities will depend, for better or for worse, on the attitude of the larger societies to them. But the tendency in the twentieth century has been for those specialized units within our society—the university, the mail-carriers' union, the retail merchants' association, the bar association—to become increasingly important in themselves and, through sheer density of population numbers if for no other reason, to become more and more self-absorbed. The Proust scholar has less and less to say to the mail carrier, and vice versa. Their dependence upon each other, and their relationship to each other, is purely economic, and for the most part rather impersonally so.

In the account that John Wade proposes, however, the relationship is not merely economic, but personal and familiar. So at the imaginary Christmas dinner, the Proust scholar tells a story that the mail carrier will find amusing, and presumably the mail carrier tells a story that the Proust scholar will find amusing, since they are both, by virtue of family and society, in a social relationship. But—to continue this tenuous probing behind the assumptions of a good essay—if we think about the Christmas gathering that John Wade sketches for us, what draws the two of them together for this social relationship is only a ceremonious occasion, Christmas dinner. The Proust scholar teaches at Vassar, the art gallery curator lives in Chicago, the female novelist lives in New Jersey; we may guess that the mail carrier works the RFD route there in Marshallville, the merchant runs the dry goods store there, the doctor practices in Atlanta, the lawyer in Macon, and so on. Their gathering, then, is a reunion, and what links them and makes them interested in each other is not what they are now, but what they were in the past, when the mail carrier and the Proust scholar and the lawyer and the art gallery director were all growing up with the others in the community of Marshallville.

I said earlier that what struck me most about the passage was its self-consciousness. What I mean is that John Wade is *asserting* in his essay that Uncle Julius the Proust scholar and Miss Mary the Chicago art gallery curator and Cousin Red the just-returned Oxford graduate are at bottom not intellectuals but just plain folk like the mail carrier and the merchant, and he is making an *intellectual argument* to support the contention. For it is not merely southern humor that John Wade was investigating in that 1932 essay. What he was doing was maintaining that in the South, Proust scholars and authorities on the sculpture of Jacob Epstein were not wandering intellectuals but members of an organic community involving people in all walks and levels of life. He was suggesting, too, that in such a community the man who studied Proust belonged equally and was equally at home with and valued with the lawyer, the doctor, the merchant, the farmer, the mail carrier.

But the truth, I am afraid, is the other way around. I suggest that the mail carrier at the dinner would hesitate not one whit in talking about delivering mail, nor the doctor about treating patients, nor the merchant about the price of eggs, because they would assume (and rightly) that all the others would know what was involved and have opinions on it, while the Proust scholar would never think to talk about the Baron de Charlus, because he would know that the mail carrier, the lawyer, the doctor, the merchant, and the farmer would have not the remotest idea who the Baron de Charlus was or why he was of any importance whatever. The best he could do, no doubt, would be to talk about the university football team's fortunes during the past fall. To the extent, then, that Cousin Julius was a Proust scholar, he was *not* part of the society. To the extent that he was an intellectual, he was cut off from it. But—assuming that Cousin Julius or someone like him was writing the essay—what he was attempting to do was to *use* his intellectual powers to set forth an interpretation of society from which he would not be separated.

I have gone into this matter because of the light it sheds, as I see it, on *I'll Take My Stand.* In his essay "Remarks on the Southern Religion," in *I'll Take My Stand,* Allen Tate asks the question, "How may the Southerner take hold of his Tradition?" by which he means the heritage of his nonindustrial, historical, concrete, community-shared attitude toward nature and man. His answer is, "by violence." The remark has been widely misunderstood. What I, at any rate, take it to mean is that the southerner, in Tate's view, must consciously and even abstractly *will himself* back into his tradition of community identity, even though the essence of such a tradition is that it is automatic and unconscious. It seems to me that there, as so often, Tate gets right at the true point of the issue and that he is simply stating what *I'll Take My Stand* is all about, and also setting forth quite clearly the anomaly involved in the whole venture. For when the Twelve Southerners set forth their Agrarian manifesto in 1930, what they were in effect attempting to do was to formulate a theory of a southern society that would still have room within it for themselves. If the South was indeed to become the Agrarian community that they favored, there would no longer exist the dissociation of sensibility that had brought about their very separateness as writers and intellectuals, for then what was now a theory of the good community would *become* the community. The very existence of *I'll Take My Stand* was emblematic of the breaking up of that once organic community; had southern society continued to provide the human identity within the southern community that had once existed, there would not have resulted the self-consciousness that led the contributors to write their essays.

Thus John Wade's imaginary Christmas dinner scene, composed as it was by someone who was aware of the extent of the separation of himself from the southern community gathered for the dinner, was an effort to will away that separation through an intellectual formulation of what that community was. It was an *assertion of identity*, an assertion made necessary precisely because the identity was, in part at least, no longer there. The separation of the southern writer from the southern community had by the 1920s proceeded to the extent that the writers who were moved to compose the essays of *I'll Take My Stand* felt impelled to formulate a view of the nature of that community in which the occasion for such separation did not exist. They took for their model the society of the Old South (and, in its less threadbare aspects, that of the late nineteenth-century South), and what they said in effect was: this is what the southern community should have been, and what it must come back to being if we are to avoid any more of the fragmentation and the dissociation that characterize modern urban life and that are already rapidly destroying the southern community. They were able to recognize that incipient disruption because they saw it within themselves: because they were already sufficiently distanced from the community to be made conscious of what that community had been and was not, in reference to themselves as writers.

It is in this light, and not as a political or economic document, that I interpret *I'll Take My Stand.* Its opposition to industrial society is based on the belief, on the part of the contributors, that man in an industrial society is involved in a progressive enslavement to economic production, which is bound to result in his dehumanization and which makes impossible through its economic specialization and social compartmentalization any individual identity and sense of "role" within a community of individuals. By contrast, to quote from the opening Statement of Principles:

> Opposed to the industrial society is the agrarian, which does not stand in particular need of definition. An agrarian society is hardly one that has no use at all for industries, for professional vocations, for scholars and artists, and for the life of cities. Technically, perhaps, an agrarian society is one in which agriculture is the leading vocation, whether for wealth, for pleasure, or for prestige—a form of labor that is pursued with intelligence and leisure, and that becomes the model to which the other forms approach as well as they may. But an agrarian regime will be secured readily enough where the superfluous industries are not allowed to ride against it.

What the Twelve Southerners were saying, in effect, is that under industrialism as it exists in twentieth-century America, society is exploitative and predatory, because it is organized with a view toward ever-increasing economic production and material consumption, and so cannot provide harmony and individuality within a stable community. In a nonindustrial society, by contrast, the organization and the direction of the society are necessarily settled and established, anchored as they are to the land, so that those who live in such a society may belong to a lasting community of individuals and can define themselves in and by its permanence.

A great deal of the impetus behind the writing of *I'll Take My Stand,* it seems to me, came out of this sense of community breakup, with its resulting collapse of the individual role within the community. Those who read the volume as an attempt to will back into existence the historical Old South by a deliberate turning toward mass subsistence-farming miss the point (though it must be said that several of the essays in the book encourage such a misreading). In its essentials the book was a protest against the kind of community that seemed all but inevitable if industrialism were allowed to transform the South into an urban-dominated, industrialized society. With the example of the urban Northeast exposed before them, the Agrarians saw the South in the process of changing into a replica of the impersonal, economically organized, soulless metropolis, in which the individual citizen was little more than a statistic of consumption and production.

From their standpoint, the southern community, which had existed during their childhood and young manhood, before the First World War, was still very much preferable to such a society, in that it afforded the citizen an individual identity, one in which relationships between individuals, because personal, were characterized by manners and the amenities. And since the southern community was historically a product of the Old South, which had avowedly been antiindustrial and had resisted, politically, socially, and ultimately militarily, the encroachment of industrial capitalism, it was only natural that the Old South would serve the twentieth-century Agrarians as a symbol for the kind of community they advocated. In addition, they were drawn, by virtue of history and community loyalty, toward a defense of the southern tradition, and they saw the historic hostility of the South toward the North in terms of the preservation of the nonindustrial, mannered, leisurely life-style, with its possibility for individual identification, against the menace of urban industrial capitalism. As Robert Penn Warren expressed it at the Fugitives' Reunion in 1956, reminiscing about how the Agrarians had become involved in their project:

The machines disintegrate individuals, so that you have no individual sense of responsibility and no awareness that the individual has a past and a place. He's simply the voting machine; he's everything you pull the lever on if there's any voting at all. And that notion got fused with your own personal sentiments and sentimentalities and your personal pieties and your images of place and people that belong to your own earlier life. And the Confederate element was a pious element, or a great story—a heroic story—a parade of personalities who are also images for those individual values. They were images for it for me, I'm sure, rather than images for a theory of society which had belonged to the South before the war. . . . For me it was a protest . . . against certain things: against a kind of dehumanizing and distintegrative effect on your notion of what an individual person could be in the sense of a loss of your role in society.

It is precisely this quality, I feel sure, that has accounted for the continuing popularity and importance of *I'll Take My Stand* over the course of some forty years, in the face of the manifest fact that neither the South nor the rest of the country was interested in holding onto an agrarian economy, and industrialism and urbanization were growing by leaps and bounds from the Potomac to the Gulf of Mexico. The volume was a protest against dehumanization, a rebuke to the mass-produced society of urban industrialism, and a plea for the retention of human values and individual identity within a community. In such a transaction the Old South and the agrarian existence served as a metaphor for the good life. Nowadays, over the distance of four decades, much of what the Twelve Southerners were saying in regard to the predatory nature of unchecked industrialism and the dehumanizing tendency of massive, unrelieved urban existence has turned out to be extremely prophetic and all too relevant. What was thought by many to be no more than the ineffectual lamentation of some impractical neo-Confederates over the passing of the golden age of slavery turns out to be the first stage of a widespread revolt against computerized, depersonalized, machine-oriented society and its ruthless exploitation of the environment and its human inhabitants. After years of being considered backward-looking reactionaries, the Twelve Southerners now begin to look remarkably like prophets.

The twentieth-century southern author's relationship to the community in which he lives is obviously very different from what it has ever been before. He writes about the community, but he does not write *for* the community. Unlike the antebellum southern writer, and unlike most of the local-color writers, he feels no compulsion to identify the premises of his art with the social and political objectives of the community. In *I'll Take My Stand*, to be sure, the traditional southern pieties were stressed, but that was a polemical work. Whatever the Agrarians may have thought as polemicists, as artists they were not concerned with prescribing for the South's future welfare. They were involved with imaging human experience, as they saw it around them, and what they focused upon was the clash of the modes of human identity. In Allen Tate's "Ode to the Confederate Dead," a poem written in the late 1920s, the central image was that of a modern southerner standing near the gate at a Confederate cemetery and finding himself unable to manage a creative identification with the dead and their Lost Cause. Each time he attempts imaginatively to cross over the wall that seals him off from the "arrogant circumstance" of the dead, his rhetoric breaks down:

> Turn your eyes to the immoderate past,
> Turn to the inscrutable infantry rising
> Demons out of the earth—they will not last,
> Stonewall, Stonewall, and the sunken fields of hemp,

Shiloh, Antietam, Malvern Hill, Bull Run.
Lost in that orient of the thick-and-fast
You will curse the setting sun.

Cursing only the leaves crying
Like an old man in a storm
You hear the shout, the crazy hemlocks point
With troubled fingers to the silence which
Smothers you, a mummy, in time.

It is the distance between a modern and the historical identity that is central to the poem. Tate's essay in *I'll Take My Stand* presented a program: to seize the tradition "by violence." The poem, imaged in what is done rather than what should be done, captures the separation. It should be noted that it is precisely this separation that we see implied in John Wade's imaginary Christmas dinner in his essay on southern humor, though that was not Wade's intention. Wade's essay represented an assertion of the Proust scholar's identity with the community that in fact did not, to the extent that he was a Proust scholar, exist. It was not a shared community experience in time present that brought him to the dinner; it was a past identity, the memory of a common experience that ended when the scholar had left the community and gone off into the world of scholarship and ideas.

The Fugitives, like the other southern writers of the renascence, were almost all born within a few years of the turn of the century. They grew up as the South began its belated entry into the modern world. From their parents, from the public and private values and loyalties of the community, they inherited the customs, manners, pieties, and beliefs of an older South. But the assumptions and the attitudes of that South were making way for new ideas, attitudes, and beliefs; the ways of thought and the modes of sensibility of twentieth-century urban, industrial America were penetrating into the hinterlands of the South. As young men and women and as southerners they were the recipients of two different and often contradictory sets of values and attitudes. What they were taught at home to think and to believe was one thing; what they saw going on around them and what they thought about it was something else again. When they left home and went off to college, what they learned there did not serve, as in general it seems to have done for their fathers and grandfathers, to reinforce what had been taught to them as truth at home. Instead, it seems to have strengthened and confirmed the forces that were separating them from the old community—forces, one must emphasize, that were already emerging within the community itself.

All in all, they were the first generation of young southerners since early in the nineteenth century to be brought into direct contact and confrontation with the vanguard of the most advanced thought and feeling of their times. Neither the rising barrier against new ideas decreed by the need to defend and maintain the South's peculiar institutions, nor the burdening weight of defeat, occupation, poverty, and emotional shock in the wake of the Civil War, served to ward off the impact of the outside world. Coming out of a society which up until their own time had been insulated against so much that was vital and epoch-making in nineteenth- and early twentieth-century thought and feeling, they found themselves living, thinking, feeling, and beginning to write their stories and poems in the United States of the 1920s. "Equipped with Grecian thoughts," wrote Ransom in one of his earliest poems, "How could I live/ among my father's folk?" Thomas Wolfe, writing back to his drama teacher at Chapel Hill to describe the experience of the 1947 workshop at Harvard, reported indignantly that one of his fellow graduate students criticized a play as "a perfect illustration of the Freudian complex," instead of saying "that's great stuff" or "rotten" as was done back home. Allen Tate published a poem in the *Double Dealer* and received a letter from Hart Crane, who told him that his poem "showed that I had read Eliot—which I had not done; but I soon did; and my difficulties were enormously increased." Thus was it with the young southerners as they discovered the modern world.

But they did not go into confrontation with that world unarmed. They took with them the experience of the southern community and the southern past, and such experience was, all in all, a formidable legacy of attitudes, presuppositions, and habits of feeling and belief, which was not to be violated without resistance. If the hold of that legacy had weakened before the onslaught of modernity, it was by no means dead. For they came to the modern world with the added increment of the defeat and shock that the war had wrought, the heritage of a history that was not merely textbook knowledge but part of the personal experience of their families and their communities, and the physical scars that had only just been erased even while the psychological markings remained. The South had lost a war. The South had experienced defeat, privation. The South had a past that could not be ignored, and the impact of that past was very real and still very potent. For the young southerners who became writers of the southern renascence, then, it was impossible to view the present without an awareness of the past that had produced them and any dream of the future would be tempered by the sobering memory of historical reality. Thus the southern writers were historically minded to an extent that was true of very few other American writers of their time. They saw things in time, and they did not discount the influence of the past upon the present.

The literature of the twentieth-century South, then, faces two ways: toward the present and toward the past. The viewpoint of each is made to interpret the other. In Allen Tate's words, "The South not only reentered the world with the First World War; it looked around and saw for the first time since about 1830 that the Yankees were not to blame for everything." Thus the exploration of the past became not merely an exercise in justification, but a search for meaning, which took the searcher down below the surface of community events into their underlying causes, and the result was a literature that at its best has illuminated what William Faulkner has called the "problems of the human heart in conflict with itself." The poems of the Nashville Fugitives are full of this kind of exploration. *I'll Take My Stand* was a way of formulating the issues topically. But it is in the poetry— and the fiction—of Allen Tate, John Crowe Ransom, Donald Davidson, Robert Penn Warren, Merrill Moore, and Andrew Lytle that the real search takes place.

Thomas Wolfe Once Again

He is not so much in vogue anymore. The young have changed; they have new heroes. The readers who found in his novels the first fine excitement of literary adventure are mostly middle-aged now, or older even. To return to the novels, as I did recently, is to try to step back into a way of looking, a way of feeling and of thinking, that is long since gone. One cannot—I cannot—read Thomas Wolfe in the way that I did when I was Eugene Gant's age. And with Wolfe that is very important.

For Thomas Wolfe is one of those writers who, in the way they interpret our experience for us and because of the circumstances in which we first happen upon them, may come to exist in a special and personal relationship to us. Particularly when we are very young and only

This essay was first delivered to the North Carolina Historical and Literary Society, Raleigh, December 1, 1972, and published in *North Carolina Historical Review*, L (Spring, 1973), 169–89. In somewhat longer form, it serves as the Introduction to Louis D. Rubin, Jr. (ed.), *Thomas Wolfe: A Collection of Critical Essays* (Englewood Cliffs, N.J., 1973).

beginning to discover the full resources of literature, we may, if we are lucky, come upon a writer who can speak to us so eloquently and so pointedly that he sets our imaginations on fire. Thereafter, no matter how many books we read, or how much we later come to appreciate and admire other and sometimes better writers, the remembrance of that first one never quite wears off. And if we try to explain what it is about such a writer's books that makes them worth reading, we can never describe it in completely objective terms, for our experience with these books has been so intense and so personal that when we talk about that writer and his work, in part at least, we are talking about ourselves.

What I find significant is the number of really good American writers who read Thomas Wolfe when they were young and first thinking about being writers and who drew from his books a sense of the dignity of writing and the determination to try it themselves. Some of these writers ultimately became far more skilled practitioners of the craft of storytelling than Wolfe was. But apparently what Thomas Wolfe was able to do was to help them believe in the worthiness of their would-be literary vocations and to make them hope that they could indeed become good writers. From the Wolfe novels they drew the inspiration of a young man wanting to write, refusing to settle for the surface denotation of American life, intent upon getting at its emotional dimensions. William Faulkner's admiration for Wolfe, for example, is precisely of this kind. Of his contemporaries, he once remarked, he valued Wolfe most because he tried the hardest to say the most. "Man has but one short life to write in, and there is so much to be said," Faulkner commented, "and of course he wants to say it all before he dies. My admiration for Wolfe is that he tried his best to get it all said; he was willing to throw away style, coherence, all the rules of preciseness, to try to put all the experience of the human heart on the head of a pin, as it were."[1] Faulkner was careful to point out that he didn't think Wolfe succeeded in what he was trying to do but that the effort he made was what mattered.

It is this sense of Wolfe striving to tell it all, rocked by sensation and emotion and searching for a way to articulate it, that has had so profound an impact on so many young authors. Encountering Wolfe, particularly if one is young and a would-be writer, has often turned out to be not merely an event; it is an emotional experience. There have been few American authors, I think, who have been capable of affording just this particular kind of intense experience. Wolfe did not merely dramatize his protagonists' lives; he also dramatized his desire to tell about those lives. Nothing could be farther from Stephen Dedalus' (but not James Joyce's) theory of the invisible artist, refined out of existence, indifferent, paring his fingernails, than the Wolfe novels. The authorial personality that is Thomas Wolfe's voice is always visible, showing and then telling, vigorously buttressing his protagonist's consciousness with external authorial rhetoric. In a sense, all of Wolfe's novels are about the feelings of a young man who wants to write, and it is to this that so many of his readers have responded.

My own encounter with the Wolfe novels has been a lifelong affair. I first came upon Thomas Wolfe in 1943, when I was nineteen years old and a private first class in the United States Army. I had taken a course in "The Modern Novel" at college a year earlier. The two modern novels we read were Samuel Butler's *The Way of All Flesh* and John Galsworthy's *The Forsyte Saga*. These had been about the extent of my acquaintance with the twentieth-century literary imagination in fiction. To say that I was enthralled with Thomas Wolfe scarcely de-

1. Quoted in the editor's preface, Richard Walser (ed.), *The Enigma of Thomas Wolfe: Biographical and Critical Selections* (Cambridge, Mass., 1953), vii.

scribes what happened. I read *Look Homeward, Angel* and straightaway was transported into a realm of literary experience that I had not known could exist. No writer, as Thoreau once remarked of Whitman, can communicate a new experience to us; but what he can do is to make us recognize the importance of our own experience, so that we become aware, for the first time, of what it is that we feel and think and what it can mean for us. That is what Thomas Wolfe did for me. He described a young man whose sensuous apprehension of life was matched by his appetite for feeling. Not only did he render the concrete details of experience in brilliant specificity, but he responded to the details lavishly and lyrically. Everything he thought, observed, and did was suffused with feeling. For a young reader like myself there could be an instantaneous and quite exhilarating identification, not only with the youthful protagonist Eugene Gant, but with the autobiographical author who was describing Eugene's experience with so much approval and pride. And it was on emotional response—not in its subtlety or discrimination, but in its intensity—that the highest premium was placed. What was depicted as most valuable and most real was the intensity with which one could apprehend and react. It was not fineness of discrimination or critical fastidiousness that counted, so much as variety, range. With such a writer as this, the potentialities for new experience seemed endless. The sound of a streetcar, the motion of an express train, the look of the street, the smell of a waterfront, the bitterness of young love jilted—the hunger was for new modes and varieties, and the more of them the better.

Here was a writer who seemed to desire nothing less than to storm the gates of heaven in frontal assault. I read, in *Of Time and the River,* his description of Eugene Gant riding on a train, standing in the vestibule between the pullmans and letting the clamorous beat of wheels on the steel rail punctuate his joy at going northward. That was just the way I had felt, traveling on a train, but until then I had not thought it could be worthy of the dignity of literary utterance. Thomas Wolfe assured me that indeed it was and that the emotional intensity I was prone to bring to such moments was not only entirely appropriate but a definite proof of superior sensibility. He subtitled his second novel "A Legend of Man's Hunger in His Youth," and he both delineated the hunger and—and this is of absolute importance—by thus depicting it in language he showed that it was worthwhile, since out of it art could be fashioned. It was not merely that Thomas Wolfe described, richly and in detail, the world of sensation, experience, and desire as it presented itself to a young man; he also made it quite clear how intensely the young man felt and thought about it and, in so doing, confirmed in rhetoric the value of the youthful perspective. The autobiographical relationship was essential to the experience of reading him; you had to recognize the experience that he showed you, and you had to realize that in thus remembering it he was giving meaning to it in language—so that presumably, since you were able to see it in the same way, you too were capable of making it into something important. Now as a matter of fact, this proposition was by no means self-evident; but the very example of the novels seemed to confirm it. What Wolfe was saying was that feeling counted for everything and that if you could feel intensely enough about the things of your world, it was all the proof needed to know that you were virtuous.

It was the description, the concrete emotional evocation of the space and color and time of a young man's developing experience of himself and his world, that gave body to the Wolfe novels, anchored the rhetoric, and ultimately helped to protect the art against the weakness of the rhetoric when, as sometimes in the early work and more frequently in the later work, it tended to dissolve into empty assertion. But for myself when I first encountered him, and for many another like me, the rhetoric presented no problem at all. I welcomed it; and the more of it the better. In my own instance it was both an easy and an exhilarating experience to identify myself with the situation of *Look Homeward, Angel,* since I too was from a medium-sized city in the Carolinas, of a thoroughly middle-class background, and given in self-defense to viewing myself as a largely unappreciated and misunderstood devotee of beauty and truth in a society governed by adult philistinism and commerce. Thus the mode of the *Bildungsroman*—the growth and maturation of the sensitive young man—fitted my estimation of the situation quite comfortably, and in my instance there was little chance that Wolfe could go too far in describing and then praising Eugene Gant's romantic renunciation of the community's commercial ethos and the Gant family's failure to appreciate the hero's artistic talents. When I read Wolfe's statement that by the time Eugene Gant was twelve "he had learned by now to project mechanically, before the world, an acceptable counterfeit of himself which would protect him from intrusion,"[2] I was enthralled with the recognition of a kindred sensibility, since that was exactly how I tended to view the matter myself.

In *A Portrait of the Artist as a Young Man,* a book that obviously meant a great deal to Thomas Wolfe, James Joyce describes Stephen Dedalus as he lectures Lynch on aesthetics: "Stephen paused and, though his companion did not speak, felt that his words had called up around them a thought-enchanted silence."[3] That is what Stephen thought; but it is not necessarily what James Joyce thought. However much the Joyce who

2. Thomas Wolfe, *Look Homeward, Angel* (New York, 1934), 201.
3. James Joyce, *A Portrait of the Artist as a Young Man* (New York, 1964), 213.

wrote *A Portrait* may have admired his young artist's intensity of spirit and honesty of vision, clearly he was well aware of the difference between the emotional evaluation that his youthful protagonist gave to his experience and the fact of an inexperienced and highly abstracted artist manqué taking himself and his pronouncements with such uncritical gravity. Wolfe, by contrast, when it came down to what Eugene Gant felt was important, never admitted to there being any such difference; and he tried to buttress the autobiographical Eugene's evaluation with authorial rhetoric asserting that, by God, it was so and anyone who said it wasn't was an unfeeling philistine.

But this is not the crux of Wolfe's art. It is not the assertions of uniqueness and claims to special sensibility that constitute the primary strength of his fiction—not even for those younger readers who, like myself, could find such claims so plausible. William Styron, whose youthful first encounter with Wolfe was much like my own, writes of the shock of his "sudden exposure to a book like *Look Homeward, Angel,* with its lyrical torrent and raw, ingenuous feeling, its precise and often exquisite rendition of place and mood, its buoyant humor and the vitality of its characters"—and then he adds, "and above all, the sense of youthful ache and promise and hunger and ecstasy which so corresponded to that of its eighteen-year-old reader."[4] What Wolfe was able to do, for readers like Styron and myself, was to render the sense of being young. He did this in part with the rhetoric, to be sure, but most of all it was the world of experience that he opened up to vision. For a young man the world is apt to seem imminently there for the taking—and Thomas Wolfe portrayed it in glowing color and brilliant detail, shot full of emotional response. You had not realized that the Negro slum sec-

4. William Styron, "The Shade of Thomas Wolfe," *Harper's,* CCXXXVI (April, 1968), 96.

tion of a southern town could be described in prose so vividly that you might recognize it instantly. Wolfe took the mundane, the ordinary, the humdrum and recreated them so sharply in language that you saw them for almost the first time. Or rather, he drew together and articulated the diffused and latent emotional impressions you had about something so that for the first time you recognized what you really saw and felt. His great subject, especially after *Look Homeward, Angel,* was America. He rendered it poetically, gave it a glamor and mystery. He made the places you were living in, and were just beginning to explore, seem full of promise and excitement. As Styron says, "he was the first prose writer to bring a sense of America as a glorious abstraction—a vast and brooding continent whose untold bounties were [a]waiting every young man's discovery." And he goes on: "It was as if for the first time my whole being had been thrown open to the sheer *tactile* and *sensory* vividness of the American scene through which, until then, I had been walking numb and blind, and it caused me a thrill of discovery that was quite unutterable."[5]

Wolfe's "discovery of America," to which Styron alludes, has been the subject of much critical discussion and more than a little dispute. After *Look Homeward, Angel,* it did become for Wolfe not merely a process but a conscious theme, and one that, as Styron says, could enchant many readers. Here Styron's, and my own, provincial, middle-class southern background is involved. In high school and in college I read, at that period, poems and fiction, but the emphasis was all on the English, and the European, scene. The Lake Country, the Scottish Highlands, the city of London, castles in Switzerland and along the Rhine, the marvels of Paris, the glories of Italy—it was appropriate to view such

5. *Ibid.,* 96, 98.

subject matter as proper objects of aesthetic contemplation. The American literature I was exposed to was mostly of the nineteenth century, with its literary diction and ideality. What Wolfe did was to bring to the contemporary American scene the same kind of intense, emotionally heightened description that I had previously encountered only in English poetry. In *Look Homeward, Angel,* he sent Eugene Gant on a walk through downtown Altamont, describing such subject matter as dentists' offices, laundrywomen, undertakers' parlors, YMCA secretaries, milliners' shops, and the like in a series of little vignettes of vivid color, and concluded each with a quotation from a poem, as much as to say that in such mundane, everyday activities the same aesthetic response was appropriate as in the more literarily respectable objects depicted by the English poets. His last stop was at a drugstore, and he made the soda fountain shine with the clarity and radiance usually reserved for Mermaid Taverns and the like. No one had ever suggested to me that a drugstore might be viewed in such fashion; that an object so familiar to me, so much a part of my everyday experience, was worthy of contemplation along literary lines was a thrilling discovery.

No one could depict a train trip with more excitement than Wolfe. The poetry of motion was his forte; it was not merely a matter of making a trip in order to arrive at this destination or that, but the experience of going for its own sake that enthralled him, and he portrayed it in a way that caught up the imagination of so many readers. When I first encountered Thomas Wolfe, I had already formed the habit of hanging around railroad stations and freight yards to watch the trains, and the discovery of a novelist who not only shared that interest, but who was able to link it emotionally and rhetorically to the way I felt about my country and about myself and my dreams of ultimate fulfillment, was a marvelous thing. Now just why it was that travel on railroad trains so fascinated Wolfe, and also readers like myself, ought not to be too hard to discern. It was the voyage out, the escape from the confines of the known and bounded, from the mundane circumstances of home and child-hood; the powerful bulk of the locomotive—so much sound and fury, harnessed for full utilization of the energy while yet retaining its explosive glamor—swiftly bears the young Eugene Gant toward his destiny, in symbolism that is at once spiritual and materialistic, aesthetic and practical, selfless and highly sexual. "'Do you know why you are going, or are you just taking a ride on a train?'" the ghost of Ben Gant asks Eugene just before Eugene is about to leave Altamont for the North. Eugene admits that he is not sure of his reasons, that "'Perhaps I just want a ride on the train.'"[6] But if Eugene is unsure at that moment, both he and Thomas Wolfe are quite intent upon making the trip, and merely to be in motion is reason enough to go.

There are voyages in *Look Homeward, Angel,* but it is with *Of Time and the River* that they seem to become compulsive. Eugene travels to Baltimore and Boston, then back to Altamont, then down to South Carolina, then to New York, then on frequent train trips up the Hudson River and back again, then finally to Europe, where he visits first England, then Paris, then the south of France. At the end he is on the ship that will take him back across the ocean to the United States. Traveling, of course, is one way of possessing new experience through an act of the will—one boards the train, looks out the window, and new towns, new countryside, new scenes appear. In a fantasy Wolfe has Eugene imagine that the northbound train he is riding leaves the tracks and soars into space:

To hell with Baltimore, New York, Boston! Run her off the Goddamn rails! We're going West! Run her through the woods—cross fields—rivers, through the hills! Hell's pecker!

6. Wolfe, *Look Homeward, Angel,* 619.

But I'll shove her up the grade and through the gap, no double-header needed! Let's see the world now! Through Nebraska, boy! Let's shove her through, now, you can do it—Let's run her through Ohio, Kansas, and the unknown plains! Come on, you hogger, let's see the great plains and the fields of wheat—Stop off in Dakota, Minnesota, and the fertile places—Give us a minute while you breathe to put our foot upon it, to feel it spring back with the deep elastic feeling, 8,000 miles below, unrolled and lavish, depthless, different from the East.[7]

But of course there is a glass window between the viewer from the train and the life that goes on beyond the window, and the only human relationship thus acquired is that of an outsider, an onlooker. Many of the most moving lyrical passages in Wolfe's work after *Look Homeward, Angel* involve just such moments in which Eugene Gant, and less occasionally George Webber, look on people from a train window and recognize their kinship and their own loneliness. Such moments, however, are transitory; the human contact is limited to the momentary glimpse, whereupon the train glides away. As John Peale Bishop declares in an essay which, though not basically favorable to Wolfe, is one of the most understanding of all writings about him:

For a moment, but a moment only, there is a sudden release of compassion, when some aspect of suffering and bewildered humanity is seized, when the other's emotion is in a timeless completion known. Then the moment passes, and compassion fails. For Eugene Gant, the only satisfactory relationship with another human creature is one which can have no continuity. For the boy at the street corner, seen in the indecision of youthful lust, he has only understanding and pity; the train from which he looks moves on and nothing is required of Eugene. But if he should approach that same boy on the street, if he should come close enough to overhear

7. Thomas Wolfe, *Of Time and the River* (New York, 1935), 71.

him, he would hear only the defilement of language, words which would awaken in him only hate and disgust.[8]

This, I take it, is in part what William Styron means in referring to an abstract quality about Wolfe's America. On the one hand we have, especially in *Look Homeward Angel,* and often elsewhere as well, a portrayal of aspects of the American scene that are concrete, evocative, enormously affective. And there is also, in the work after *Look Homeward, Angel,* a deliberate and cumulative attempt to depict the idea of America itself—an attempt which, though involving much itemization and often long catalogs, is usually singularly impersonal in nature, in that the numerous specific items are chosen as typical examples rather than for themselves. The human contact, in other words, is as viewed through a train window, and neither lasting nor individualized. Wolfe seeks to give them meaning through emotional rhetoric, the emotion belonging to his protagonist as he views them and to the novelist as he remembers viewing them. In page after page of *Of Time and the River* Eugene Gant is shown "experiencing" America, both while traveling across it and afterward through memory while in France. His longing for it while abroad is agonizing, his view of it as seen from train windows is full of love, compassion, desire. But when viewed in this way, as "America," it consists entirely of lists, catalogs, assemblages of examples. It is, in other words, almost entirely quantitative, a collection of items, scenes, themes, names. There is little or no sorting out, no choosing of some of the items as more or less uniquely or typically American, more or less beautiful or meaningful, than others. And at the end what has been given is an abstraction, "America," along with a display of items that are proposed as typical examples of its makeup.

It will not, however, suffice to leave the matter there.

8. John Peale Bishop, "The Sorrows of Thomas Wolfe," in Edmund Wilson (ed.), *The Collected Essays of John Peale Bishop* (New York, 1948), 135.

The passages and episodes in which Wolfe writes his long catalogs to express his protagonist's sense of America have another function. They serve that function imperfectly, and perhaps the method used to achieve it is not among the most efficient available artistic strategies. But it is one that helps to account, in large part, for the tremendous impact that the Wolfe novels can make upon younger, romantically attuned readers. What the "America" episodes do is to dramatize both the Wolfean protagonist's and, importantly, the authorial personality's yearning for experience. The very fact that the emotional hunger is there in such abundance and that it cannot quite make contact with—or, to continue the metaphor, find adequate spiritual nourishment in—the substance at which it is being so urgently directed is itself a device for imaging the sense of loneliness and spiritual yearning that lies at the heart of the experience of reading the novels. And we go wrong, I think, if we refuse to accept that dimension and dismiss such a viewpoint as an example of the so-called "imitative fallacy." For the experience of fiction is a subtle and complex affair, and if we try to leave out the "rhetoric" of the art, the formal function of the presence of the storyteller in our reading of the story he is telling, we may impoverish our relationship with a work of fiction.

What I am getting at is that, whatever else may be said, what Wolfe did in his fiction was to *dramatize himself as author,* warts and all. Or more precisely, what he did was to dramatize himself in the act of looking at himself. What is involved here is a biographical matter and, more importantly, very much a formal, literary relationship. Not only was Wolfe's protagonist a dramatized version of himself when a bit younger, but the rhetoric of the interpretative description serves to set up a myself-when-younger relationship between the storyteller and the protagonist.

For example, in *Of Time and the River* Eugene Gant is

at Harvard, studying drama, and he receives a telegram summoning him home to the bedside of his father, who is dying. He borrows money for the train fare, hurries to the South Station, boards a train, and watches from the window as it moves out of the station:

Then the great train, gathering now in speed, and mounting smoothly to the summit of its tremendous stroke, was running swiftly through the outskirts of the city, through suburbs and brief blurs of light and then through little towns and on into the darkness, the wild and secret loneliness of earth. And he was going home again into the South and to a life that had grown strange as dreams, and to his father who was dying and who had become a ghost and shadow of his father to the bitter reality of grief and death. And—how, why, for what reason he could not say—all he felt was the tongueless swelling of wild joy. It was the wild and secret joy that has no tongue, the impossible hope that has no explanation, the savage, silent, and sweet exultancy of night, the wild and lonely visage of the earth, the imperturbable stroke and calmness of the everlasting earth, from which we have been derived, wherein again we shall be compacted, on which all of us have lived alone as strangers, and across which, in the loneliness of night, we have been hurled onward in the projectile flight of mighty trains—America.[9]

Note how the last, lengthy sentence, though it begins in the past tense—"It *was* the wild and secret joy,"—shifts the center of experience away from Eugene's sudden trip homeward and into the time of writing, in which the author, no longer the homeward-bound Eugene of the past, interprets what the joy *is*. Eugene, riding homeward from Boston on the train, first felt the joy; the authorial voice telling us about it re-creates the moment; and how he feels about it as he describes it is precisely how Eugene felt when he experienced it. The aesthetic and emotional distance between Eugene going home and the author describing it is all but obliterated by the author's rhetoric, which bridges and unites the two experiences. With his rhetoric he injects himself

9. Wolfe, *Of Time and the River,* 246.

into the narrative, ends up speaking directly to us, and the story becomes, as it has been doing from the first page onward, almost as much a demonstration of the recreating storyteller's sensibilities as an account of the protagonist Eugene Gant's youthful adventures.

This dual identity as character and chronicler, enforced through rhetoric and attitude, is both the strength and the weakness of the Wolfe books. It enables Wolfe to bring to bear on his youthful protagonist's experience the impressive powers of his rhetoric. He can recognize, explore, and delineate the particularities of that experience. He can use the affective possibilities of rhetoric to intensify the meaning of the experience and guide our response to it. He can, in other words, both show and persuade; and because the persuasion is coming from a formally established point of view, a re-creating authorial personality, it takes on an authority that would otherwise be missing if it were merely arbitrary authorial embellishment.

But just as surely, it can work only if we are willing to believe in the validity of both the youthful protagonist's experience and the re-creating interpreter's delineation of it. Let us once feel that what the interpreter is telling us about the meaning of what happened is exaggerated, or confused, or actually inaccurate, and the whole relationship breaks down. For the rhetorical stance of this remembering sensibility has got to be plausible, too. When the author says that Eugene did or thought such and such, we accept that; but when he insists that what Eugene did or thought signifies this or that about human experience, and we believe that it doesn't so signify, he is in trouble; and when he tries to enforce his interpretation by cascades of affective rhetoric, what results is something very different from what he intends. Let me cite another example, from the material posthumously published as a novel, *The Web and the Rock.* Wolfe is describing young George Webber's feeling and behavior at a time when he had been quarreling with his mistress. His novel has been rejected, he is in bad shape emotionally, and sometimes, when he telephones his mistress' home to find her not in, he imagines that Esther is betraying him.

And he would leave the phone to drain the bottle to its last raw drop, then rush out in the streets to curse and fight with people, with the city, with all life, in tunnel, street, saloon, or restaurant, while the whole earth reeled about him its gigantic and demented dance.

And then, in the crowded century of darkness that stretched from light to light, from sunset until morning, he would prowl a hundred streets and look into a million livid faces seeing death in all of them, and feeling death everywhere he went. He would be hurled through tunnels to some hideous outpost of the mighty city, the ragged edge of Brooklyn, and come out in the pale grey light of morning in a wasteland horror of bare lots and rust and rubbish; of dismal little houses flung rawly down upon the barren earth, joined each to each in blocks that duplicated one another with an idiot repetition.[10]

Here there are two levels of experience. One is that of George Webber in love, as he suspects his mistress and suffers. However, by use of the conditional tense the author tells us that George "*would* leave the phone to drain the bottle," and "*would* be hurled through tunnels," and so makes it clear that the experience is one that happened to George on characteristic occasions, rather than just the time being described. Clearly, therefore, it is the authorial personality who is speaking to us, recapitulating and summarizing his protagonist's experience over a period of time. Now presumably what the author is doing is showing us how it was with young George Webber at a bad time. It is not that Esther Jack is really betraying George; rather, George, in his pain and torment, imagines that she is, and on such occasions goes off like a madman into the night to wander about

10. Thomas Wolfe, *The Web and the Rock* (New York, 1939), 554–55.

the city in his anguish. Under such conditions, his behavior could hardly be termed inexplicable. Nor would it be improbable that at such a time, drunk, distraught, despondent, George might well envision the city through which he is wandering in just such fashion as described.

But exactly who is it that sees the walk as a "prowl" along "a hundred streets," during which George looks "into a million livid faces seeing death in all of them"? To whom does "the ragged edge of Brooklyn" appear as "some hideous outpost," as "a wasteland horror of bare lots and rust and rubbish," and of "dismal little houses flung rawly down upon the barren earth"? Is it the distraught young protagonist or the supposedly more objective authorial personality interpreting what happened? The answer, syntactically and emotionally, is that both of them see and evaluate it that way. As with the train trip, there is thus little or no difference between the two perspectives. At such moments, all too frequent after *Look Homeward, Angel,* what happens is that the reader is thereupon likely to refuse to accept the interpretation of George Webber's experience which the author is insisting upon. He can go along with the notion that young George Webber may have felt this way about the city at the time and may indeed have imagined he was prowling a hundred streets and looking into a million livid faces, but when the story-teller, the remembering author who as interpreter and judge ought not still to feel betrayed and overcome with a sense of failure, also interprets and evaluates the experience in such fashion, without irony or humor or reservation of any sort, it is something else again. The sympathy and understanding the reader might have for the youthful George Webber at such times of torment is seriously undercut when he realizes that the author is in complete agreement with his protagonist, that he sees nothing excessive, nothing pathological, nothing childish or histrionic in George's attitude, but is recounting it with complete approval and endorsement.

The experience of Thomas Wolfe's fiction, therefore, involves two factors. One is the way in which the doings of the protagonists of the novels are described and communicated to us. The other is the way in which the authorial voice interprets and evaluates those doings. But these two factors cannot be separated from each other and considered in isolation. The impact of the first, as we have seen, is made possible in part by the second. The success of *Look Homeward, Angel* is based on the characterizations of the Gant family and especially of Eugene, and it is the presence of the remembering author that makes possible the rich, emotion-laden concreteness of such characterization. *Look Homeward, Angel* has not the single focus of the apprentice artist-protagonist's consciousness that we find in Joyce's *A Portrait of the Artist as a Young Man;* we see the Gant family before Eugene is born, and throughout there are frequent chapters devoted to W. O. Gant, Eliza, and others of the family, chapters which are not part of the youthful Eugene's experience at all. But it is the remembering artist's re-creation and interpretation that unifies the novel. When W. O. Gant comes back from his western trip (in Chapter 7), there is no way that his infant son Eugene can know what is going on in his mind; but the fact that the son is, as remembering author, re-creating what went on in his father's mind gives this Joycean chapter a double function in the novel itself. Wolfe calls him "Gant the Far-Wanderer," and tells us what he does in a way that Gant himself could not do. And toward the end of the episode he thrusts his own authorial voice directly into the narrative to explain, in his own language, what W. O. Gant and, briefly, Eliza are doing and thinking, and what it means. The episode ends up being fitted into the sensibility and the consciousness of the remembering storyteller, and it draws its ultimate significance in the novel from what that remembering storyteller can make of it. At the close of the novel, the fact that the protagonist is about to turn away from the place where all this has happened and that as experience it is concluded for him combines with the reader's knowledge that what he has been reading is a re-creation and ordering of what has happened and gives the novel its conclusion and its meaning.

The early reviews of *Look Homeward, Angel* all remark on the vividness of the characterization of the Gant family and on the presence, throughout, of the sense of loneliness and lostness. The latter is certainly there not because of what the characters themselves say and think, so much as because the remembering author keeps interpreting their experience in that way and keeps stressing that quality. And, by and large, it works. The reader is willing to accept that rhetorical interpretation of the experience. The loneliness of a young man, the sadness over the dissolution of his family in time, the sense of deprivation and loss—these are not inappropriate or extraneous to the experience being described. And if, to a reader who is unable to take the emotions of the adolescent Eugene Gant with quite the seriousness that the author does, the importance placed on Eugene's sensibility in the latter chapters begins to seem a bit overdone, there is still enough vivid experience in *Look Homeward, Angel,* and enough believable emotional content in the rhetorical interpretation by the narrator, to make this book an impressive, original work of art. One may weary of the incessant reiteration of the *O lost!* motif, may come to feel that Eugene Gant's loneliness is being insisted upon too stridently, but it is the reitera-tion, and not the attitude itself, that is overdone. The author, that is, may be using his rhetoric to exaggerate the attitudes he is expressing, but the attitudes are be-lievable. Generally speaking, the reader can feel that what the rhetoric says the story means is what the story does mean, even if overstated. With *Of Time and the River,* however, it is another matter. To guide us in our apprehension of Eugene's post-Altamont adventures we get, in Wolfe's second novel, a great deal more authorial rhetoric than was previously offered. Not only is *Of Time and the River* a much longer book than *Look Homeward, Angel,* but it also contains far more direct assertion by the author. In his famous critical attack on Wolfe, "Genius Is Not Enough," the late Bernard De Voto objected to what he called all the "placental material" in the novels. There had been a good deal of such material in *Look Homeward, Angel,* he said, along with some fiction of altogether superb quality. But in *Of Time and the River* the placental material had taken over and, in addition, had been given a rationalization: it was supposed to connote the "voiceless and unknown womb of Time" and "dark and lonely and lost America." The writing that De Voto termed placental, and which he felt should have been discarded en route to the story itself, was no more and no less than the authorial rhetoric, which De Voto described as "long, whirling discharges of words, unabsorbed in the novel, unrelated to the proper business of fiction, badly if not altogether unacceptably written, raw gobs of emotion, aimless and quite meaningless jabber, claptrap, belches, grunts, and Tarzan-like screams."[11] But while many readers will agree with the burden of De Voto's strictures, which is that *Of Time and the River* is an overwritten and unstructured book that would have profited by a great deal more cutting and revising than the author was willing to give it, it should be recognized that De Voto's memorable assault fails to comprehend how the Wolfe novels actually work as fiction.

11. Bernard De Voto, "Genius Is Not Enough," *Saturday Review of Literature*, XIII (April 25, 1936), 3–4.

De Voto's theory of fiction dismissed absolutely what we have seen is a necessary dimension to the art of fiction as practiced by Wolfe—that conscious presence of the authorial voice interpreting the doings of the protagonist. "A novel *is*—it cannot be asserted, ranted, or even detonated," De Voto said. "A novelist represents life. When he does anything else, no matter how beautiful or furious or ecstatic the way in which he does it, he is not writing fiction."[12] But the truth is that a novelist can, if he is good enough, use all those methods and yet be representing life in so doing. For part of the representing—in Aristotelian terms, the imitation—happens to be the act of giving order and meaning; and when Wolfe uses his authorial rhetoric to reinforce, interpret, comment upon his protagonist's actions and thoughts, we object not when the rhetoric as such shows up, but only as it fails to enhance our interpretation and evaluation of what the protagonist's life means. When it does fit the occasion, when what the authorial personality says about the protagonist seems believable and appropriate, then, far from being disconcerted by the presence of the rhetoric, we accept it and let it help us take part in the experience of the fiction. What I think De Voto really objected to was not the asserting, ranting, or detonating rhetoric of the novelist; it was the inappropriateness of such rhetoric as an accurate and believable interpretation of the experience being chronicled. When Wolfe goes off on a long lyrical flight about Eugene's train trip northward as representing an expression of the soul of America, and the interpreting narrator poeticizes for pages about what Eugene Gant is doing and feeling, it isn't the rhetorical presence as such that annoys, but the sense that the author is attempting to exaggerate the emotional ardor of the youthful, drunken Eugene Gant into a triumphant, rhapsodic

12. *Ibid.*

insistence upon the poetic virtue of Eugene's superior
sensibility. We can't and don't believe that the experience signifies or proves all that; and the more the author goes on about it the less convincing he seems; until
at the end we think—not, "what has all this to do with
the story?" (as De Voto says we do)—but "he's trying to
make far too much out of the whole thing."
The difference, I think, is essential, for it has to do
with how the Wolfe novels work as fiction. The intense
experience that reading Wolfe can be for the young is
possible precisely because of the ability and the willingness of a certain kind of younger reader to accept, at
face value and as a version of the truth, just the sig-
nification that the narrator is attaching to it. This reader
identifies with the author. For this reader a rhetorical
exercise such as that involving the spirit of America isn't
"placental," as De Voto would have it; rather, it is an
important part of the experience of reading *Of Time and
the River,* because it pronounces the meaning and significance of the train trip and reinforces the feelings of
the younger Eugene Gant who made the trip with the
more "mature" rhetorical approval of the author telling
about it. And *that* is the way *Of Time and the River* works:
it is a kind of alternation of viewpoint between the
younger Eugene and his older writing self in which
the younger man acts and feels and thinks, and then the
older man not only expresses his approval but confirms
the verdict in emotive rhetoric. The charm, for the
younger reader, lies in the fact that although the older,
commenting narrator is, by dint of his rhetorical skill
and the obvious fact that he wrote the book, no mere
youth first undergoing the experience, he nevertheless
not only accepts and ratifies the younger viewpoint but
extols it as being even more significant than the younger
protagonist himself had realized. The verve, the self-
importance, the romantic insistence upon uniqueness of
sensibility, the essentially uncritical, quantitative hunger

for sensation of the adolescent and postadolescent, far from ever being qualified or viewed ironically by the older narrator, are enthusiastically received by many younger readers. My own copy of *Of Time and the River* is inscribed 1944, when I was twenty; it is the copy that I used a little more than a year later when I gave a report on Wolfe in an English class I was enrolled in after the war was over, and its margins are marked to indicate the passages I chose for reading aloud on that occasion. It must have been quite a performance I put on that day, for the passages I selected back then were almost uniformly those with the greatest amount of rhetorical bombast, the most enraptured expressions of loneliness and exhilaration, the most arrogant and impassioned assertions of uniqueness and superior sensibility! Clearly the rhetoric did not faze me; obviously I considered those rhapsodic catalogs, that now seem so empty and self-deceiving, to be profound statements about the nature of reality. Here, for example, is one passage that apparently I marked for reading aloud, from the train episode early in *Of Time and the River:*

What is it that we know so well and cannot speak? What is it that we want to say and cannot tell? What is it that keeps swelling in our hearts its grand and solemn music, that is aching in our throats, that is pulsing like a strange wild grape through all the conduits of our blood, that maddens us with its exultant and intolerable joy and that leaves us tongueless, wordless, maddened by our fury to the end?

We do not know. All that we know is that we lack a tongue that could reveal, a language that could perfectly express the wild joy swelling to a music in our heart, the wild pain welling to a strong ache in our throat, the wild cry mounting to a madness in our brain, the thing, the word, the joy we know so well, and cannot speak! All that we know is that the little stations whip by in the night, the straggling little towns whip by with all that is casual, rude, familiar, ugly, and unutterable. All that we know is that the earth is flowing by us in the darkness, and that this is the way the world goes—with a field and a wood and a field! And of the huge and secret earth all we know is that we feel with all our life its texture with our foot upon it.[13]

Why that passage appealed to me when I was one-and-twenty, I can now only dimly surmise. For one thing, it asserts that the condition of very young manhood is one of a tremendous urgency of feeling and emotion and that the cause, the locus, of such feeling is essentially indefinable. Furthermore, and most importantly, it asserts that there is really no need to have to understand and define it, for the feeling itself is all that matters. The passage is violently and hugely romantic; it predicates, as the norm, an infinite capacity for feeling, without any real need at all for attempting to understand the nature of the feeling, or any necessity for the feeling being grounded in an object or a situation. There is no requirement that the emotion be used, no suggestion that until or unless it is made part of the design and purpose of one's life, it will remain unanchored, useless, and ineffective. Quite the contrary; it insists that "all that we know" is the intensity of the emotion itself. The implication is clearly that any attempt to make anything more or different of it than that would be to cheapen the emotion.

Now to have someone say that, to say it in words that pile up one upon the other in a massive rhetorical progression that reproduces the vague but intense feeling being described, is quite likely to have a powerful appeal for a young person who thinks he can recognize in it his own portrait, done largely as he likes to conceive of himself. It is this that accounts for the tremendous feeling of identification that so many younger readers have with the Wolfe novels and their author. It is indeed the "shock of recognition" that is involved: the discovery that one's inmost feelings have been articulated by other, so that presumably they are worth having after all.

13. Wolfe, *Of Time and the River*, 34.

But the trouble with such feelings, as James Joyce recognized about the young Stephen Dedalus, is that that is all they are: unanchored, unused, and, in the form presented to us, unusable emotion. In the diary that culminates *A Portrait of the Artist as a Young Man,* Stephen records, for April 10, a rhapsodic passage about the sound of hoofs on the road, but on April 11 he records, "Read what I wrote last night. Vague words for a vague emotion."[14] There are no such passages as that latter entry in the litanies of Eugene Gant, for there is no such qualitative distance between Eugene Gant and Thomas Wolfe; the young man's attitude toward his own importance is fully endorsed by the somewhat older novelist writing about him. Wolfe seems to have had none of Joyce's Thomistic zeal for precise significa-tion, none of Joyce's insistence upon defining his terms. The difference, to be sure, is not always in Joyce's favor. Placed alongside Eugene Gant's sensuous apprehension of his experience in *Look Homeward, Angel,* the emo-tional apprehension of life of Stephen Dedalus in *A Portrait* seems impoverished, narrow. But what for a boy and a very young man is appropriate and in its way admirable becomes for an adult something less than that. We will allow, even encourage, the youth and the young man to go after his experience hungrily, uncriti-cally; later on will be time enough to sort things out and decide which parts of it he wishes to use. But when the young man moves on into full adulthood, and it is time for his emotional apprenticeship to be done with, we grow impatient with a continued refusal to sort out, criticize, choose, and select; as De Voto put it, "If the death of one's father comes out emotionally even with a ham-on-rye, then the art of fiction is cockeyed."[15] The difficulty for the adult reader of the Wolfe novels, in particular after *Look Homeward, Angel,* is that not only

14. Joyce, *A Portrait of the Artist,* 251, 252.
15. De Voto, "Genius Is Not Enough," 4.

does the autobiographical protagonist insist upon holding on to his immaturity, but the interpreting author equally insists upon the entire appropriateness of his doing so and upon the spiritual insensitivity of all who refuse to go along with him when he does it. Furthermore, the authorial commentator, for all his approval, appears to become increasingly apprehensive that others may not share his approbation, and his response is to double and treble his own rhetoical assertion of the rightness of Eugene's behavior, attempting to sweep away all possible objections, including perhaps his own, in a torrent of words. This is the material that De Voto calls placental. It is not that so much as it is simply superfluous.

If Wolfe had lived to revise the material published as his last two novels (they were put together by his editors from among his manuscripts), would he as a writer have changed in any significant way? Was he working, as some commentators have claimed, toward a much greater maturity and objectivity—toward the social rather than the lyrical novel? One is not at all sure. In 1938, after Wolfe had broken with Maxwell Perkins and Charles Scribner's Sons and had signed a contract with Harper and Brothers, he wrote his new editor, Edward C. Aswell, about the plans for his new book. The choice of the protagonist, he informed Aswell, would be crucial. He was done with "lyrical and identifiable personal autobiography" such as had characterized his first two novels:

> In other words, the value of the Eugene Gant type of character is his personal and romantic uniqueness, causing conflict with the world around him: in this sense, the Eugene Gant type of character becomes a kind of romantic self-justification, and the greatest weakness of the Eugene Gant type of character lies in this fact.
> Therefore, it is first of all vitally important to the success of this book that there be no trace of Eugene Gant-i-ness in the character of the protagonist, and since there is no longer a

trace of Eugene Gant-i-ness in the mind and spirit of the creator, the problem should be a technical one rather than a spiritual or emotional one. In other words, this is a book about discovery, and not about self-justification.[16]

All this sounds very good, but when Wolfe proceeds to tell Aswell what it is that he intends to do, it turns out that the main change he has in mind will be to make his new protagonist a short, stocky, long-limbed man rather than a tall one, and that in the course of the narrative he will learn to accept his physical variance from the norm. And after he descibes the prologue he will write, he goes on to say that the narrative itself will begin in a railroad station:

For the purpose of this beginning—this setting—is to show the tremendous and nameless Allness of The Station—ten thousand men and women constantly arriving and departing, each unknown to the other, but sparked with the special fire of his own destination, the unknown town, the small hand's breadth of earth somewhere out upon the vast body of the continent—all caught together for a moment, interfused and weaving, not lives but life, caught up, subsumed beneath the great roof of the mighty Station, the vast murmur of these voices drowsily caught up there like the murmurous and incessant sound of time and of eternity, which is and is forever, no matter what men come and go through the portals of the great Station, no matter what men live or die.[17]

Will the new work, then, really be very different from what has come before? Is the Eugene Gant-i-ness really banished, both from the protagonist and from the mind of the creator? One doubts it very much. For what lies at the center of the Eugene Gant-i-ness and gives it its special quality is not the youthful protagonist's romantic self-justification so much as the authorial storyteller's romantic self-justification. It has been the remembering narrator's inability to distinguish his perspectives from

16. Thomas Wolfe to Edward C. Aswell, February 14, 1938, in Elizabeth Nowell (ed.), *The Letters of Thomas Wolfe* (New York, 1956), 714.
17. *Ibid.*, 719.

those of his autobiographical protagonist's, and his insistence upon asserting, in pyramiding rhetoric, the validity and the wisdom of his protagonist's view of himself, that has given the first two novels the quality of youthful self-justification. And nothing in what Wolfe wrote about his future work gives much indication that the author's attitude toward his autobiographical protagonist would be one whit more distanced than with the earlier work. He still envisions his protagonist as existing at the center of the universe. What is important about the railroad station, he says, is "not lives but life"—which, since his protagonist is going to be in the station, means that the protagonist's experience will be thought of by the narrator as absolutely archetypal, possessing the significance of Everyman. Not for a moment does it occur to him that his protagonist's experience may possibly be less than that, that it may be one man's life only, and not Life in general. An unkind critic, reading that outline, might well remark that seeing one's protagonist as archetypal is fully as arrogant as is seeing him as unique.

So I doubt that toward the end of his career Thomas Wolfe was moving significantly away from that romantic self-justification and that the books he would have written had he lived would have been importantly less egocentric than his earlier work. Indeed, the single clue I see toward any such eventuality ever occurring lies not in his posthumously published fictions, which are more or less the same thing as before, but in one sentence in the last thing he ever wrote, the letter to Maxwell Perkins written on August 12, 1938, from the hospital in Seattle during Wolfe's final illness. Writing at a time when he thought he had a chance for recovery, though he knew he was critically ill, he told his first editor:

So much of mortality still clings to me—I wanted most desperately to live and still do, and I thought about you all a thousand times, and wanted to see you all again, and there was the impossible anguish and regret of all the work I had not done, of all the work I had to do—and I know now I'm just a grain of dust, and I feel as if a great window has been opened on life I did not know about before—and if I come through this, I hope to God I am a better man, and in some strange way I can't explain, I know I am a deeper and a wiser one.[18]

"I know now I'm just a grain of dust," not "Man is just a grain of dust," but that one man, Thomas Wolfe, is: here we have a note different from anything found in any of the millions of words published or unpublished that Wolfe had written up to that time. Whether, if he had lived, that note would have been developed and sustained, we shall never know, for in just over a month's time, at the age of thirty-seven, he was dead.

What we have in the Wolfe fiction, then, is the dramatized record of a talented and romantic young writer's encounter with the experience of being an artist in America, as it forced itself upon him. He described it happening, and he told us what he thought it meant. Especially after his first book, what he said it meant is often not what we think it really did mean, but there can be no mistaking the earnestness with which he presented his case or any questioning of the artistic honesty of the attempt. We may disagree with the interpretation, may feel sometimes that he is trying to justify what cannot and should not be justified, and sometimes even that he is using his rhetoric to cover his own uneasy suspicion that what he has been saying means something other than he intends. But let this be said: he never spares himself, never hides behind cheap deceits or clever, modish poses. His aim, as Faulkner says, was to tell it all, and though by no means always sure of what it was he was telling, he did his best. This is why it seems to me that even *Of Time and the River,* for all its excess

18. Wolfe to Maxwell E. Perkins, August 12, 1938, *ibid.,* 777.

and its attitudinizing, comes out as a pretty good book. This is to say, we may not like all of what we see in it, but there can be no doubt we have experienced something very formidable and very honest. What we have experienced is Thomas Wolfe trying to tell about himself as Eugene Gant; and I submit that this is worth having, and we should let no theory of the effaced narrator prevent us from recognizing that this is the formal experience of the encounter with *Of Time and the River*. What one may think about the experience may change a great deal over the decades, but there can be no doubt that the transaction is there to be read, with no tricks, shortcuts, or evasions in the telling. It is the story of the archetypal young American would-be artist, grotesqueries, awkwardness, self-deceptions, and all, in search of his subject. Those who have dismissed that search as mere fustion and rhetoric—De Voto, Clifton Fadiman, Stanley Hyman, Randall Jarrell, Caroline Gordon, John Donald Wade, many others—may have deprived themselves of a precious experience. One is moved to quote what the great artist Elstir says in Proust's *Within a Budding Grove* when the young Marcel asks him, in effect, whether he was once the foolish little painter who had frequented the salon of the Verdurins:

"There is no man," he began, "however wise, who has not at some period of his youth said things, or lived in a way the consciousness of which is so unpleasant to him in later life that he would gladly, if he could, expunge it from his memory. And yet he ought not entirely to regret it, because he cannot be certain that he has indeed become a wise man—so far as it is possible for any of us to be wise—unless he has passed through all the fatuous or unwholesome incarnations by which that ultimate stage must be preceded. . . . We are not provided with wisdom, we must discover it for ourselves, after a journey through the wilderness which no one else can take for us, an effort which no one can spare us, for our wisdom is the point of view from which we come at last to regard the world. . . . I can see that the picture of what we once were, in early youth, may not be recognisable and cannot, certainly, be pleasing to contemplate in later life. But we must not deny the truth of it, for it is evidence that we have really lived." [19]

For many readers such as myself, the glory of Thomas Wolfe, I think, is that he can still show us that.

19. Marcel Proust, *Remembrance of Things Past,* trans. C. K. Scott Moncrieff (2 vols.; New York, 1934), I, 649.

Southern Literature:
A Piedmont Art

It is hard to say where the South begins or where it ends. When you drive down from New York, if you turn directly southward just below Wilmington, Delaware, and travel along the coast instead of toward Baltimore and Washington, you will not get fifteen miles distant from Wilmington before the countryside suddenly turns southern. There will be pines, the sandy soil, the houses and barns sprawling unpainted and untrimmed in horizontal proximity to the earth, in general the somnolent, relaxed attitude—it could be coastal Carolina, yet you are scarcely 100 miles below New York City. On the other hand, if you drive southward along the Valley Pike, coming down through the Pennsylvania Dutch country across Maryland and the eastern arm of West Virginia and into Virginia via Winchester and Harrisonburg, you can get all the way to Staunton and

This essay was prepared as part of a program on the Piedmont South for the 1968 meeting of the South Eastern American Studies Association at Clemson University, Clemson, South Carolina, and subsequently published in *Mississippi Quarterly*, XXIII (Winter, 1969–70), 1–16.

even Lexington, more than 150 miles within the Old Dominion, and it will still look and feel like Pennsylvania—big, gabled barns painted red houses of rouge-red brick and of stone; a sober, well-cropped appearance to everything. Or so it has always seemed to me. But when I consider the matter logically, I realize that I am not talking about South and North, I am talking about the difference between Piedmont and Tidewater. For since I come from the coast, I think of pine flats, salt marsh, water oaks, and a rundown landscape as the South, when it is really only that part of the South to which I am accustomed. And I realize, too, that it is this, and not a magical difference between two states, that can account for a phenomenon I used to notice and meditate about every time I drove southward from the mountains of Virginia, where until recently I lived. It is that along U.S. Highway Number One, a few miles below the town of Rockingham, North Carolina, there is a place where the country seems abruptly to change, to become at once flat, lazy, gentle, the foliage less intensely green and paler, the very air heavier and more somnolent— and this point is precisely at the border between North and South Carolina, and yet there is no river or line of hills observable on the map to demarcate the boundary. What was happening was simply that I was leaving Piedmont North Carolina and entering the South Carolina coastal plain, which swings down from Cape Hatteras. So that all the time, what I had thought of as North, and as opposed to South, was Piedmont, as opposed to Tidewater, or as we say it in South Carolina, Low Country as opposed to Up Country.

It has been the custom for the Low Country to think of itself as the South and to condescend to the Piedmont, for a good many years. History happens very rapidly in America, so that the fact that the Tidewater cities were settled some few decades before the communities in the upstate regions began to take shape has been enough to create a kind of cultural and historical distance that in Europe was many centuries in the making. Thus the Low Countryman is likely to consider his relationship to the Up Countryman as roughly comparable to that between, say, a citizen of Dublin and a man from the West of Ireland, or between a Parisian and a resident of the Landes country, when the fact is that both Charleston and the Up Country were settled, as Europeans measure time, almost simultaneously. Yet the differences between Low Country and Up Country, Tidewater and Piedmont, are not imaginary; they are real and genuine, and the culture of the Southeast is in large measure what it is because of the differences. However much South Carolinians may, for example, speak as one voice in response to what goes on in Washington, within the state itself they tend to view many things very differently (including, for example, the interpretation of liquor law enforcement).

I remember an incident that occurred while I was a student at the High School of Charleston. A group of professional education officials from Columbia came down to inspect and evaluate the high school. Even though I was only a student, I was able to sense a feeling among my teachers that what was being done represented something of an invasion, reminiscent of the Vandals entering Rome, so to speak, and there was general uneasiness lest the education specialists of the state university prove insensitive to the subtle qualitative superiority of the High School of Charleston's faculty and make unfavorable comments concerning the educational facilities of the city of Charleston. (Some of the resentment had to do with the fact that they were education officials, of course, but it was doubtless considered characteristic of the Up Country that it believed in education officials.)

The resentment existed on both sides, however, because I remember that when the chairman of the visiting inspection committee spoke to the student body at assembly, he pointed out, in an aside, that for many years Charleston County had demanded the right to elect two senators to represent it in the state legislature, while the other South Carolina counties had to be content with one apiece. This struck me as not very democratic of Charleston, but what was most surprising was the manner whereby it was revealed to us—something like that of an American being informed for the first time about the Mexican side of the Texas Revolution. If that was the intention, it obviously succeeded, because twenty-five years later I still recall the incident.

Certainly there has been an assumption of cultural superiority on the part of the Low Country, and perhaps there still is, though I cannot say for sure, not having lived in the Tidewater South for a quarter of a century. But if there is, then in my particular field of professional interest, which is literature, the phenomenon I have had to confront is the extent to which the important literature of the South has tended largely to be a Piedmont rather than a Low Country product. To be sure, this is not particularly true for South Carolina, for the simple reason that not a single one of the more important southern writers of the last four decades is a South Carolinian, either from Low Country or Up Country. Ours have been writers of considerable less magnitude, and while several of them came out of Charleston, no especially stunning distinction is thereby conferred upon Charleston.

Almost all of the really major southern writers of the 1920s and 1930s were raised above the fall line. In North Carolina Thomas Wolfe was from the mountains. In Georgia neither Carson McCullers nor Erskine Caldwell came from Savannah. Most of the good southern poets have been from Kentucky or Tennessee. William Faulkner was from northern Mississippi. And so on. Even among the more recent writers, those of the 1950s and 1960s, this has tended to be the case. Though Flannery O'Connor was born in Savannah, she grew up upstate. Madison Jones, Shelby Foote, Reynolds Price, Peter Taylor, Walker Percy, and Randall Jarrell are all inland folk. William Styron alone is from Tidewater, and—an important qualification—he comes not from the old Virginia seaboard communities of Norfolk or Hampton, but from the New South industrial community of Newport News.

By all rights, one would think, this should not be so. Culture is traditionally an affair of cities, not rural regions, and the Tidewater cities were places of considerable sophistication for many decades before the Piedmont developed its urban centers. There was a professional theater in Charleston when most of the cities of Up Country South Carolina were not even villages. There was a literary review published in Charleston which was read on two continents when Nashville, Tennessee, was a trading post, and Oxford, Mississippi, was inhabited by the real-life counterparts of William Faulkner's Ikkemotubbe and his Chickasaw braves. Literature was published in Charleston before people living in the vicinity of Asheville, North Carolina, could read. Yet when one thinks of literature in the South, he thinks not of Charleston, but of Yoknapatawpha County, the Fugitives of Vanderbilt University, Altamont in Old Catawba. And rightly so.

Why is this? Why do almost all of the South's writers of the twentieth-century renascence come from places a hundred miles and more distant from the seacoast? I wish to propose an explanation, which may be considered, since I am from the Low Country, to be a form of sour grapes, but which I think is true. It is that the South's writers come from the Piedmont precisely *because* the formal culture of the South has been principally a Low Country, Tidewater affair.

Writers are odd creatures. They do not come, apparently, from places where there is a great deal of artistic culture immediately available—if they did, New York City would produce the best American writers, which it does not. Neither, however, do they come from Montana or Wyoming or North Dakota—from places only sparsely settled and mostly agricultural. Apparently they come more often out of societies in the process of transition from one kind of culture to another. They come—I speak, of course, of groups of writers, not the occasional lone sport—when a society has been one kind of society and is changing into another. Late nineteenth-century Ireland was such a society; so was middle and late nineteenth-century Russia, and so was Elizabethan England, and eighteenth-century England, and so was the South of the twentieth century—and, within the South, the Piedmont above all.

Consider the instances of two twentieth-century southern writers, both now dead, one of them from the Up Country, the other from the Low Country. Both Thomas Wolfe and DuBose Heyward were young men of much talent and energy. But whereas Wolfe grew up in a mountain community, and his father was a stonecutter and his mother operated a boardinghouse and speculated in property, DuBose Heyward's family was of the Charleston aristocracy. His great-great-great-grandfather had been a signer of the Declaration of Independence and his grandfather a prosperous planter. Though his father died when he was a child, and the family was impoverished, the Heywards were interested in and very much a part of Charleston social and cultural activity. Indeed, Heyward's mother was a part-time poet and writer. And when after the First World War DuBose Heyward grew interested in the writing of poetry, he found in Charleston some kindred poets—Hervey Allen, John Bennett—to talk with and form a literary circle. When they decided to organize a poetry society, as Frank Durham tells us in his biography of Heyward, they drew up a list of persons to ask by going through the Charleston telephone directory! Can anyone imagine Thomas Wolfe being able to do that in Asheville? The picture of Eugene Gant's youth as given in *Look Homeward, Angel* is one of great loneliness. Save for his teacher Margaret Leonard, there is absolutely no sense of anyone or anything in Altamont providing him with an outlet or an audience for whatever artistic interests and sensibilities he possesses. The only cultural event described in *Look Homeward, Angel* is a ludicrous pageant staged in honor of Shakespeare's death three hundred years earlier. Like Wolfe, Eugene Gant went away from home, to the state university, to develop his dawning literary talent; his brother Ben, who could not go, was stifled and suffocated. At Pulpit Hill Eugene found a theater group and a literary society; even so, Wolfe's description of his college years is one that continued to involve much loneliness and solitude.

We will find no such pervasive loneliness or limitation in the early life of DuBose Heyward. He sketched, wrote poetry, and was read to; though poor and often ill as well, he cut a figure in Charleston society. When as a young man he wrote a one act play, it was produced in the South Carolina Society Hall and reviewed enthusiastically in the *News and Courier*. Though in *Mamba's Daughters* he tells us that his autobiographical character Saint Wentworth "was sensitive and took refuge from humiliating realities in a dream world of his own" and that "he spent most of his time roaming the waterfront," there is little sense of cultural deprivation, of the abiding loneliness of the young artist, either in Heyward's novel or in his life.

If I seem to be basing too much of my argument on a comparison between what after all are two individuals, then let me make a group comparison, between Heyward and his fellow poets of the Poetry Society of South Carolina and the group of young apprentice poets in the Up Country South who became known as the Fugitives of Nashville. In the 1920s these two groups were generally considered to be the two most notable examples of the quickened interest in poetry of a South which was finally "reawakening." We find the same division here, too. The Poetry Society of South Carolina, its membership selected as we recall from the Charleston telephone book, was a community activity, with hundreds of members. It gave prizes, staged readings and lectures, published a yearbook in which the literary doing of the community of Charleston were reported at length. The editors of the city's newspapers served as presidents. Poetry was socially respectable in Charleston during the 1920s; the best people in town attended the meetings and the readings, just as they attended the dramatic performances and the concerts at the Academy of Music and later at the Dock Street Theater.

Contrast the Charleston poets with the young Fugitives of Nashville, almost all of whom were teachers or students at Vanderbilt University. They too began meeting to read each other's poems, and soon they decided to publish a magazine. There was a certain amount of local newspaper notice, not all of it favorable by any means, but even though they somehow managed to secure financial help from the Associated Retailers of Nashville, the group remained small and private. Their meetings were working sessions, not public events. The Fugitives meant business, and there was nothing social or public about their affair with the muse.

At one point a poem by one of the Fugitives, John Crowe Ransom, was adjudged winner of one of the Poetry Society of South Carolina's many prizes. There was much embarrassment among the society's leadership, because the directors of the group were fearful that if Ransom's poem, "Armageddon," were to be published in the yearbook, as was the custom with the prize poems, its apparent irreverence would create a scandal and cause the good Charlestonians to resign from the society in droves. So they reached a compromise; "Armageddon" was not published in the yearbook but as a separate booklet, for distribution among those members of the society who "express a desire to have it." Can anyone remotely imagine such a consideration playing a part in the decision to publish or not to publish a poem in the *Fugitive*? The difference was that the poets of the Poetry Society wrote *about* Charleston, and *for* a Charleston audience, while the Fugitives seldom wrote *about* Tennessee and never *for* a Nashville audience. Their subsequent adventure at Agrarianism, indeed, was in part an attempt at conscious identification with their region, an attempt which the Charleston writers would never have considered necessary.

Most of the leading figures in the Poetry Society of South Carolina, all of whom needed money, became popular novelists and playwrights. Heyward's success with *Porgy* is well known. Hervey Allen's *Anthony Adverse* was a tremendous best seller. Josephine Pinckney wrote a group of novels, the best known being *Three O'Clock Dinner*. Before and after the 1920s John Bennett was a writer and illustrator of children's books. Several of the other members also produced popular fiction. The Fugitives were no more wealthy than the Charlestonians, but even so, none of them became really popular writers. They stayed within the university and continued with poetry for the most part. Eventually Robert Penn Warren enjoyed wide readership with his fiction, but not at the expense of his artistic integrity; his most popular novel was also his best.

The best writers of the twentieth-century South have been university trained. Wolfe at Chapel Hill, the Fugitives at Nashville, Faulkner at Ole Miss (his father was its treasurer), Eudora Welty at Wisconsin—most of the best writing to come out of the South has been the product of minds exposed to university ways. The reason that the poetry of the Nashville Fugitives has lasted, while that of the Poetry Society of South Carolina is all but forgotten, is in part because the Nashville poets had formidably trained intellects and were strongly interested in language and form, rather than picturesque subject matter. The only poetry by the Charlestonians that stands up well today, in my opinion, is that of Beatrice Ravenel, who underwent an impressive if irregular education at Radcliffe and Harvard and who was never closely associated with the Poetry Society writers, as Morris Cox points out in his study of the group.

Has it ever been remarked that from Virginia to Mississippi, until very recently, there was not a single university of even second-rate status in the Tidewater regions of the South? In every instance, the state and private universities of any reputation are located well in from the ocean. Only in recent years have there been any universities at all in seaport cities, and most of them are branches of other universities. The leading southern universities—Virginia, Virginia Tech, North Carolina, Duke, North Carolina State, South Carolina, Clemson, Georgia, Georgia Tech, Emory, Alabama, Auburn, Vanderbilt, Tennessee, Mississippi, Mississippi State—are every one of them Piedmont institutions. This is not because historically there were no colleges within the Tidewater from which universities might eventually have evolved. Charleston has had a municipal college since Revolutionary War times and a military college for almost as long. In Virginia the College of William and Mary was producing statesmen in the mid-eighteenth century, yet it has never developed into a university.

Of course the reason that the state universities of the Southeast are almost all located in the Up Country is that in each instance their location was the result of

political compromise. But this is not a sufficient explanation. When the decision to establish most of these
schools was made, the Tidewater South still held the
major share of political and economic power within
each state. Had the seaport cities really wanted universities located within their midst, it is doubtful that their
demands could have been resisted. The conclusion is
inescapable that the universities were located upstate
because the people chiefly demanding state-supported
colleges in the antebellum South were the people of the
Piedmont regions, and also because the Low Country
people did not consider it very important that the new
colleges and universities be located close to home.

If I seem to be suggesting that higher education was
held in greater esteem and was of greater importance to
the Up Country than to the Low Country, that is not
what I have in mind. Paradoxically, quite the reverse, it
seems to me, is true. From earliest colonial times, college
was an accepted part of the training of a young Tidewater gentleman. We are told that before 1860, two-
thirds of the American students at the Inns of Court in
London were southerners. I should be interested in
seeing this figure broken down into geographical regions; I suspect that the large majority of them, both
actually and in proportion to relative population, were
from the seaport cities of the Old South. If half the
students at Princeton before the Civil War were southerners, and if Harvard, Yale, Pennsylvania, and the
other universities of the northeastern states were heavily populated by southern students, I would guess that a
majority of them were from the Tidewater. The reason
is simple: not only did the seaport cities have the money,
but they were, especially in a day before railroads
existed, accustomed to travel beyond the borders of
their regions. In the old Low Country there was a formidable tradition of study in New England and Europe.
Society in a city such as Charleston was stratified, estab-

lished clearly along caste lines. It was the aristocracy, the upper class, that possessed much of the wealth and also the tradition of higher education for its sons. For Rutledges and Pinckneys and Randolphs and Pages and Harrisons and Elliotts and the like, education automatically meant travel, whether to the North or abroad. They did not think in terms of college at home; their children were, as part of their training, expected to go to Boston, Hew Haven, England, Scotland, the Continent, or at the very least the new state university up in the Piedmont.

In short, there was little pressure for the universities to be located in the port cities themselves. In South Carolina, for example, when it became time to send young Hugh Swinton Legaré to school, his mother, we are told, "perhaps under the sound idea that he had now reached the age where the effeminacy of a home education should be broken—determined to send him to a distance," and young Legaré was therefore placed in the Reverend Moses Waddel's academy, near Abbeville, then sent to the South Carolina College in Columbia, and after that to the Continent and to Edinburgh for the study of the law. Why would a Legaré have wanted a university to be founded in Charleston?

What I am suggesting, therefore, is that colleges and universities did not flourish in the Tidewater *because* higher education was habitual, an affair of caste and class, and best pursued elsewhere. The Up Country, however, remote from the seaports, less cosmopolitan and less cultured, aspiring to sophistication, demanded the state universities and got them. I rather think that even to this day, it will be found that the proportion of Tidewater students relative to total population in attendance at state universities is lower, and at out-of-state institutions is higher, than that for Piedmont students.

Though the universities of the Southeast were and are located principally in the Piedmont, I think it is undeniable that historically the general level of cultural sophistication has been higher in the old seaport cities than in the towns of the Up Country. Easier access to Europe and to the Northeast, a more cosmopolitan population, greater extremes of wealth, an Episcopalian rather than a Calvinistic religious heritage—these are among the factors at work here. I mentioned before that there was a theater in Charleston in the early years of the eighteenth century. Savannah, Wilmington, and Mobile likewise had theaters early in their histories. It is precisely the arts of the theater that have flourished best in Charleston and in most of the old seaport cities, for the reason that the theater is by nature a public art form, a community affair. Theaters, orchestral concerts, and the like are possible only when there is an audience, a community sufficiently tolerant of and interested in such activities to provide the patronage needed to support them. Even the renowned St. Cecilia Society of Charleston began as an organization sponsoring musical concerts. Can anyone imagine a flourishing professional theater in much of the Up Country before the Civil War? It would have been thought sinful, scandalous.

The young writer-to-be growing up in a seaport community is thus likely to have enjoyed a local audience from the start and to have received recognition and a degree of understanding that his counterpart in the Piedmont did not enjoy. This made for a social art, one not importantly detached from the community. Thus the arts of the Tidewater have been respectable, genteel; the apprentice novelist or poet has been nurtured upon such attitudes. He has inherited a tradition of interested gentility, an audience of gentlefolk. The major writers of the modern South, however, almost all of them Up Countrymen, enjoyed no such understanding. Their artistic interests set them apart from the Piedmont communities in which they were born, and with the solitude came the detachment, the alienation even, that ultimately made for important literary art. Their art was the act of ordering, of asserting a meaning and perhaps an identity as well, that so-called Real Life did not provide. As Thomas Wolfe wrote, "One finds among a great number of our people, I mean the laboring, farming sort of people from which I came, a kind of great wonder and doubt and romantic feeling about writers so that it is hard for them to understand that a writer may be one of them and not a man far away like Lord Byron or Tennyson or Percy Bysshe Shelley." In part, of course, this is a matter of class, caste, and economics, as Wolfe suggests, but I think it is also a matter of geography. Had Wolfe been born in one of the old Tidewater cities, his literary ambitions might not have seemed so strange to his family and their friends.

This brings us to still another factor in our speculation. It has to do with the history of the South since the Civil War and in the first several decades of the twentieth century. The southeastern seaport cities were urban centers for decades before most of the Up Country towns became cities. The Up Country's growth has been primarily post– Civil War in time. Much more so than in the Tidewater cities was the inhabitant of the Piedmont towns, and the surrounding countryside, exposed to swift, even violent transition in the community life around him. What had once been tranquil and agricultural became metropolitan and industrial.

If literature is the writer's attempt to give form and order to his experience, then how different has been the experience of Low Country and Up Country in the years when the southern writers were born and grew up. From personal experience I can testify that it has been only since the coming of the Second World War that life in Charleston importantly differed from what it had been for generations. The northern city limits of

Charleston in the 1930s ran along Mount Pleasant Street, which was where they were in 1865. Comparing the city I knew as a child to that which I visit nowadays, I find a tremendous difference. I doubt that the difference was nearly so striking to DuBose Heyward when he came back to Charleston in the middle 1930s. In his lifetime his native city increased in size hardly at all. Its population remained pretty much the same. Anyone who knew Charleston in the 1930s and who reads a novel such as, say, Owen Wister's *Lady Baltimore,* which was written in the early 1900s, can easily recognize almost everything there. The names in the Charleston guidebooks published during the 1880s are not much different from those published during the 1920s and 1930s. Indeed, in the generations after the Civil War there was not money enough in the city to tear down the antebellum homes and substitute the currently fashionable Victorian monstrosities, with the result that with the coming of the automobile and the tourist trade, Charleston began enjoying all the benefits of a colonial Williamsburg economy without having needed a John D. Rockefeller to recreate it.

For the writers of the southern renascence, then, the Tidewater South has been a fairly settled, orderly place. The young writer growing up in a city such as Charleston found life conducted pretty much along the traditional lines. He inherited, to a degree that his Up Country compatriot could not have known, a considerable amount of cultural activity and the like—theaters, concerts, even an indigenous literature (for there has been an actual Charleston literature for many years, and for most of that time it has been a very self-conscious literature, capitalizing on local color, and written with an eye for the local and tourist trade). The young Tidewater writer, therefore, has tended to have very little of the rebel in him; he has not known the loneliness and isolation that produced the detachment needed to force him to question the prevailing civic values. Add up the names of the southeastern Tidewater writers of recent years. There is not an iconoclast in the crowd. In the Piedmont South, there has indeed been change, of every sort and in every direction. If life was settled and fixed in the nineteenth century, it has hardly remained so in the twentieth. The Piedmont became the manufacturing region, with the South's major commercial centers. From the farms the people came into the towns, and the towns became cities. The vigorous Calvinism of the Up Country, in its Baptist and Methodist as well as Presbyterian manifestations, made its strident claims upon the consciousness of the young—and lost out, if one is to judge by how the writers eventually turned out. It was the Piedmont, not the Tidewater, that was caught up in the economic and political turmoil of the Populist era; it was in the Piedmont that the Klan flourished, and where most of the lynchings took place; it was the Piedmont counties in every state that voted prohibition into existence, and today resist local option. The foremost political demagogues of the Solid South have not been citizens of the Tidewater. They bear Up Country names: Ben Tillman, Cole Blease, Gene Talmadge, Tom Heflin, Huey Long, James K. Vardaman, Tom Watson, Theodore G. Bilbo, and so on. The battles over labor union organization took place where the textile industry largely was—in the Piedmont. Whatever there has been of change, confusion, economic and social turmoil in southern life has been, until recent years at least, most characteristic of the Piedmont, not the seaboard South.

For the young southerner with literary talent who grew up in the Piedmont South, then, the task of finding order and stability in a society very much in transition has been more than ordinarily difficult, and the literary image he has therefore given to his experi-

ence has been one of sharp contrasts, dramatic high-
lights, men and women caught up in the stress and the
violence of human definition amid chaotic times. Consider the figures who people the fiction of Wolfe,
Faulkner, McCullers, O'Connor—they are made larger
than life, both greater and less than human at the same
time; their grandiose rhetoric, their violent actions,
their wild gestures are exaggerated to the towering dimensions of lofty tragedy and wild, furious comedy.
What Warren said of Faulkner will serve, to greater or
lesser degree, for them all: "He has taken our world,
with its powerful sense of history, its tangled loyalties, its
pains and tensions of transition, its pieties and violences,
and elevated it to the level of a great moral drama on
the tragic scale. We can be proud of that fact."

The literature of the Piedmont South, then, embodies
that aspect of southern literature which embodies the
change from one kind of life to another, from a settled,
fixed agricultural economy to a changing, tumultuous
industrial economy, from a closed society of farms and
towns to an open society of cities, from a narrow but
fervent Calvinism to an urbane eclecticism, from the
Old South to the New. It represents, in short, almost
everything that is important and interesting in southern
literature. For to all intents and purposes, and with only
one or two exceptions, the literature of the Piedmont *is*
southern literature.

However difficult it may have been for the young
writer growing to maturity amid the turmoil and stress
of the changing Up Country South, then, it was a fortunate heritage for him, so far as the nurturing of his
creative imagination was concerned. Whatever the difficulty and lack of understanding that may have rested
in the fact that Thomas Wolfe's mother ran a boardinghouse and bought and sold property, while DuBose
Heyward's mother wrote poetry, there seems little question that it is the Altamont boardinghouse that seems

destined for literary immortality. The fountain in Asheville's Pack Square, not that in Charleston's Hampton Park, has proved to be the sign and symbol of time and change in the South. So that if to a Low Country southerner like myself, the image of the southern landscape tends sometimes to be confused with the particularities of the Tidewater scenery, to the world at large, which knows the South principally through what its great writers have shown of it, the South wears an Up Country look, and will be remembered most vividly and lastingly in the changing shape of the Piedmont South.

Everything Brought Out
into the Open:
Eudora Welty's *Losing Battles*

I

Miss Welty when last seen, in 1955, published *The Bride of the Innisfallen,* her third collection of short stories (fourth if you count *The Golden Apples*). Thereafter, and for fifteen years, silence, the only exceptions being a little privately printed essay, *Place in Fiction,* and a few magazine pieces. So it has been a long time between books.

Then came, in 1970, the author's sixty-first year, her longest novel, *Losing Battles,* an affair of some 436 pages all told, being the story of a family reunion in the northeastern Mississippi community of Banner. This particular place in fictional Mississippi is too small even to be a town, and most of what happens does so on a farm up a hillside several miles away from the post office and the general store. The elapsed time is something more than twenty-four hours of a summer day and night in the 1930s. Most of what takes place is talk. The talk begins

This essay was originally published in the *Hollins Critic,* VII (June, 1970).

when Miss Beulah Renfro, granddaughter of Elvira Jordan Vaughn, "Granny," puts in an appearance on the second page, after some five hundred words of place-setting, shouting, "Granny! Up, dressed, and waiting for 'em! All by yourself! Why didn't you holler?" Thereafter everybody talks, all the time. It ends with a hymn, "Bringing in the Sheaves."

When Eudora Welty's people talk, it is a special kind of talk. They do not talk *to,* they talk *at.* Part of the reason that they talk is to communicate, but part of the reason is to dissemble, to mask, to hide. They converse obliquely, chattering away all the time but never entirely revealing themselves or saying what they think; and the barrier, the mystery that results, lies at the center of the high art of Eudora Welty.

I say high art because the more I read and think about Miss Welty's fiction, the more I suspect that she is not merely a good writer, one of the very best of the half-a-dozen fine women writers that the South has produced in the past half century, but a major author, one of the three or four most important writers to come out of twentieth-century America. Her best fiction—*The Golden Apples,* some of the stories, now *Losing Battles*—goes beyond storytelling, beyond people and places, to those truths of the human heart that only the greatest art can reveal. There is only one other southern writer of her generation in her league: her fellow Mississippian William Faulkner.

Eudora Welty does it the hard way, and what is happening and what it means has to sink in, in retrospect, after reading the story. The writer she most resembles, I think, is Thomas Mann. That is to say, she is not technically experimental to any notable degree, and when you read her books you have to let the story pile up, until it is done. Then when you think over what you have read, you begin to perceive the ramifications, the events begin to link up, the people take on their meaning *sub specie aeternitatis* as it were, and the depth, the profundity of what you have seen happen in the story now begins to emerge. It isn't like the searing, tragic art of a Faulkner, for example, which holds you enthralled and breathless as a great elemental drama thunders toward climax and conclusion. The surface of her fiction is always deceptively mundane, matter-of fact, usually funny. The difference between Miss Welty's fiction and that of less-gifted authors is that her fiction doesn't lie on the surface, and the surface is anything but superficial, yet, paradoxically, everything is contained right there in the surface.

This is the chief difficulty with *Losing Battles,* one that may prevent it from attaining the massive popularity of so many lesser novels by lesser but more flamboyant novelists, and that gets in the way of immediate recognition for its author. What must be overcome, if the wisdom of *Losing Battles* is to be savored in its fullness, is its density of surface. Every line must be read carefully. It cannot be skimmed. *Losing Battles* is not difficult in the way that many novels are difficult. It hasn't an opaque surface that hides the story and the meaning behind a texture of dense language and obscure reference. Everything is out on the surface, but the art *is* the surface, and every inch of the surface must be inspected. This means that you have to follow the conversations and note the narrative directions and take in every word, every phrase, holding it all in suspension, letting it accumulate. Many of us don't like to read that way; we haven't the patience to follow every footpath and byway in a novel that takes approximately the same amount of time to read as it does for the events themselves to happen. So we tend to go racing through, and we miss the detail and so the story; and we can, if we want, say that this constitutes a criticism, an adverse judgment, a limitation of the art. Fiction that demands more attention than one is willing to give, we can say, is to that ex-

tent unsuccessful art. To which Miss Welty might reply
(along with Lawrence Sterne, James Joyce, Thomas
Mann, and one or two other artists with the same
shortcoming), "Oh, but you see, what I have to show
you can't be shown in any other way than this, more's
the pity, so that you'll have to choose whether *you* want
to know what I have to tell you, in which case you'll have
to let me show it to you the only way I know it, or
whether *you don't* want to know it. For if I tried to show it
any other way, *it* wouldn't *be.* You would instead be
getting something else, something other. I'll do my best
to divert and amuse and please you all along the way,
but it must be along *this* way, for there isn't any other."

Of course Eudora Welty wouldn't say that. She would
let her art, at whatever risk and at whatever cost, speak
for itself, as she has always done. But she might point
out, as she has in *Place in Fiction:*

The business of writing, and the responsibility of the writer,
[is] to disentangle the significant—in character, incident, setting, mood, everything, from the random and meaningless
and irrelevant that in real life surround and beset it. It is a
matter of his selecting and, by all that implies, of changing,
"real" life as he goes. With each word he writes, he acts—as
literally and methodically as if he hacked his way through a
forest and blazed it for the word that follows. He makes
choices at the explicit demand of this one present story; each
choice implies, explains, limits the next, and illuminates the
one before. No two stories ever go the same way, though in
different hands one story might possibly go any one of a
thousand ways; and though the woods may look the same
from outside, it is a new and different labyrinth each time.

II

Losing Battles begins with the wait for the various grand-
children of Granny Vaughn and their families to arrive
at the family residence, now the home of her granddaughter Beulah Beecham Renfro and her husband

Ralph, and located way up at the end of a winding road north of the town of Banner. Among the most eager of those who are doing the waiting is a daughter-in-law, Gloria Renfro, whose husband Jack has been away at the state penitentiary at Parchman since the day of their wedding. All are certain that Jack will get home for Granny's birthday reunion, however, not only to honor Granny and rejoin his wife but to see his little daughter, Lady May, for the first time. And soon Jack arrives, in good spirits, not at all resentful or embittered at his incarceration. He is overjoyed at seeing Gloria again, delighted with Lady May, and properly attentive to everyone present (though he does find time to get Gloria off by herself and renew relations properly). All the other relatives arrive, too, and everyone is in high spirits, remaining so for the entire occasion.

Unexpected guests at the reunion, and most reluctant to be there, are Judge Oscar Moody and his wife Maud Eva. It was Judge Moody who had sentenced Jack to his two years in prison, for fighting with Curly Stovall, the storekeeper at Banner, but nobody seems to mind that, Jack least of all. The judge and his wife are present because their fancy Buick automobile has, hilariously and improbably, become lodged against a tree, far up on a hillside, after the judge swerved off the road to avoid running over Lady May and Gloria. For the ensuing twenty-four hours the Buick remains there, teetering over the edge, its motor still running, with Aycock Comfort, a friend of Jack's, seated in it to keep it balanced. Not until the next morning, in just about as wild and as comic an episode as Miss Welty has ever created, is the Buick rescued, somewhat the worse for wear, and taken, tied between a school bus and a truck and with a pair of mules harnessed behind to do the braking, down the hillside and into the community of Banner.

At the reunion, people talk, sing, play, gossip. Among the numerous topics discussed are Granny's youth, the family's history, the obscure antecedents of Jack's wife Gloria, and the life, death, and influence upon the men and women of the Banner community of Miss Julia Mortimer, longtime teacher at the Banner school. Miss Julia has just died, at the nearby town of Alliance, but she is to be buried in the Banner cemetery. Gloria had been Miss Julia's protégé and had married Jack against her wishes.

All the Vaughns and Renfros and Beechams and the related descendants and cousins and kin at the reunion, and all the other townsfolk of Banner community as well, have been Miss Julia Mortimer's pupils, and she has vexed them all. In the mingled rage, guilt, and nostalgia with which they speak of her, whether oblique or direct, the nature of their vexation becomes apparent. For in what she was, what she wanted them to do, what she sought to force them to learn about the world and themselves, she was a threat to the entire Banner community. It was her objective to make the people of Banner, her pupils, realize and confront the ultimate consequences of their humanity.

What all these generations of men and women want to do—do, indeed, succeed in doing for the most part—is to go about their lives and their family and community doings innocently and unthinkingly, meeting birth, life, love, and death as they arise, without the dread and the knowledge of anticipating or asking why. In so doing, they are not only helpless against time and change but unable to deal with their circumstance. Miss Julia Mortimer had sought to force them to see who they were and what they were doing. As Gloria Renfro, who has come closest to being marked by Miss Julia's imprint, expresses the matter, in a rare moment of confrontation, "Miss Julia Mortimer didn't want anybody left in the dark, not about anything. She wanted everything brought out in the wide open, to see and be known. She wanted people to spread out their minds and hearts to other people, so they could be read like books." That statement, uttered by Gloria after the funeral, and as she sees that she may not be able to win her husband Jack away from the family and into a life of their own, amounts to a confession that Gloria has been marked by Miss Julia's determination, even though by marrying Jack she had done her best to escape the mantle placed upon her.

Gloria's statement, I suggest, comes very close to being a statement of Eudora Welty's artistic credo. For in *Place in Fiction* we find her saying much the same thing. She is writing about the importance of place in grounding fiction in reality. "The good novel," she says, "should be steadily alight, revealing. Before it can hope to be that, it must of course be steadily visible from its outside, presenting a continuous, shapely, pleasing, and finished surface to the eye." For place "has a good deal to do with making the characters real, that is, themselves, and keeping them so."

The reason is simply that, as Tristram Shandy observed, "We are not made of glass, as characters on Mercury might be." Place *can* be transparent, or translucent: not people. In real life, we have to express the things plainest and closest to our minds by the clumsy word and the half-finished gesture; the chances are our most usual behavior makes sense only in a kind of daily way, because it has become familiar to our nearest and dearest, and still demands their constant indulgence and understanding. It is our describable outside that defines us, willy nilly, to others, that may save us, or destroy us, in the world; it may be our shield against chaos, our mask against exposure, but whatever it is, the move we make in the place we live has to signify our intent and meaning.

Thus the novelist, by selecting and defining people in a place— "the more narrowly we can examine a fictional character, the greater he is likely to loom up"—can through his focus provide awareness, discernment, order, clarity, insight— "they are like the attributes of love." The novelist seeks, hopes to write so that "the exactness and concreteness and solidity of the real world achieved in a story correspond to the intensity of feeling in the author's mind and to the very turn of his heart," since "making reality real is art's responsibility."

III

It is from just that kind of searching recognition that people seek diligently and determinedly to hide, and in Eudora Welty's fictional world, families and communities exist to enable their members to hide from reality. For as Gloria Renfro understands and tells her husband Jack, "People don't want to be read like books," whether by others or by themselves. In Miss Welty's work, we sometimes come upon people who realize this. We find characters who shrink from such knowledge and also a precious few who, like Miss Julia Mortimer, do not thus shrink.

In Miss Welty's first novel, *Delta Wedding*, Laura McRaven travels to Shellmound, the family seat of the Fairchilds in the Delta country. For the Fairchilds (except for one of them, Shelley) everything that happens is gentled, humanized, incorporated into their ordered world. Violence, death, terror—a cyclone, a shooting, a train that runs over and kills a girl—are denied; the Fairchilds pretend that such things never exist and that the protected, comfortable family world that is Shellmound can go on forever. The community existence, the constant coming and going in company with each other, protects the private loneliness of each participant by being carried on as if such secret knowledge did not exist. In the family, certain things are known, thus avoiding inquiry into private matters. As Shelley Fairchild records in her diary, "We never wanted to be smart, one by one, but all together we have a wall, we are self-sufficient against people that come knocking, we are solid to the outside. Does the world suspect? that we are all very private people? I think one by one we're all more lonely than private and more lonely than self-sufficient."

Shelley, who knows this but for the time being at least will take part in the pretense, and little cousin Laura McRaven, who is from Jackson and knows things about the outside world that will not fit into Shellmound's version of life, realize what is going on. "My papa has taken me on trips—I know about geography," Laura insists. But she goes unheard: "In the great confines of Shellmound, no one listened." Yet Shellmound is doomed, for change is inevitable, and the vague uneasiness that the peaceful, contained version of reality that Shellmound comprises will soon disintegrate is present throughout the book. Only Shelley, and Laura, will not be entirely helpless in its face; for only they, of all the Fairchilds, know that it is bound to happen.

The Golden Apples, published in 1949, is the masterpiece of all the books. In a set of seven closely related narratives, together comprising forty years of human experience in the town of Morgana, Miss Welty sets forth a profound and hauntingly beautiful account of human beings in time, banded together to screen out the knowledge of their mortality. The inhabitants of Morgana—King MacLain, far-wanderer, Morgana's favorite fertility symbol; his twin sons Ran and Eugene, marked for life (and for death) by their father's heritage; the Morrison children, Loch, who can leave Morgana, and Cassie, who can stay; Miss Eckhart, the German music teacher who brought "*the* Beethoven" to Morgana and thus left her impress on those able to receive it (or unable to escape it); and, most of all, Virgie Rainey, who dueled with time, place, and Miss Eckhart all the way—these are unforgettable people; and so, to only a lesser degree, are a host of minor characters.

"Time goes like a dream no matter how hard you

run, and all the time we heard things from out in the world that we listened to but that still didn't mean we believed them," declares Virgie's mother, Miss Katie Rainey, to a stranger at the outset (and *only* to a stranger, for like Prufrock and Guido, Miss Katie Rainey would not dare say what she did to anyone who might report it in Morgana). It was not that Morgana did not believe the news from the world outside, so much as that its citizens strove not to believe it. King MacLain left town for years—and left his wife Miss Snowdie to raise the twins—but he always came back, usually at key moments, and at the end he attends Miss Katie Rainey's funeral, knowing he will be the next to die. Yet King never "left" Morgana; though separate from the town, he was never separate from its ways. He played by its rules and, operating within them, took what he wanted. Those rules were: never remind us that time, death, and art exist and are not accountable by Morgana's ways of measurement. Do not, in other words, tell us that we do not control our fate.

Poor Miss Eckhart—Lottie Elisabeth Eckhart, who taught Virgie Rainey to play "Für Elise" and to master the Liszt concerto, and who said that "Virgie would be heard from in the world, playing that"—never learned those rules. She set a metronome in front of her piano pupils, let it tick away remorselessly, timelessly, in absolute disdain of Morgana clock-time; Virgie Rainey, outraged, demanded it be put away. When a terrible thing happened to her—attacked, raped—she would not leave town and take from Morgana the knowledge that desperate things did happen, and that people survived as people even so. When the man she loved so timidly and inchoately was drowned, she nodded her head in helpless rhythm at the graveside, and then sought to throw herself into it—and Morgana could not countenance the evidence that there was grief that terrible or feeling that desperate.

At the end of her story— "June Recital," the heart of the book, Miss Welty's supreme creation—she comes back to Morgana from her place at the county poor farm, goes inside the old MacLain house where she had once lived and taught, and while her erstwhile pupil Virgie Rainey and a sailor boy cavort around and upon a mattress upstairs, sets her metronome to ticking and tries to set fire to the house. She fails at it, as with all she ever attempted; she is led away, back to the poor farm, and when Virgie Rainey, racing out of the still-smoking house, runs past her, they do not say a word or exchange a glance. For they were both, as Cassie Morrison divines, "human beings terribly at large, roaming on the face of the earth. And there were others of them— human beings, roaming, like lost beasts."

But Loch Morrison, too young to understand what was going on, retrieves the metronome, fetches it up to his room, waits to hear it begin ticking of its own volition: "All by itself, of its own accord, it might let fly its little door and start up."

"You'll go away like Loch," Cassie calls out to Virgie many years later, after Virgie's mother's funeral. "A life of your own, away—I'm so glad for people like you and Loch, I am really." Loch has long since departed, but not before, in the story entitled "Moon Lake," he has successfully given artificial respiration to a drowned orphan, tirelessly, rhythmically, with no heed to clocks, the steady in-out, in-out rhythm of elemental life-giving itself—and of generation, of sex, as the scandalized Morganans sense instinctively while they watch him at work. They must bring him down to their size; Jinny Love Stark, already a determined citizen though still a child, will "tell on him, in Morgana tomorrow. He's the most conceited Boy Scout in the whole troop; and's bowlegged." But Loch Morrison is one of those who will leave, because he cannot pretend that Morgana is the world.

Yet it is Virgie Rainey—the gifted one, who battled Miss Eckhart all the way, sought to deny her own self, took a job playing "You've Got To See Mama Every Night" at the movie house rather than going on with "*the* Beethoven," went away briefly but came right back, sought fulfillment in a succession of lovers—who was most marked by Miss Eckhart. At the close, forty years old, unmarried, alone, ready at last to leave for good, she realizes that like the old music teacher, she too saw things in their time, in the rhythms of art and life and of ultimate human existence. Miss Eckhart had "offered, offered, offered—and when Virgie was young, in the strange wisdom of youth that is accepting of more than is given, she had accepted *the* Beethoven, as with the dragon's blood. That was the gift she had touched with her fingers that had drifted and left her."

So brief a summary, and of only the main plot-relationship at that, can do little justice to what is in *The Golden Apples*. It is, I think, an even more successful work than *Losing Battles,* but perhaps I say this for having known *The Golden Apples* for two decades, while *Losing Battles* is still to be lived with. But one recognizes at once, in the new novel, that Miss Julia Mortimer, with greater success, and Miss Lottie Eckhart, with lesser success, fought the same battle, representing for their fellow townsfolk the possibility, and the threat, of a greater and more ultimate discovery and self-revelation, and so were both feared and shunned. And similarly, Virgie Rainey and Gloria Renfro are of the same kind: both have been touched with the dragon's blood, and neither may put aside the legacy, struggle though they do. When the family accepts Gloria that day at the reunion, it is only with suspicion. They want her to become part of their common conspiracy, even down to the way she wears her clothes. As Aunt Beck says to Gloria, "You're just an old married woman, same as the rest of us now. So you won't have to answer to the outside any longer." But they ought not be so sure as that; "some day yet," Gloria tells her husband, "we'll move to ourselves." That is not what Miss Julia Mortimer had in mind for her; but neither is it what the Renfros and Beechams and Vaughns want, either. Miss Julia Mortimer is dead when the family reunion that constitutes *Losing Battles* takes place, and she never appears as a character, but increasingly her presence comes to dominate the story. At the last, as the inhabitants of Banner watch the long funeral procession from Alliance and the burial in the Banner cemetery—there are hundreds of persons present, former students from distant states, a governor, a Catholic priest, a judge (for that was what Judge Moody was doing in the neighborhood), dignitaries and plain folk both—we realize that the spinster schoolteacher had been a worthy adversary indeed to the family, and to all that makes human beings seek to flee themselves and others. She has, in her time, made time run.

All of this is not told, or pointed out, as one goes along; it is realized as the reader begins putting together the experience of the bright, thick-textured surface of people, doings, and talk that constitutes this novel. *Losing Battles* is not, as it moves along its way, a somber book. It is alive in humor and merriment and, especially after we get into it well, filled with almost constant humor and diversion. But there are no shortcuts. It demands that the reader invest time and attention without stint, for as long as it takes to read it through. What it requires is sentence-by-sentence participation. What it provides, for those willing to take part, is delight ending in wisdom.

William Styron
and Human Bondage

I

"If this is true, from my soul I pity you."
—Judge Cobb, sentencing Nat Turner

Styron was off to a good start. "A wonderfully evocative portrait of a gifted, proud, long-suppressed human being."—Alfred Kazin in *Book World*. "The most profound fictional treatment of slavery in our literature."—C. Vann Woodward in the *New Republic*. "One of those novels that is an act of revelation to a whole society."–Raymond A. Sokolov in *Newsweek*. "A first-rate novel, the best that William Styron has produced and the best by an American writer that has appeared in some years."–Philip Rahv in the *New York Review of Books*. There were a few dissents, to be sure, but it was clear that *The Confessions of Nat Turner* was making its way from the outset.

In that respect it was in startling contrast to *Set This*

This essay was originally published in the *Hollins Critic*, IV (September, 1967), 1–12, and subsequently included, together with the appended Afterword, in R. H. W. Dillard, George Garrett, and John Rees Moore (eds.), *The Sounder Few: Essays from the* Hollins Critic (Athens, Ga., 1971), 305–24.

House on Fire, which, when it appeared in 1960, was jumped upon by almost everybody. That novel had the misfortune to be the long-awaited second novel by a man whose first book was a tremendous success. In the nine years that followed *Lie Down in Darkness* (a novella, *The Long March,* didn't really count), the critics grew tired of waiting. Almost everyone had predicted great things for William Styron, and the longer it took for him to produce a second big book, the more exasperated everyone became. So that when Styron finally managed to complete his second novel, its publication was almost certain to be anticlimactic. In addition, *Set This House on Fire* was very long, it was filled with much soul-torment, and there was no neat tragic pattern such as characterized Styron's first novel. Thus when *Set This House on Fire* finally appeared, all the journalistic reviewers began scolding at once. Supposedly the new book was wind-blown, self-indulgent, sentimental, bathetic, overwritten, and so on—the chorus of castigation rose to an impressive decibel volume. Only a corporal's guard of reviewers dared to disagree, to insist that while *Set This House on Fire* wasn't a flawless novel, it was nevertheless a very impressive accomplishment, a moving work of fiction, in every way worthy of if not superior to *Lie Down in Darkness,* so that its author need in no way feel that he had failed to live up to his notices.

During the seven years between *Set This House on Fire* and Styron's new novel, however, critical opinion has pretty much come around to the viewpoint that Styron's second book was a quite respectable performance. Once the reviewers in the critical quarterlies, who are notably unswayed by journalistic reviews, began writing about the book, the initial verdict was reversed. Critical essays and chapters of books appeared which treated *Set This House on Fire* as a work which, though flawed in parts, contains some of the better writing of our time. For example, a good critic, Frederick J. Hoffman, has this to say about *Set This House on Fire* in his *The Art of Southern Fiction*: "Styron's most recent novel sets the imagination agoing, in the expectation of an American literature of existentialism. . . . But it is perhaps best not to name it that, for fear of weighing it down with labels and classifications. The important fact is that Styron has used his talents mightily and to a good effect in this novel."

Set This House on Fire is the story of Cass Kinsolving, an artist unable to paint. A World War II veteran, married and living in Europe, he must undergo a terrifying stay in the lower depths before he can win his way back to sanity and creativity. The leading characters, very unlike most southern fictional folk, engage in long, probing psychological analyses of their inner souls. There are no Negroes (though there is a memory of them), no First Families going to seed, no church services, no blood-guilt of generations, no oversexed southern matrons. It is thoroughly, completely modern, even cosmopolitan. Cass Kinsolving is a man in bondage; in Paris, Rome, and Sambuco he lives in an alcoholic daze, tortured by his inability to paint, drinking, wandering about, pitying himself, doing everything except confronting his talent. He had sought to find a form for his art outside of himself; he could not put up with his creative limitations, and he looked to the society and people surrounding him for what could only be found within himself: the remorseless requirement of discovering how to love and be loved, and so to create. Only through violence and tragedy could he win his way through to self-respect and attain an equilibrium with the world that enables him to function effectively.

All very odd and strange, this sort of thing: Styron wasn't supposed to write that kind of a novel. What also perplexed many reviewers was that this process and this outcome were not presented ironically or obliquely; there wasn't the self-conscious distrust of high rhetoric and ultimate judgment that characterizes much "existential" fiction today. The language was unabashedly resounding and rhetorical. And because it was the kind of book it was, the form of the story was restless, groping, searching, and not at all neat and tidy. The difficulties inherent in any attempt to use the high style to deal with contemporary life are of course obvious. Our sense of irony is too strong to permit it to function without severe qualification. Faulkner, for all his greatness, could never successfully handle an intelligent modern man learning how to cope with contemporary urban society: his Gavin Stevens is among his less-convincing characterizations. Robert Penn Warren managed it in *All the King's Men*, but to do so he had to filter the rhetoric through a wisecracking, hard-boiled type of narrator who could protect his more sounding declarations from irony by getting there first himself. Few other contemporaries even dare to try it; they fear, and with reason, that they will come out of it talking like the later prose of Carl Sandburg.

Styron's attempt, in *Set This House on Fire*, was not completely successful either. There is a shift of character focus in the novel, to the effect that part of the true explanation for Cass Kinsolving's plight lies not in his own past experience but in that of his friend Peter Leverett. This isn't ultimately fatal; such is Styron's artistry that we accord Kinsolving the right to feel and think as he does, in defiance of the strict logic of plot. The main thing is that *Set This House on Fire* works; one way or another, it adds up. There are moments when Cass's believability seems to be in jeopardy, but each time Styron comes through.

Styron, Hoffman remarks, "moved away [in *Set This House on Fire*] from the special moral dimensions of the southerner looking at portraits of colonels, or addressing himself to the landscape of his youth, or to the special qualities of feudal vengeance or pride. . . . He has assumed a larger risk, moved into a more competitive field, entered a tradition of psychological and moral analysis that has been occupied by Kierkegaard, Mann, Sartre, and Camus before him." So concluded many another critic after reading *Set This House on Fire,* though usually without Hoffman's ability to perceive that in so doing, Styron had written an excellent novel. Yet the implication, voiced by numerous other critics as well, that in *Set This House on Fire* Styron had ceased to be a "southern writer," in the way that Faulkner, Warren, Wolfe, Welty, Lytle had been southern writers, was unwarranted, I think. For the so-called "southern quality" in modern American fiction is not at bottom a matter of subject matter or theme, so much as of attitude; it is a way of looking at the nature of human experience, and it includes the assumption that to maintain order and stability the individual must be part of a social community, yet that the ultimate authority that underlies his conduct is not social but moral. It is, in short, a religious attitude, though most often it does not involve the dogmas of revealed religion. This attitude, not the presence of the particular institutions and events that customarily embody the attitude, is what has enabled the work of the better southern novelists to seem so "meaningful" in our time. It is precisely this attitude, too, that has made possible and believable the use of the full, unstinted, high rhetorical mode that so marks much of the work of Faulkner, Warren, Wolfe, and others. We will not buy rhetoric unless we believe in the absolutes that justify it, and the southern writers do believe in them. In many ways Styron's second novel represents a kind of examination into the soundness of such a view, ending in a confirmation. Cass Kinsolving's emotions and ideals are examined and tested in the furnace experience of Paris and Sambuco and are finally pronounced sound. Whereupon Cass may come home.

He comes back, however, not to the community in

which he grew up, but to another place, where he is ready to install himself—another southern community, but one without historical and social links with his own past. It had been necessary for him to leave the scene of his past behind him, to travel to another continent and there ratify the individual and social worth of those attitudes and ideals, independent of their institutions and for himself, in order to make them *his*, and not merely something automatically bequeathed to him.

Thus for Styron, *Set This House on Fire* represented a clearing away, as it were, of the debris of the southern fictional texture—all the accustomed artifacts of setting, history, community that have for several generations provided the experience out of which southern fiction has been created. But the underlying attitude toward the nature of human experience in time remains; and far from representing any kind of abdication of what has come to be recognized as the southern literary mode, *Set This House on Fire* is an extension, perhaps the only possible extension, of that mode into a new day and a different kind of experience.

Toward the close of the novel Cass Kinsolving hears his family stirring about the house in the morning light and thinks: "I didn't know what it was but there they were sort of strutting face to face and soundlessly clapping their hands together, like Papageno and Papagena, or something even more sweet, paradisiac, as if they were children not really of this earth but of some other, delectable morning before time and history." As if there could be any possible doubt of the literary mode out of which that style of rhetoric comes!

II

*It might offend Negroes that I as a white man have
presumed to intrude on the consciousness of a Negro.*
—William Styron, interview in *Book World*

Which brings us, seven years later, to *The Confessions of
Nat Turner.* This time the scene is again the South—the
Commonwealth of Virginia, scarcely more than an
hour's ride by automobile from the very city in which
Peyton Loftis, Peter Leverett, and William Styron were
born and grew up. Furthermore, *The Confessions of Nat
Turner* is an historical novel, based squarely on the
single most complex and pervasive theme of all southern history, the presence and role of the Negro. The
central character and narrator is a preacher, whose
thoughts and deeds are based on biblical admonition
and whose language is charged with scriptural rhetoric.
So that Styron would seem to have come full circle—
starting out with Peyton Loftis from Port Warwick in
Tidewater Virginia, then north to New York City; then
eastward across the ocean to Paris and Italy with Cass
Kinsolving, and at length back home to the South. Now
it is Tidewater Virginia once more, the year is 1831, and
there is the selfsame Black Shadow that has darkened
the pages of southern literature from the romances of
William Gilmore Simms on through to Mark Twain,
George Washington Cable, and Thomas Nelson Page,
and more recently William Faulkner, Robert Penn Warren, and every other southern writer of the twentieth
century so far.

But there is a difference. The story is told both by and
about a Negro. Styron has sought to put himself into the
mind and heart of a slave preacher who in August of
1831 led a bloody insurrection in Southampton County,
Virginia. No southern writer has ever really done this
sort of thing before with much success. The faithful
Negro retainers who relate in such ornate dialect

Thomas Nelson Page's idylls of Virginia plantation life "Befo' de War" were stereotypes, designed to exhibit the graciousness and romance of antebellum society. Joel Chandler Harris' Uncle Remus was also a delightful old darky, but he knew his place, and his creator was careful most of the time to keep to the surface of things. Even Faulkner, who Ralph Ellison says has written more accurately and truly about the Negro than any other writer living or dead, black or white, shows us not the Negro so much as the white man learning to see the Negro—learning to see him more sharply and honestly than ever before.

Styron goes further. He is satisfied with nothing less than to try to *become* Nat Turner. Now it seems to me that, from the standpoint of the developing cultural history of the South, this very attempt is important of itself. In the years after 1865, writers like Page and Harris created Negro narrators to tell their stories under the naïve belief that this was a comparatively easy thing to do, since their notion of what it was like to be a Negro was itself something quite simple. Their Negro was the "Old Time Darky," faithful, true, obedient, whose every thought and allegiance was for Massa (sometimes spelled Marster, sometimes Mars', occasionally Maussa). A Thomas Nelson Page was confident that he understood the Negro; it never occurred to him that he might not. The great southern novelists of the 1920s, 1930s, and 1940s—Faulkner, Warren, Wolfe, the others—made no such easy assumptions; rather, they focused upon the difficulty, the impossibility even, of the white man knowing what Negroes really thought and felt. This recognition that the complaisant pastoral figure that a Thomas Nelson Page could so naïvely accept as a "true" representation of the Negro was in fact a vast oversimplification symbolized a long step forward in the white South's willingness to accord the Negro full human status. Now comes a fine novel by a

leading southern writer of the post–World War II generation, essaying to portray the innermost thoughts of a
Negro, and doing so without very much self-
consciousness. One cannot help but see this as emblematic of an important social breakthrough. For the point
about Styron's characterization of Nat Turner is that
Nat's existence as a Negro is not seen as making him in
any recognizable way importantly "different" from what
a white man might be in similar circumstances. Nat
Turner comes eventually to hate all white men; but this
emotion is not portrayed as an inherent racial characteristic. Rather, it is a response, a desperate and tragic
one, to the social inhumanity of slavery. A Negro as seen
by William Styron is in no important or essential way
different from a white man. Social conditions, not he-
redity and biology, set him apart. The walls of separateness are man-made.

Nobody, of course, knows "who" the real Nat Turner
was. Except for a twenty-page "confession" dictated to a
white lawyer and read before the trial court as evidence,
there is little to go on. Not much additional information is to be found in the only book written about the
Nat Turner Insurrection, William Sidney Drewry's *The
Southampton Insurrection,* published in 1900 by a long-
since defunct publishing house dedicated to defending
the Confederate heritage and racial segregation.

That Styron's Nat Turner is surely not the "real" Nat
Turner is indisputable—in the sense that every human
being is a unique personality, so that nobody could
possibly reconstruct anything resembling the real Nat
Turner without abundant evidence. In any event, *The
Confessions of Nat Turner,* as the southern historian C.
Vann Woodward says, is "not inconsistent with anything
historians know" and is "informed by a respect for history, a sure feeling for the period, and a deep and
precise sense of place and time." This seems to me
likewise indisputable.

Yet at least one other southern historian, and a good one, has told me that he felt that Styron had committed a grievous historical mistake, in that he makes Nat Turner, a slave preacher on a southside Virginia plantation thirty years before the Civil War, think and talk exactly like a modern Black Power advocate; Styron's Nat Turner, he believes, sounds not like a slave, but like Stokely Carmichael. This is a severe criticism. Though I think it is not true, I confess that there are certain moments in Styron's novel in which one gets something of this feeling. Nat's reiterated insistence on the need of all Negroes to strike the Happy Darky pose when dealing with whites— "I replied in tones ingratiating, ministerial—the accommodating comic nigger"—tends to make the reader uncomfortably aware on such occasions of the author laboring to present the "Negro point of view." Doubtless Virginia slaves learned to do exactly what Nat says, but Nat's self-conscious theorizing about it would seem somewhat anachronistic. Similarly there are several passages in which Nat and other slaves talk at some length about the "smell" of white people—we glimpse the author waxing ironic about certain often-echoed white shibboleths. (Cf. Thomas Jefferson, in the *Notes on the State of Virginia:* "They secrete less by the kidneys, and more by the glands of the body, which gives them a very strong and disagreeable odor"—as if there were bathrooms available for slaves at Monticello!)

But these instances are relatively few, and are unimportant. So is the argument that by making Nat Turner into a much more intellectual and reflective person, possessing a much more complex vocabulary than the real-life Nat Turner could probably have had, Styron violates the historicity of the situation. This seems to me to overlook the fact that Nat Turner could never have been a "representative" Negro slave of the 1830s. A "representative" slave could not possibly have led the Nat Turner Insurrection. Furthermore, it is not required or fitting that Styron's Nat Turner be "representative," "typical"; on the contrary, he *must* be an exaggeration. His thoughts, his emotions, his language must be plausible only to the extent that the reader must feel a slave preacher in southside Virginia in the year 1831, given the admitted uniqueness of Nat Turner's situation, could conceivably have thought and felt and spoken as he does. Besides, what is really involved here is the reader-writer relationship; for after all, is not the reader already engaged, by the mere fact of reading the book, in an "illogical" activity, inasmuch as he is being asked to imagine that he is reading the thoughts and words of a long-dead Negro preacher about whom almost nothing whatever is known? To echo Johnson, surely he who imagines this may imagine more. What matters is that Negro slaves (and Negro freedmen) *did* have to play roles in order to deal with the whites, and Nat's awareness of the role differs from that of most Negro slaves only in that it is made conscious and articulate. The truth is that Styron's Nat Turner is nothing more and nothing less than a tragic protagonist, and we ask representativeness and typicality of such a character no more than we ask that Sophocles show representative and typical Greeks of ancient Thebes in *Oedipus Rex.*

III

"To a mind like mine, restless, inquisitive and observant, there was nothing that I saw or heard to which my attention was not directed."
                    —Nat Turner, "Confession"(1831)

The Confessions of Nat Turner is told in the first person present. The language purports to be that of Nat, but not as spoken to anyone. Nat is thinking, "explaining" himself—to the reader, to "posterity," to himself. Though in point of strict logic this is quite impossible, it is an acceptable literary convention, much as the Shakespearean soliloquy is a literary convention.

The use of Nat as narrator affords Styron several advantages for telling his story. First of all, since Nat is a preacher, and deeply immersed in the language and style of the King James Bible, we will accept from him a high rhetorical style which we might otherwise not permit, especially from a Negro slave in antebellum Virginia. More importantly, we soon become aware that when Nat actually talks, whether to whites or Negroes, his language is much more idiomatic and colloquial. The reader's awareness of the difference in language and voice, of the contrast between the manner in which Nat thinks or remembers and the way that he talks, is essential to the form and meaning of the novel. For not only must Nat, despite his learning, continue to play the role of humble, barely literate slave before his betters, but the very fact of his intelligence and learning serves to isolate him all the more. The whites, no matter how sympathetic (and some *are* quite sympathetic), must by reason of time and place inevitably view Nat as an inferior, a freak—a slave, less than human, a bond servant, one who surprisingly can read and write but is still an inferior creature.

This of course is the true horror of slavery for Nat. He is considered less than a man, and open, human contact with his peers is utterly forbidden him. The result is loneliness and rage. He comes to *hate* the whites because they have placed him and kept him in this position, and his rage is most keen at those times when he is being most patronized. For those whites who are kindest to him—in particular the girl Margaret Whitehead—inevitably do most to reinforce his consciousness of his inferior status, since they believe they are *not* patronizing him while still expecting him to remain safely in his place. In her romantic, naïve way Margaret Whitehead means only the best for Nat and genuinely likes and admires him, yet she fails utterly to comprehend the nature of his position and cannot for a moment grasp what torture is involved for him. In part her good intentions are only an aspect of her sentimentality; in being "frank," she condescends. Yet she *does* mean well; she does, in her own way, even love Nat, and before he dies he comes to realize that.

The contrast between what Nat thinks and can think, and what he must say and appear to be to whites whether of good intentions or bad, enforces the sense of isolation and loneliness that characterizes Nat's life. With the slaves, he does not have to pretend in the same way; in their company he can be himself as he cannot with white people. But his fellow bondsmen, being without his literacy and intelligence, cannot communicate with him either, especially after he has conceived his plan for a revolt and must bend every effort to manipulate and direct them toward his ends. Not even Hark, his closest friend and his chief lieutenant in the insurrection he organizes, can understand or imagine what Nat is thinking or feeling. Thus Nat Turner as depicted by Styron is cut off from whites and blacks alike, and the violence of his protest is his insurrection.

There is still another advantage in Styron's use of Nat as narrator. In the very contrast between the complex, subtle diction of Nat's thoughts and the verbally crude language he must use to express himself aloud, there evolves a tension which grows more and more acute as the narrative develops and as Nat increasingly comes to comprehend the nature of his enforced isolation. The gulf between Nat's private self and his role in time and place builds up toward a point at which language itself will no longer suffice to provide order. There must then be the explosion of action, whereby language and deed are unified through violence—and the tragedy is accomplished.

Why did Nat Turner stage his insurrection? This, after all, is the question that Styron sets out to answer by writing his novel. Because slavery was evil, and for a slave capable of a high degree of thought and feeling, intolerable—yes. Because Nat in particular had been promised his freedom by his first owner, only to be betrayed into renewed and hopeless bondage—yes. These are the topical answers. But because William Styron is the fine novelist that he is, they are not the full or even the most important answers.

Nat Turner, a human being, rebels because he is deprived by his society of the right to love and be loved. I do not mean by this merely that Nat rebels because he is denied sexual fulfillment, though he is (save for one youthful homosexual experience, Styron's Nat Turner is an ascetic, thereby providing psychological grounding for his messianic religious visions). The question is larger than that. Nat cannot love—physically or spiritually. The world he inhabits is such that at best he can expect from whites only pity, and at worst outright hatred, while from his fellow slaves he can expect only inarticulate admiration at best, and at worst envy and contempt. Thus he cannot *give* himself to anyone. No one wants him for what he is. For everyone, white and black, friend and foe, he must play a role. For his first owner, who educated him, he is a noble experiment, an object of benevolence, a salve to the slave-holding conscience. For Margaret Whitehead he is a sympathetic auditor to whom she can pour out her girlish fancies and exhibit her broad-mindedness. For his last owner he is a clever, valuable mechanic, a source of financial profit. For his fellow slaves he is a leader, one who can plan and organize their revenge. Even to his fellow conspirator Hark, who does indeed love and admire him, he cannot be fully himself, for Hark's imagination and intelligence are too limited to enable him to share Nat's innermost thoughts. Denied, therefore, the right to give himself, to love, Nat can only hate, and the result is destruction.

What good, the interrogating lawyer asks Nat, did his insurrection accomplish? The lawyer answers his own question:

"Here's what it got you, Reverend, if you'll pardon the crudity. It got you a pissy-assed record of total futility, the likes of which are hard to equal. Threescore white people slain in random butchery, yet the white people firmly holdin' the reins. Seventeen niggers hung, including you and old Hark there, nevermore to see the light of day. A dozen or more other nigger boys shipped out of an amiable way of life to Alabama, where you can bet your bottom dollar that in five years the whole pack of 'em will be dead of work and fever."

"One hundred and thirty-one innocent niggers both slave and free cut down by the mob that roamed Southampton for a solid week, searching vengeance," the lawyer continues. And finally, the Nat Turner Insurrection will mean much more harshly repressive laws for the slaves:

"When the legislature convenes in December they're goin' to pass laws that make the ones *extant* look like rules for a Sunday School picnic. They goin' to lock up the niggers in a black cellar and throw away the key." He paused, and I could sense him leaning close to me. "*Abolition*," he said in a voice like a whisper. "Reverend, single-handed you done more with your Christianity to assure the defeat of abolition than all the meddlin' and pryin' Quakers that ever set foot in Virginia put together. I reckon you didn't figure on that either?"

"No," I said, looking into his eyes, "if that be true. No."

There was and is no happy ending for the Nat Turner Insurrection. Styron knew this, and his novel shows it. It did not bring Negro slavery one whit closer to an end; if anything it retarded progress. The harsh Black Codes enacted throughout most of the South in the decades before the Civil War were due at least in part to the fear of servile revolt that the Nat Turner Insurrection had triggered.

IV

This attempt to separate truth from fiction has been exceedingly difficult, owing to the numerous misrepresentations and exaggerations which have grown up about the subject.

—Drewry, *The Southampton Insurrection*

In staging his insurrection Nat Turner believed that he was doing the Lord's bidding, as it had been revealed to him in a series of supernatural visions. Styron was careful to give these moments of revelation a solid psychological basis: they come always after Nat has gone without food for several days and is weak and feverish. Yet *The Confessions of Nat Turner* is not primarily a psychological study. The limits of Nat's personality are not defined by the science of abnormal psychology. He represents, and is, the strong man in bondage, a human caught in a situation not originally of his making but ultimately requiring his total commitment. Faced with evil, Nat cannot hide from it, but his appalling attempt to right matters only brings defeat and greater suffering. In other words, it is a tragic situation, and the resolution of it is tragedy.

The specific events of Nat Turner's life which impelled him toward the Southampton Insurrection are unknown. As a novelist, Styron had therefore to give him a history, and it was the task of his creative imagination to make the personal history contain the meaning forced upon the subject by history. Thus Styron represents Nat during his youth as having been favored and set apart by his owner, imbued with much hope and optimism. When instead of being freed he is sold into renewed bondage, Nat's sense of personal rage and helplessness forces him to take account of the wretched lot of his less-gifted fellow slaves, for whom he had once felt contempt and disdain. It is at this stage in his life that the conviction of religious mission comes upon him (in which respect Styron departs from the 1831 "Confession," for Nat Turner says there that from his childhood onward he had felt himself "intended for some great purpose"). Nat then begins mapping out his plan to lead an insurrection. The growth of the spirit of rebellion in Nat is charted by Styron with calculated deliberateness; the calm, carefully chosen language with which Nat tells his story only serves to intensify the sense of impending crisis and explosion.

In *The Southampton Insurrection* Drewry repeatedly expresses astonishment over the fact that Nat Turner himself had been treated with kindness by his owner and had stated as much in his "Confession." Drewry insists that not only Nat but almost all the slaves in antebellum Virginia were kindly treated. This is proved, he declares, by the fact that so few slaves joined Turner. Most remained loyal to their owners, and some distinguished themselves by their bravery in defending their white families against the insurgents. Thus the only explanation Drewry can suggest for the insurrection is that abolitionist propaganda had inflamed the mind of Nat Turner, already crazed by a fanatical belief in his supernaturally prophetic destiny.

The true explanation, as is obvious, is that it was precisely *because* Nat Turner himself was treated well and had so distinguished himself in education and intelligence that he was prompted to lead his revolt; as Styron shows, his superior attainments and status only made more clear to him the hopelessness of servile bondage. Thus nothing could so madden Nat as the occasional expression of pity on the part of a white man or woman. In one of the finest episodes in the novel, Styron depicts Nat's sensations upon seeing a northern-born wife of a planter break down and weep at the sight of a particularly wretched and abject Negro. This unusual passage cannot be satisfactorily excerpted; suffice it to say that it is a masterful portrayal of complex emotions of hate, lust, love, and shame contending within a man's heart. "I was filled with somber feelings that I was unable to banish," Nat remarks afterward, "deeply troubled that it was not a white person's abuse or scorn or even indifference which could ignite in me this murderous hatred but his pity, maybe even his tenderest moment of charity."

The point is that in this and numerous other instances, *The Confessions of Nat Turner* is a very *wise* book. Styron's understanding of his material is most impressive. When one thinks about it, the possibilities for melodrama and easy pathos inherent in the subject matter of this novel are very broad. What a less-gifted novelist might have produced, one shudders to think. Styron, for example, barely mentions the period of ten weeks that actually elapsed between the suppression of the insurrection and the capture of Nat Turner, during which Nat himself hid out in the woods and fields. Another novelist might have attempted to make this episode the occasion for a long, pseudophilosophical meditation by Nat on the meaning of what has happened. But Styron lets Nat's thoughts about what he has done arise in the actual retelling of the story—in, that is, his confession—so that by the time the actual insurrection takes place, what it means has been convincingly anticipated and prepared for us. The events of the insurrection, therefore, bloody as they are, are not merely horrible; they are the motivated, terribly meaningful violence climaxing an intolerable situation.

One could make many other observations about William Styron's new novel. Most of them have already been made or will soon be; publication of the novel is obviously one of the more noteworthy literary events of recent years. Its importance lies simply in the fact that a dedicated and talented American novelist has written a book dealing with one of the most fateful and pressing concerns of our country's history, one that is by no means fully resolved. The topical relevance of this book is obvious—so much so that one need not comment on it.

This observation should be made, however: at a time when many influential critics have been saying that the day of the novel is done, Styron has produced a first-rate work of fiction while working very much within the traditional novel form. By bringing his intelligence and imagination to bear upon an important and deeply human situation, he has reinvigorated the form and shown that it is still quite alive. He has thus given the lie to all those tired critics who have been going about lamenting the death of the novel and proclaiming the superior merits of this or that substitute. It is time, therefore, that we cease bewailing the passing of the demigods of an earlier generation and recognize the fact that with such writers as William Styron, Saul Bellow, and John Barth regularly producing prose fiction for us, we have no occasion for complaint. A novel as good as Styron's can hold its own in any company.

Afterword: The Nat Turner Controversy

The best thing I can do to indicate what has happened to William Styron since my piece on *The Confessions of Nat Turner* first appeared is to append a review that I wrote for the Washington *Sunday Star* for September 1, 1968, under the title "The Literary Attacks on Styron's *Nat Turner.*"[1]

Those of us who, last fall, read and admired William Styron's *The Confessions of Nat Turner,* and said so in print, have subsequently been treated to as odd a literary—or, more properly, a cultural and socio-

---

1. John Henrik Clarke (ed.), *William Styron's Nat Turner: Ten Black Writers Respond* (Boston, 1968).

logical—phenomenon as has recently existed in American letters.

For Styron's *Nat Turner* got good reviews at first—and not by journeyman reviewers alone, but by such respected literary critics and historians as Philip Rahv, C. Vann Woodward, Alfred Kazin, and others. What Styron was especially praised for was the way in which he, a white man, had been able to get so thoroughly into the personality of a Negro slave of the 1820s and 1830s, so that without stereotype or condescension he made a believable tragic hero out of the leader of the Nat Turner rebellion of 1831.

It soon developed, however, that Styron wasn't going to be let off so easily. Led by the historian Herbert Aptheker, a chorus of advanced reviewers began jumping on Styron's book, and soon various Negro intellectuals joined in, until by the late winter of 1967–1968 Styron's supposedly antiracist novel was being condemned as an insult to the memory of Nat Turner, an embodiment of traditional white stereotypes of the Negro, a flagrant perversion of history, and—I quote from the introduction to the volume under review here—a "deliberate" attempt to distort the true character of Nat Turner because of the author's "reaction to the racial climate that has prevailed in the United States in the last fifteen years."

This book, a collection of attacks on Styron and his novel by ten Negro writers, will surely go down in literary history as one of the most curious documents ever compiled. It reminds me, in miniature, of nothing so much as the barrage of novels produced by southerners during the 1850s in answer to the "lies" and "distortions" of Harriet Beecher Stowe's *Uncle Tom's Cabin.* And, I might add, the present-day refutations are just about as relevant as the antebellum models.

The question that comes to mind upon reading these

essays is, Why? What is it that has prompted so many Negro critics—and these ten essayists are not the only or even the best objectors to the novel—to rise in anger at Styron's book? Is it because, as several of the essayists say, Styron has demeaned a great man, portrayed an authentic Negro hero as a neurotic, and so forth? I don't think so, really. The novel that I read and admired made an obscure, little-chronicled Negro slave preacher into a tragic hero of great stature, and made the remorseless, irresistible current of events that led him toward bloody rebellion into the tragic drama of a strong man caught up in the demands of an intolerable social and moral situation. How anyone can see Styron as degrading or stereotyping Nat Turner is still quite unaccountable to me.

Is it because Negro writers resent the fact that Styron, a white man and a Virginian to boot, produced the first really important literary work about a Negro slave insurrectionist? There is a little of this feeling in these essays, though several of the contributors go to some pains to deny it: as for example when John W. Williams begins by saying, "Since I do not believe that the right to describe or portray or in other ways delineate the lives of black people in American society is the private domain of Negro writers, I cannot fault Styron's intent," and then concludes with the remark that "black writers, it appears, have lost the race, if ever there was one, to air the truth. The likes of Styron are already past the finish line."

Yet I do not feel that the fact that Styron, and not Ralph Ellison or James Baldwin, wrote *The Confessions of Nat Turner* is what is behind the current furor. Just now the prevailing attitude is that white writers are not supposed to be able to understand how a Negro—any Negro, rich or poor, intelligent or stupid, intellectual or nonintellectual—thinks and feels, but I feel that there were ways that Styron might have written his book and portrayed Nat Turner that would have won him the admiration, however grudging, of almost all Negro critics. The real trouble with Styron's novel, in the eyes of Negro critics, is not that it is a racist document, I think, but paradoxically that it isn't racist enough. In other words, Styron did things with the characterization of a Negro slave preacher and revolutionary that no one who was a racist could or would have done, and which he could do only because he did not himself even consider the possibility that most of the racist shibboleths and dogmas were to be taken seriously.

In his novel, for example, Styron makes Nat Turner a celibate, who desires several white women, one of whom in her naïve and sentimental way actually returns his love. To Styron's critics this is an example of racist thinking: it supposedly embodies the racist doctrine that all Negro males secretly want to rape white women.

What Styron was instead trying to show was that in setting Nat Turner apart from his fellow slaves, making him into something special, encouraging him to think of himself as not only better than but different from his less-favored brethren, white racist antebellum society was in effect robbing Nat Turner of his virility. It was setting up an artificial barrier between Nat and his own race. It was placing him in an impossible situation, in which he was permitted to exist on the fringes of the dominant white society but without being allowed to enter it fully, and at the same time so isolating him from the enslaved black society that he could find no membership and fulfillment there either. This, Styron was saying, was what slavery (and, by implication, racism of any sort) does. The whiteness of Nat Turner's imagined lovers is a measure of the distortion that slavery (and racism) produced in him.

Styron's depiction of Nat Turner's sexual fantasies in this way, then, constitutes not racism, but an attack upon racism, and exists because he considered the

whole folklore about all Negroes inherently desiring
white women so absurd that it was impossible to take it
seriously. But the difficulty is that Styron's Negro critics
do take it seriously—seriously enough to fear that any
suggestion that Nat Turner, or any Negro leader, might
desire a white woman is the repetition of a dangerous
racist shibboleth.

Most of the criticism of Styron's treatment of Nat
Turner in this collection of essays is of this order and
based on these assumptions. At one point, for instance,
Styron depicts a free Negro starving in a time of
drought. Because he isn't anyone's "property," he is
allowed to starve. Styron's critics object that this is an
example of the old racial dogma that slavery had its
good side and that Negroes were really better off as
slaves than as free men. What Styron was showing instead was that in a society that was based on race, and
which considered men worthy of being kept as chattels
because their skin was dark, mere political freedom
could mean little. Again, an attack on racism, not a
defense of slavery, and one based on the assumption
that there could obviously be no truth in the notion that
anybody was really better off as a slave. Apparently,
however, to the Negro critics of his book the claim that
Negroes were inferior creatures who were better off
protected and cared for like animals is all too serious to
be ignored. It must be refuted.

And that is what is at the heart of the whole business.
The ten Negro intellectuals who object to Styron's portrayal of Nat Turner in his novel don't want racial
absurdities ignored. They want them refuted, and they
want Nat Turner, or any other Negro chosen for the
hero of a novel, designed specifically as a refutation
of the various racial clichés and shibboleths and
stereotypes.

Styron might have produced such a novel. There
have been such; some are singled out for praise in the

course of these essays. But they are inferior works of fiction, in part because their authors thought it more important to present their characters as Negro heroes than as tragic protagonists. Styron didn't want his protagonist to be an exemplary Negro; he wanted him to be a great man. It is my belief that when the smoke of controversy blows away and important fiction about a Negro slave leader can be read as fiction and not as either pro- or anti-Negro propaganda, the best critics both white and Negro will recognize how fine a characterization, and how great a man, William Styron's Nat Turner is.

Second Thoughts
on the Old Gray Mare

When we presume to talk about the South, and what the
future may hold for its writers, we ought first to ask
ourselves what it is that we wish to know, and why.
Novelists themselves seldom ponder such questions; I
doubt for example that William Faulkner ever spent
much time consciously brooding over the present and
future of southern writing. Indeed, many southern
writers are actively uninterested in being known as
southern writers; they go to some lengths to deny that
they are anything known as a "southern writer." And
one can understand why. No good writer likes the notion of provincialism and limitation implied thereby; he
doesn't care to think of himself grouped along with
John Trotwood Moore, Augusta Evans Wilson, and
Harry Stillwell Edwards as exemplars of the literary
genius of Dixie. And he doesn't like the implied

This essay was prepared for delivery as part of the Reynolds Symposium on
"Southern Fiction Today" at Davidson College, Davidson, North Carolina,
March, 1968, and subsequently included in George Core (ed.), *Southern
Fiction Today: Renascence and Beyond* (Athens, Ga., 1969), 33–50.

chauvinism, the lingering aura of the United Daughters of the Confederacy literary tradition, whereby mediocre poets and shallow storytellers are pridefully extolled because they are "Ours." To the extent, therefore, that the question of whether the southern renascence will continue into the future notably involves motives of sectional patriotism, so does it seem not merely distasteful but indeed dangerous to good critics and readers as well. We who theorize about southern literature ought constantly to bear that difficulty in mind. To what extent are we, in however erudite and scholarly a fashion, engaged in waving the Confederate flag when we talk about writers as southerners? Are we, if less naïvely and ingenuously perhaps than our predecessors, nevertheless engaged in composing our contemporary version of that once-desired nonpartisan history of the War Between the States written from the southern point of view?

The difficulty we face in this respect is that, as southern readers and critics, we read and we think out of a tradition that for many years was strongly patriotic, based on deep sectional needs and regional loyalties that arose out of what were not literary so much as political and social conditions. The demand for a southern literature, as distinct from an American literature, first made itself felt during the decades preceding the Civil War, when the South was engaged in insisting on its own separate political identity. There is all too much truth to the jest that when the southern states met in convention in Nashville in 1850 to discuss sectional needs and tactics, the effect was: "*Resolved*: that there be established a Southern Literature. *Resolved*: that the Honorable William Gilmore Simms be requested to write it." Afterward, in the years following the war, when the local-color movement was at its height and southern writers seemed to some critics to dominate the American literary scene, considerable patriotism was mixed into the motives of both the writers themselves and the southern critics who wrote so proudly about them. And when the vogue of local color passed, and southern letters receded into a state so comatose and feeble-blooded as to elicit H. L. Mencken's famous indictment in "The Sahara of the Bozart," much of the criticism written by southerners about southern writers was pathetically chauvinistic and insular, seeking to convince a dubious world that shallowness was admirable because it was southern. You will find the sentiment entombed in so many of the biographical sketches introducing the work of now-forgotten southern poetasters and sentimentalists in that vast compendium of patriotic mediocrity, *The Library of Southern Literature.* Little wonder, then, that in 1923, when *Poetry* magazine called upon southern poets to "accept the challenge of a region so specialized in beauty, so rich in racial tang and prejudice, so jewel-weighted with a heroic past,"[1] the Nashville Fugitives strongly dissented, with Allen Tate declaring that "we fear very much to have the slightest stress laid upon Southern traditions in literature; we who are Southerners know the fatality of such an attitude—the old atavism and sentimentality are always imminent."[2]

The question might have been permitted to recede into the past, along with the aging veterans of the onetime Confederacy, had it not been that not only those Fugitives of Nashville but a host of other southerners as well began publishing, in the late 1920s and in the 1930s and thereafter, literature of such signal accomplishment and importance that it became impossible to ignore considerations of time and place when dealing with it. In the year 1929 alone, for example, Faulkner published *Sartoris* and *The Sound and the Fury,*

1. Harriet Monroe, "The Old South," *Poetry,* XXII (May, 1923), 91.
2. Allen Tate to Marjorie Swett, June 22, 1923, quoted in Louise Cowan, *The Fugitive Group: A Literary History* (Baton Rouge, 1959), 116.

Wolfe *Look Homeward, Angel,* Cabell *The Way of Ecben,* Glasgow *They Stooped to Folly,* Heyward *Mamba's Daughters,* Merrill Moore *The Noise That Time Makes,* Tate his biography of Jefferson Davis, Warren his biography of John Brown, and Erskine Caldwell his first collection of short stories. The roster of important southern writers between the two world wars, including not only those just mentioned but Ransom, Davidson, Porter, Welty, McCullers, Green, Lytle, Roberts, Stribling, Hellman, Gordon, Bishop, Brooks, and others, was such as to make critics and readers everywhere conscious not only of their existence but of their regional identity. For clearly there *was* a common identity; there were certain recognizable characteristics to their work, traits, interests, and attitudes that all of them seemed to share, none of them peculiarly southern perhaps but, taken in the aggregate and in their recurrent presence within the novels, stories, and poems, more than enough to make people talk and think about a distinctly *southern* kind of writing.

Precisely what is this southern quality (or qualities) that characterizes the South's writings has been a matter of some dispute. For Allen Tate it is "a literature conscious of the past in the present."[3] For Robert B. Heilman it is "the coincidence of a sense of the concrete, a sense of the elemental, a sense of the ornamental, a sense of the representative, and a sense of totality."[4] Frederick J. Hoffman believes it has to do with a literature of "place," with all the historical, cultural, and social factors thereto appended.[5] I prefer to think of it as at bottom an attitude toward the nature of man in

3. Allen Tate, "The New Provincialism," in *Collected Essays* (Denver, 1959), 292.

4. Robert B. Heilman, "The Southern Temper," in Louis D. Rubin, Jr., and Robert D. Jacobs (eds.), *Southern Renascence: The Literature of the Modern South* (Baltimore, 1953), 3.

5. Frederick J. Hoffman, *The Art of Southern Fiction: A Study of Some Modern Novelists* (Carbondale, Ill., 1967), 12–28.

society that can best be described by the word "religious"—though, I hasten to add, by no means sectarian. But whatever the quality, this much seems undeniable: the South, as it was and is, was deeply involved in the work of these writers. When so many good writers appeared within the matter of a decade or so, while in the decades before them so little important literature had been produced by southerners, and when so much of their work had an identifiable and recognizable shared quality, mere coincidence could not be a sufficient explanation. Something about the bounded geographic region in which they were born, and about the specific history and culture of that region, must of necessity be involved.

To come to grips with this body of literature, however, which of itself no longer demanded any impulse involving chauvinism, the southern critic has labored under a long heritage of flag-waving—southern literature for the sake of southern pride—and an equally long heritage of conscious political sectionalism—southern literature as the antithesis of, and existing in contrast to, "northern" literature. And for the southern critic the job has been to divest himself of this excess historical baggage, in order to deal with literature which not only stands in no need of sectionalism in order for its excellence to be appreciated but which demands for its proper understanding a disinterested criticism which can identify and evaluate for what it is the impulse toward sectionalism that has been so important a feature of southern life and is therefore embodied in the literature.

And yet, having said that, one must at once enter a demurrer to the effect that not only are novelists intensely human, but so are literary critics, and it would be useless to pretend that there are not mixed in within the complexity of motives that lead men to write novels and lead other men to read and to criticize them just such impulses toward sectional identification and assertion.

In few of the southern writers, perhaps, did the desire for regional identity reach the level of conscious statement that it did for the Agrarians of Nashville, but in one form or the other it was and still is present among them all. So that among the equipment which the southern critic can bring to the task of analyzing and understanding southern literature, sectional identity and sectional pride are not to be despised. It is not, for example, merely the critical intelligence of a Cleanth Brooks that makes his study of the novels of William Faulkner the best guide to the accomplishment of that writer; it is also his intense emotional engagement with the novels and with the region. Brooks's pride in Faulkner, tempered as it is by an acute critical intelligence and a shaping imagination, plays no insignificant part in his critical success. Not, therefore, the denial of the complex factors of identification and pride, but the disciplined harnessing of such impulses, so that they do not dominate but are placed at the service of the intelligence and the understanding, is what is needed. When, to choose another example, Hugh Holman so masterfully interprets Thomas Wolfe in terms of the particular characteristics of Wolfe's Piedmont southern heritage, he is able to do so not because he denies that he too is a product of the Piedmont South, but because he is able to recognize, in himself and therefore in Wolfe, just what that heritage has made possible.

I have gone into what might seem to be a long digression on the past and present problems of the critic of southern literature because we cannot make much sense of the problem we address ourselves to today unless we realize the extent to which, merely by phrasing the question in the way we have done, we are involved in its answer. Will the southern renascence continue into future generations? To make any kind of meaningful answer, we must decide not only what the question means, but why it is asked.

We ask it, I think, not merely because as readers and as critics we are curious as to whether an interesting phenomenon will continue to exist. More than mere curiosity is involved. Most of us who have admired the work of the southern writers of the last quarter century and more would *like* for it to continue. We would like for the South to continue to be one of the leading forces in the literature of our country, and we have been gratified at its having been so. There are certain issues on which our region has not shown up to very good advantage. The South has been caught up in a process of transition which has been marked by considerable turmoil and ugliness. Its literature has been one of the happier products of this process. Not merely along with, but indeed *directly out of* the turmoil and even the violence of the changing South, there have come novels and poems which have fixed the image of the South in art and have given to it the imaginative dignity of tragedy and comedy. In particular William Faulkner has created high tragedy out of the southern experience. Not only does this afford southerners the occasion for much understandable pride, but it also constitutes assurance that what has been going on in the region during Faulkner's lifetime and our own is not simply ugly, but also highly meaningful, so that the confused positions we have occupied add up finally to a drama of definition, with the contending forces representing not merely sordid self-interest but profoundly important human needs and aspirations.

Previously I suggested that I thought that the distinguishing characteristic of the literature of the modern South was its essentially religious nature. I mean by this that the image of human life that it represents is one in which the values embodied in it—love and honor and pity and pride and compassion and sacrifice, to adopt Faulkner's memorable assessment—have not been relativistic, arbitrary, materialistic, but absolute, unswerving, spiritual. Its human confrontations have not been the clash of ignorant armies by night, but the high drama of the soul. The southern writer has habitually seen man as by nature a creature of society and has seen his alienation from society as tragic, and he has also depicted the base of human action as essentially moral. He has seldom ascribed the test of his behavior as one of social efficacy alone. In the novels of Faulkner and his fellow southern writers, what men do and think *matters*, and this has given to the characters a dignity and importance that transcends the merely biological and economic.

With this attitude toward human experience have gone a number of literary characteristics, some of which might at first glance appear to be purely formal in nature, but all of which ultimately depend for their validity upon that attitude. The historical sense, the assumption that what human beings have done in time is meaningful and that men are creatures of time and are molded by what has transpired before them, rests absolutely upon the conviction of the importance of what men can achieve; for if human life ultimately means nothing, and if there are no values which transcend the requirements of the moment, then the past is indeed a bucket of ashes, and only what *is*, and not how it came to be or what it may some day turn out to be, is of any interest.

Not only Robert Heilman but numerous other critics have recognized in southern literature a devotion to the concrete, the specific, along with a distrust of the abstract. It has been the rich texture of the southern novel and the southern poem as well, "things as they are in their rich and contingent materiality," [6] as Ransom put it, that has given body and form to the artistic image. The sodden grays, the drab surfaces of the

6. John Crowe Ransom, "Poetry: A Note on Ontology," in *The World's Body* (New York, 1938), 116.

naturalistic novelists, for example, have found little counterpart in southern writing, for the reason that the southern writer has characteristically been unwilling and unable to subordinate the complexity of human life in time and place to the demands of any ruling thesis or theory that would oversimplify or unduly limit his experience. Systems, theories, dialectics tend to reduce the complexity and variety of human responses, in that they would isolate certain factors and attempt to judge and interpret the actions and experience of men in terms of those factors alone. Just as men resist the impoverishment of such systematizing, so the southern writer has insisted upon complexity and has habitually delighted in the particular, the concrete, even the eccentric. The well-known southern addiction to rhetoric, for the full resources of language in its connotative as well as denotative potentialities, is grounded in this passion for specificity of detail; the southern writers' addiction to the high style of discourse, his susceptibility to excess of diction, is a natural consequence both of his traditional belief in the complexity of experience and of his willingness to invoke moral and ethical values in order to define and judge the experience of men. Rhetoric becomes ludicrous the instant we cease to sympathize with it; it depends upon the ultimate importance we are willing to give to what men say and feel and to the individuality of their own particular ways of expressing it. The language of *Absalom, Absalom!* would seem empty and meaningless if Faulkner did not believe that what Thomas Sutpen did and sought was *important,* and if he did not make us think so too.

Thus when we find ourselves asking whether the South will continue to produce important fiction, it is in part a question of whether the meaning that the writers of the southern renascence have given to our experience will remain applicable and whether the moral and ethical values that they have ascribed to human experience will continue to be valid. Inherent in the literature of Faulkner, Wolfe, Warren, and the others is a judgment of the nature and the importance of human life in time and place, and in particular of our lives in our time and place.

We do not like to think this estimate of human potentiality is inadequate and outdated, and so, not surprisingly, we find ourselves examining the work of the writers of the generation following that of Faulkner, Wolfe, and the other writers of the 1920s and 1930s, to see whether there has been a slackening, a falling off in quality. Has the southern renascence run its course, and is the remarkable upsurge in the creative vitality of a region that began manifesting itself after World War I a thing of the past, with the yield steadily dwindling as the South advances further and further into the second half of the twentieth century? And if so, what does this mean about the southern experience of our own day?

For many of us, the problem has involved something of a dilemma. On the one hand, we have fervently desired a change in some of the South's most traditional attitudes. In particular the place of the Negro in the South has seemed to us to merit considerable revision. The inhumanity and injustice of the South's treatment of the Negro have weighed heavily upon the southern conscience. Yet paradoxically, the presence of the Negro in the South and the position he has occupied in the South have been closely associated with a kind of rural society and with an attitude toward the nature of man in society and the human values by which we seek to order our lives that we are loath to surrender and that the literature of the South has distinctively embodied. We face, therefore, the prospect of seeing the Negro accorded the full and unrestricted participation in our society that he merits as part of the change of that society to one that is predominantly urban and industrial—one in which many of the aspects of southern life that we have cherished seem to be threatened with imminent extinction. And if this is what is happening, then it would seem to follow that a literary mode based upon that kind of society and embodying its values and beliefs will likewise become obsolete and outdated.

All this, therefore, is implied in the question of whether the so-called southern literary renascence is over. Consequently, when we read the fiction of Styron and O'Connor and others of the post–World War II southern writers to see whether the creativity of the southern literary imagination remains alive and unimpaired, our curiosity is more than merely that of literary historians. What we are asking is, can a region which has been changing—and in certain important ways changing to better advantage—continue to afford its writers, and by extension ourselves as well, the quality of human definition in time, and the attitude toward human potentiality and limitation, that in the past it has managed so well?

It is in this light that I interpret the almost uniformly favorable reaction of southern critics and reviewers to the recent publication of William Styron's novel *The Confessions of Nat Turner*. For here was a novel by a leading post–World War II southern writer of fiction, which was clearly and undeniably constructed and told in the old southern tragic mode, with all the familiar attributes—the rhetorical high style, the strong man engaged in a struggle against time, the religious attitude toward human experience on both the protagonist's part and the author's, the complexity of a dense social texture, the individual seen as irretrievably a man in society, yet possessed of his own solitude and capable of the exercise of his own free will. Yet there was one telling difference between this novel and those of Styron's great predecessors. He told his story not merely from the point of view of the Negro slave Nat Turner, but in so doing he assumed the Negro slave to be fully equal, capable of every moral impulse and every complex thought that a white man could know, so that the only difference existing between Nat Turner and any white man was what society had decreed. In other words, it was the first major southern novel in which a Negro protagonist was depicted as a fully equal individual, the first "integrated" southern novel, so to speak. Thus Styron had at once continued the best of the old human values of the southern novel, and yet on the quintessential southern political and social question had written his book squarely out of the attitudes of the enlightened contemporary urban South. It was hardly surprising, then, that book reviewers and critics throughout the South received his work with a tremendous sense of satisfaction; for what Styron had in effect told them was, "See, it can still be done, just as before; we can combine the best of our old way with the best of the new way, so that we need not give up the human values of the southern community in order to live in the modern world."

Perhaps I overrate *The Confessions of Nat Turner,* and if so it is doubtless for precisely those reasons; but to me it is a major work of fiction and demonstrates conclusively what I have long contended, which is that the South's potentiality for continuing to nurture important literature is still far from exhausted and that if indeed the cultural conditions which made possible the literature of the generation of Faulkner and Wolfe are fated to disappear as the South urbanizes, it will take a great deal more urbanizing than has thus far occurred. Of course I am aware that it is possible to point to significant differences between Styron's art and that of his predecessors, but it seems to me that the similarities are still fully as important as the differences and that the differences represent the necessary accommodations of a succeeding generation's attitudes to the facts of its own experience—an experience that in some important respects remains essentially continuous.

Yet I face, in that assertion, the argument to the contrary, advanced some thirty years ago by Allen Tate and developed with so much insight and persuasiveness by Walter Sullivan.[7] The argument is that as the South has changed from one kind of society into another—and the words *rural* and *urban* are perhaps only the · best possible approximations for what the change has been—the breakdown of the moral and ethical social structure that was the Old South has advanced to such an extent that the so-called "historical dimension"—the contrast between the religious and social order that the Old South made available as an image for its writers and the secular, materialistic mass society of modern America that is now our experience is no longer possible. Thus the collapse of the old order that was going on throughout the western world in the nineteenth and early twentieth centuries, which permitted to the artist the momentary individual solution and the undeniable artistic achievement of the so-called "novel of growth" wherein the old absolutes of religion, nationalism, and ethical progress were supplanted by the new divinity of art, took the form, in the early twentieth-century South, of the collapse of a myth, the myth of the "Old South." Now that the myth no longer can be taken sufficiently seriously to make possible even the meaningful rejection of it, the particular focus of consciousness, the meeting of past and present, the "looking two ways"[8] as

7. Mr. Sullivan and I have been happily debating this matter for close to a decade now, and neither of us has succeeded remotely in convincing the other. In more morbid moments I sometimes fear that in both instances there is more than a little generalization from personal needs going on; that is, as a novelist he has been trying manfully to come to grips with the difficulties he faces in writing fiction, while as a somewhat less persistent novelist I have been desperately trying to pretend the difficulties aren't there! (Of course, I don't really believe this.)

8. Allen Tate, "The Fugitive, 1922–1925: A Personal Recollection Twenty Years After," *Princeton University Library Chronicle,* III (April, 1942), 83.

Tate has termed it, can no longer give to the writer's work the important image of particularity that made possible the southern renascence.

This is a very formidable argument. In one sense there is no way to refute it. But let us recognize it for what it is. It is not in essence a literary argument. It is a cultural, perhaps even a religious argument and one that I associate, in its nonsouthern manifestations, with T. S. Eliot, Oswald Spengler, Henry Adams, and that host of profound thinkers who view the events of the past six or seven hundred years as representing a "Decline of the West," the breakdown of civilization and culture as western man has known them, the recrudescence of a new age of barbarism attendant upon the collapse of Christianity. In the nineteenth century Matthew Arnold stated the premises about as well as anyone in "Dover Beach":

> The Sea of Faith
> Was once too at the full, and round earth's shore
> Lay like the folds of a bright girdle furled.
> But now I only hear
> Its melancholy, long, withdrawing roar.

Surely there are times when the most optimistic among us feel like that; and if Matthew Arnold could experience such a devastation because of the London dock strikes, what must we feel, when each morning's newspaper and each evening's television newscast bring the tidings they have been bringing us these last several decades?

Do not think that I exaggerate when I say that the "decline and fall of the myth of the Old South" argument is part and parcel of the general cultural position about the collapse of western Christian society. The assumptions are precisely the same. I quote Mr. Sullivan himself, from an extremely fine essay of some fifteen years ago about the Civil War in southern fiction:

In the Old South the honor and the pride were there, not as individual virtues in isolated men, but as a part of the public consciousness, the moral basis on which the culture was constructed. That is the reason that the War has been used so often by so many Southern writers. It is the grand image for the novelist, the period when the "ultimate truths," with which Mr. Faulkner says the writer must deal, existed as commonly recognized values within a social framework. It is the only moment in American history when a completely developed national ethic was brought to a dramatic crisis.[9]

Whether or not Mr. Sullivan is right in that assertion about the civilization of the Old South, this much is true: one can point to numerous passages in the work of Faulkner, Warren, Tate, and many of the other leading writers of the sothern renascence that more or less say the same thing. This much, it seems to me, is undeniable: the sense of decline and fall, of the collapsing moral order of the Old South in crass modern times, has indeed constituted a theme of striking literary efficacy for many fine southern writers. But that this particular measuring device is by any means the only or even the most important theme or attitude that the southern experience has afforded to its writers, I would emphatically deny. And I would also deny any basis in actual fact for the idea, which for convenience I shall call the "decline and fall of the Old South" position. The whole argument, it seems to me, is based on a series of premises which I see no reason to take for granted, either in their general cultural assumptions or in their specific application to the question of whether a distinctively southern, regional literary art is or is not dead.

The first premise is that the Old South furnished a superior moral ordering, however temporary, the breakdown of which provided a legitimate and actual

9. Walter Sullivan, "Southern Novelists and the Civil War," in Rubin and Jacobs (eds.), *Southern Renascence,* 125.

basis for a sense of decline and fall, of a descent into crass times. I do not think that it did, and nothing that I read in southern history makes me believe in the actual existence of any such superior moral structure in the Old South. I do not deny that many of the South's best writers have believed it did, but what they believed was a myth. And if so, then there is no reason for me to suppose that either the particular myth or others equally usable may not continue to be just as possible to the southern writer as in the past. The notion of a "decline and fall" having taken place is an omnipresent, ever-renewable notion. One finds it throughout the correspondence of Jefferson and Adams, for example. I imagine that Charlemagne and Queen Elizabeth of England likewise felt so. The times are *always* getting worse. The past is always nobler than the present. It was in the time of the Book of Samuel, I believe, that the sister-in-law of Samuel named her son Ichabod, saying, "The glory is departed from Israel."

The second premise implicit in the "decline and fall of the Old South" idea is that the qualities of imagination responsible for the excellence of so much southern writing in the decades following the First World War were dependent for their availability upon the specific historical occasion of a South that was in the process of changing from a rural, agricultural society to an urban, industrial society. That these qualities, which I have contended are the product of an essentially religious attitude, and which derive from a view of men as capable of the heroic and the tragic stature, may well have grown out of that specific historical occasion, I do not deny. But that is no reason to assume that they will not survive once passed. That they must and will be modified to fit a different circumstance is undeniable; but my own belief, from what I see of the region and from reading the work of not only Styron but numerous other southern writers of a new generation, is that they are so very deeply engrained within southern experience that they will continue to assert themselves almost indefinitely.

At bottom, I admit that this comes down to a conviction that the religious values thereby represented remain available because they remain valid. In other words, I do not think we are dealing merely with literary conventions and relative strategies; I think we are ultimately dealing with the image of truth out of which great literature must be constructed. I do not see those values as either verifiable by or dependent purely upon a specific belief in the Protestant Christianity that gave them their particular form and shape in the South; in my belief they transcend any such sectarian origins.

The third premise that I feel goes along with the "decline and fall" notion of southern literature is that in changing from a rural, agricultural to an urban, industrial society, life in the South has changed so utterly that it no longer is, or will soon no longer be, recognizably and identifiably southern experience as previous generations have known it. I do not think that is true. I am perfectly well aware that the suburbs of Nashville physically resemble those of Detroit; but I do not believe that all of the essential qualities of southern life have disappeared just because the South has become urbanized. I do not find the human attitudes and values of life in the South as I see it today so enormously different from what I knew as a child growing up in a small southern city, nor do I find them completely different from those of the life described in the novels of writers much older than myself. An important difference that I *do* see involves the South's attitude toward the place of the Negro in the southern community. This *is* changing, and it seems to me that what is really happening is that the Negro is being brought *into* the community. The essential community is still there. Of course there have

been changes—but there have also been important sur-
vivals. The way the southerners think and act and talk
remains in numerous important ways essentially un-
changed. The southern city as I see it is very much a
southern city, and not merely a city located in the South.
So, as far as I am concerned, there has been considerable continuity along with the change, and I think that
the South as a distinct place is still very much available to
the writer.

The fourth and final premise I wish to note in the
"decline and fall" argument is the notion that it is possible to point out a significant decline in the quality of
southern writing since the years of the renascence. I
deny that any such drastic decline exists. There may be
some falling off in quality, but no more than might be
expected as the literary generations change. The level
of attainment with such things is never uniformly constant. There are still numerous fine southern novels
being written.

I will try to be specific. I have been reading and reviewing books by southern authors for perhaps twenty
years. During that time I have seen publication of *The
Golden Apples,* by Eudora Welty; *A Good Man Is Hard to
Find,* by Flannery O'Connor; *A Death in the Family,* by
James Agee; *The Confessions of Nat Turner* and two other
fine novels by William Styron; two excellent novels by
Walker Percy; and *The Sot-Weed Factor,* by John Barth,
among many other books. That is a pretty good showing.
Nothing I have seen has convinced me that there has
been any alarming overall decline in the quality of the
writing by southerners during this period. Nor does it
seem to me that these books, and many others as well,
lack the abundant presence of most of the qualities we
have come to associate with the literature of the modern
South. The writers *differ* markedly among themselves, of
course: like their predecessors, these writers are highly

individualistic and original in their artistry. They represent, too, the experience of a new generation, which must find its own language. To the extent that the southern experience is changing, its writers must change with it. Yet their work remains distinctive and recognizable, the change has been taking place very much on southern terms, and the books of Styron, Barth, Percy, O'Connor, and the other writers of the post–World War II generation constitute, in their imaginativeness and individuality, an undeniable continuation, into a new time and place, of a tradition of remarkable literary achievement.

So I cannot see any compelling reason to write off the southern literary renascence as something which flowered brilliantly for several decades but is now finished. It may well be that the particular image of the decline and fall of the Old South that proved so useful to some of the best writers of the 1920s and 1930s has lost much of its usefulness, though I am by no means sure even of that. But this has been only one of the themes and the attitudes of modern southern literature; it accounts for some writers but not for others, for some books but not others. It has little or nothing to do with, for example, *Look Homeward, Angel,* or *Light in August,* or *As I Lay Dying,* or *The Heart Is A Lonely Hunter,* or *A Death in The Family,* or *The Golden Apples.* These books, and many others like them, are not less distinctively of the southern literary mode for not being based on the sense of decline and fall. And the books of the younger writers seem just as identifiably regional even though they come out of an experience that supposedly is crucially different. For one thing, novels such as Barth's *The Sot-Weed Factor* give promise of the continuation and even the intensification of what from Cabell to Faulkner to Wolfe to Welty has been an important comic inventiveness, very much a part of the southern literary mode throughout the region's history even though not nearly so often remarked on as the literature of high tragedy. It would not be too startling to see the counterparts of Don Quixote come riding out of the Deep South and into Virginia and the Carolinas in the years ahead. Urban though it may be, the South still has a goodly quantity of its historical experience left to it. The southern community has changed, but it is by no means close to extinction. Meanwhile, it seems to me that neither the fear that it has gone nor the hope that it survives is as relevant to our purposes as the obvious fact that the region still exists and that its writers continue to thrive. I see no reason for doubting that the continuing drama of the southern experience is likely to remain the nurturing ground for a literature that will clearly be, in John Crowe Ransom's felicitous phrase of some years ago, "modern with the Southern accent."

Index

271